Learning-Centred Curriculum Design

Learning-Centred Curriculum Design

Anne Hørsted, John Branch
and Claus Nygaard

THE LEARNING IN HIGHER EDUCATION SERIES

First published in 2017 by Libri Publishing

Copyright © Libri Publishing

Authors retain copyright of individual chapters.

The right of, Anne Hørsted, John Branch and Claus Nygaard to be identified as the editors of this work has been asserted in accordance with the Copyright, Designs and Patents Act, 1988.

ISBN 978-1-911450-15-3

A CIP catalogue record for this book is available from The British Library

Cover design by Helen Taylor

Design by Carnegie Publishing

Libri Publishing
Brunel House
Volunteer Way
Faringdon
Oxfordshire
SN7 7YR

Tel: +44 (0)845 873 3837

www.libripublishing.co.uk

Contents

Foreword

"I want you to imagine that you have been asked to form a new department of ...... Given the rare opportunity to write without constraint, would your curricula bear much resemblance to most of the formal courses of study to be found today? With any luck your answer will be something like, good grief no! If your answer is something else ... there is not much hope for the future!" (Gould 1973, 253).

"the academic community, alongside developing a scholarship of its own towards learning and teaching, should also develop a scholarship of curriculum." (Barnett and Coate 2005, 159).

"faculty knowledge about course design is the most significant bottleneck to better teaching and learning in higher education." (Fink 2003, 24).

Enhancing the quality of curriculum design is one of the key things that we can do to benefit student learning. Too often curriculum design is focused on meeting quality assurance needs to uphold the standards specified by various national, institutional, and professional bodies; rather than focusing on quality enhancement and designing transformative leaning experiences. Moreover, many curriculum designs are more teaching-centred than learning-centred, focused on the interests of the teachers, rather than on the needs of the learners. This book is a breath of fresh air in that it provides a scholarly and highly contextualized discussion of the nature of a *learning-centred* curriculum design.

It is as well to remember, as Jenkins (1998, 3) reminds us, that when considering the curriculum we should distinguish between:

- the curriculum which is *intended* by staff and designed before the student enters the course;

- the curriculum that is *delivered* by the staff/learning materials (including books and software);

- the curriculum that the student *learns and experiences*; and

- the curriculum that the student *makes part of herself/himself* and remembers and uses some years later.

This book primarily deals with the first two forms of the curriculum, but by taking a learning-centred approach, most chapters also address the last two as well. This book makes a significant contribution in five main areas:

Firstly, it brings together literatures and approaches on curriculum design with those on student learning. These are often treated separately. The key framework for the book is a 2x2 matrix in which each chapter is located in terms of its primary contribution. The vertical axis focuses on learning process (*how* students learn) at one end and learning outcomes (*what* students learn) at the other; while the horizontal axis stretches from curriculum design process (*how* we designed) to design outcomes (*what* we designed). This framework provides a simple, but stimulating and memorable, model. Some readers will know how I like 2x2 models (Healey, 2005); and I predict that, as with mine, this may be the most reproduced and cited part of the book.

Second, the introductory chapter recognises that curriculum design in higher education is not restricted to the module/course and programme levels, but is also important at the academic and university levels. Although I would not go as far as the authors and argue that in designing a curriculum we need to start at the institutional level and move down to the module/course level; it is important to recognise the interaction between the levels. More attention in higher education, I feel, needs to be placed at the programme level, and the potential of designing programme-level assessments, such as portfolios, which assess the learning over several modules/courses at once. Where the portfolio covers learning over more than one year, students could select their best work as a showcase portfolio, and hence allow them to take risks in their learning knowing that not everything they do will count.

Third, the book teases out what a learning-centred approach to curriculum design means as against a teacher-centred approach. I particularly liked the distinction that Bartholomew and Curran make between a tutor-centric and a student-centric approach to enacting curriculum alignment. They suggest that the sequence of events is critical. Whereas in the former, the sequence sees students being taught, and then being tested on how well they have received the instruction; in the latter, the assessment, along with the assessment criteria, are designed directly from the learning outcomes. This, they argue, forces the designer to decide 'what good learning looks like'.

Fourth, a theme running through several of the chapters is the importance of engaging students in curriculum design. Where this is done most effectively, it means going beyond the student voice and collecting data on their likes and dislikes, and involving them as partners in the design of their courses. In this approach students are recognised as producers and co-creators of knowledge, and not simply consumers and recipients of instruction. Hayes provides a fascinating account of a negotiated curriculum on an MEd course, where both learning outcomes and assessment are shaped by each participant.

Finally, and sensibly, the book does not suggest there is single approach to designing a learning-centred curriculum, but rather that what is appropriate is context- and culturally-specific. Hence each of the chapters explains carefully the local context in which their initiative is embedded. However, variation not only occurs between chapters, it is also apparent within some course designs, where students are given choices in, for example, the form of the assessment. This recognises the differences in motivation and needs between students taking the same course and begins to move us towards a more individualized model of higher education.

The authors of the 11 chapters are to be congratulated for producing a stimulating, and, in places, challenging, discussion of the nature of a learning-centred curriculum design, which is well illustrated by detailed case studies. Together the chapters point to the importance of 'doing better things' and not only 'doing existing things better'. I commend this book.

Mick Healey
Managing Director, Healey HE Consultants
and Emeritus Professor, University of Gloucestershire
August 2017

Bibliography

Barnett, R. and Coate, K. (2005) *Engaging the curriculum in higher education.* Open University Press: Maidenhead.

Fink, L. D. (2003) *Creating significant learning experiences: An integrated approach to designing college courses.* San Francisco, CA: Jossey-Bass.

Healey, M. (2005) Linking research and teaching exploring disciplinary spaces and the role of inquiry-based learning, in Barnett, R (ed) *Reshaping the university: new relationships between research, scholarship and teaching.* (pp. 30–42). Maidenhead: McGraw-Hill/Open University Press.

Gould, P. (1973) The open geographic curriculum, in Chorley, R. J. (ed.) *Directions in geography.* (pp. 253–2840. London: Methuen.

Jenkins, A. (1998) *Curriculum design in geography,* Cheltenham: Geography Discipline Network, Cheltenham and Gloucester College of Higher Education.

Chapter 1

Four Perceptions of Curriculum: Moving Learning to the Forefront of Higher Education

Claus Nygaard, Anne Hørsted & John Branch

Introduction

We open this book, *Learning-Centred Curriculum Design in Higher Education*, with an introduction chapter in which we present a broad introduction to the theme of the book, and position its chapters in relation to a general model of curriculum design. The aim of the book itself is to inspire its readers—whom we believe to be instructors at universities around the world—to design proactively curriculum which engage, motivate, and inspire students in their learning activities...ultimately enhancing their learning outcomes and improving their employability. Our introduction chapter has three main sections. In section one, we explore four different perceptions of curriculum which correspond to four different levels of higher education. In section two, we propose a four-phased curriculum design process, which draws on these four perceptions of curriculum, and which moves learning to the forefront of higher education. In section three, we overview each of the chapters of the book, according to a central organising model.

Four Perceptions of Curriculum

We open this first section of our introduction chapter by looking at curriculum theory in a historical perspective. It is clear from the academic field of curriculum design theory—which has evolved since the 1940s—that there is no uniform definition of either curriculum or curriculum design (Lynch, 1941; Eisner, 1965; Tanner, 1966; Beauchamp, 1972, 1982; McCutcheon, 1982; Vallance, 1982; Goodson, 1992). In 1965, however,

Eisner proposed a typology for categorising curriculum design in terms of different perceptions of curriculum which correspond to four different levels of higher education: 1. course curriculum, 2. subject-matter curriculum, 3. academic curriculum, and 4, school curriculum. Although his focus was on elementary schools, his typology is both relevant and interesting for researchers and practitioners of curriculum design in higher education. Inspired by Eisner (1965), and considering other perceptions of curriculum through time (Herrick, 1965; Macdonald, 1965; Beauchamp, 1972; Bernstein, 1975; Fogarty, 1998; Biggs, 1996; Ramsden, 1998), we have developed Figure 1, which characterises four perceptions of curriculum design.

Perceptions of curriculum	Course curriculum	Subject-matter curriculum	Academic curriculum	University curriculum
Focus of attention	The microcosmos of student learning.	The clustering of student learning.	The academic range of student learning.	The holistic understanding of student learning.
Definition of curriculum	The course curriculum is the description of content, instructional methods, and assessment methods of a specific course.	The subject-matter curriculum is the description of a cluster of curricular activities tying together a number of closely-related courses within a particular academic discipline.	The academic curriculum is the description of the entire array of curricular activities which constitute the course offerings.	The university curriculum is the description of all ends for which the university is responsible... all activities which are sanctioned by the university.

Percep-tions of curriculum	Course curriculum	Subject-matter curriculum	Academic curriculum	University curriculum
The make-up	The course curriculum is made up from the point of view of the individual course designer/owner.	The subject matter curriculum is made up from a clustering of course curricula.	The academic curriculum is made up from a range of subject-matter curricula.	The university curriculum is made up from all curricular and extra-curricular activities, including sport, culture, and social life which are not directly tied to any academic course or discipline, and which are not necessarily course-based or credit-based.
The design agent	The course curriculum is typically designed by a instructor who is considered a certified domain expert within that specific course.	The subject-matter curriculum is typically designed by a group of instructors who work closely together within an academic discipline.	The academic curriculum is typically designed by an internal governing body at the university which consists of instructors with expertise in the academic discipline, administrators, and students.	The university curriculum is typically designed by an internal governing body at the university which consists of university- and faculty-level administrators, and sometimes members of the university advisory board.

Figure 1. Four Perceptions of Curriculum and Their Characteristics.

Curriculum as Course Curriculum

The narrowest perception of curriculum is the course curriculum. It refers to curriculum for one specific course within an academic discipline, such as a semester-long chemistry course, an intensive week-long economics course, or a year-long language course. Note that in some parts of the academic world, what we refer to here as a 'course' is called a 'module', and the term 'course' means an entire degree programme. The course curriculum consists of the content, instructional methods, and assessment methods of a specific course. As such, we can say that the focus is on the micro-cosmos of student learning...that is to say, what the student must learn by taking a course. The course curriculum is most probably seen from the point of view of the instructor. And the course curriculum is typically designed by an instructor who is considered a certified domain expert within that specific course. The instructor has the choice of teaching and learning activities, and therefore has responsibility for the structuring of students' learning processes. Each course has its own curriculum. Each course, in a way, is its own isolated entity, not linked to other course curricula within the academic discipline. An instructor who is responsible for a course curriculum might well see the course as the most important part of the overall educational offering within the academic discipline, and consequently think about students as 'my students'. As an example, a course curriculum could be for a Developmental Psychology course which is part of the academic discipline of Early Childhood Education. Course curriculum design often has a strong focus on the development of a syllabus, which is the 'physical' manifestation of the content, instructional methods, and assessment methods of the specific course.

One advantage of the perception of curriculum as course curriculum is that instructors are usually experts in the course content, owing to their scholarly research and their academic or practical experiences. They are also the most obvious choice for conducting research-based education within their own courses. One disadvantage of the perception of curriculum as course curriculum, however, is that the broader picture of the entire discipline of study is lost in the micro-cosmos of the specific course. Indeed, the link to other courses might not be not apparent...for instructors, or for students. The responsibility then falls on students alone to integrate the learnings from each course. In our experience, curriculum in most universities is linked strongly to the perception of curriculum as course curriculum.

Curriculum as Subject-Matter Curriculum

Another and broader perception of curriculum is curriculum as subject-matter curriculum. It describes the activities which are planned within a particular academic discipline. Holding this perception, instructors focus on clustering teaching and learning activities within the academic discipline which ties together a number of closely-related courses within a particular academic discipline. For example, it could be the clustering of the curricula of political economy and public finance within the academic discipline of public policy. The focus of attention, therefore, is how to cluster student learning. Each cluster has a subset of courses which all address learning activities which integrate and add up to the broader subject-matter. The subject-matter curriculum is typically designed by a group of instructors who work closely together within an academic discipline.

One advantage of the perception of curriculum as subject-matter curriculum is that with this perception in mind, courses are not left as isolated entities in the wider academic offering. Indeed, they are clustered and related to each other, based on identified subject-matters, which might lead to academic activities adding up to a broader and more integrated learning. The subject-matter curriculum is most likely defined by a group of instructors who know the umbrella of courses within their subject-matter curriculum, and who can refer to learning objectives and learning activities from other courses during their own courses. The learning process is not left to students alone, but is facilitated and guided in a focused way by a larger group of instructors.

One disadvantage of the perception of curriculum as subject-matter curriculum is that the identification of subject-matters within the academic disciplines creates an unhealthy polarity between the clusters of courses. It could be an unproductive division between 'hard courses' and 'soft courses', for example. Consider the common polarisation in the academic discipline of business administration between subjects such as economics, finance, and statistics on the one hand, and human resource

finding its way into higher education, and at an increasingly rapid pace. That said, it is rare to see curriculum design processes themselves conducted from this perception. Indeed, it is common to see universities appreciate and acknowledge the 'student experience', but in turn see curricula which appear as seemingly random patchworks of individually-designed course curricula which are driven by front-running instructors.

The Sum of Its Parts

In summary, the four perceptions of curriculum can be viewed (See Figure 2.) in two dimensions: 1. the focus of the curriculum, and 2. the view on student learning. With respect to focus of the curriculum, the four perceptions of curriculum range from a partial view with curriculum as course curriculum, in which the curriculum is focused very narrowly on a specific course, to a summative view with curriculum as university, curriculum, in which the curriculum is the sum of its parts. Likewise, the four perceptions of curriculum range from a micro-view with curriculum as a course curriculum, in which student learning occurs in and about the specific course only, to the holistic view with curriculum as university-curriculum in which learning is considered integrated throughout the entire student experience.

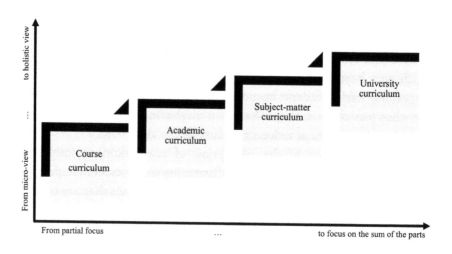

Figure 2. A View of the Four Perceptions of Curriculum

With a partial focus and a micro-view, the tendency is for curricula to be instructor-driven and output-oriented. With a focus on the sum of the parts and a holistic view, the tendency is for curricula to be more student-driven and experiential in nature. But with either extreme, moving student learning to the forefront of higher education is imperative, suggesting the need for a more purposeful approach to curriculum design.

A Four-Phased Curriculum Design Process

We suggest that curriculum design ought to have four phases, which correspond to the four perceptions of curriculum which we explored above (See Figure 3.). With each phase, the curriculum moves in reverse from a focus on the sum of the parts to a partial focus, and from a holistic view to a micro-view. Let us outline each of the four phases as we see them.

Phase 1. Design the University Curriculum

We suggest that curriculum design ought to start with the design of the university curriculum. It is with the university curriculum which has the broadest focus and most holistic view on student learning. Questions ought to include: What is the university known for? What characterises its brand? What is the role of technology? What is the role of society? What is the life of students like? Which extra-curricular activities govern the engagement and identity of the students? In which ways do the students learn?

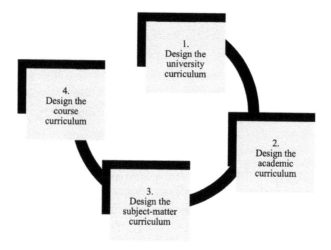

Figure 3. A Four-Phased Curriculum Design Process

Asking such broad questions forces curriculum designers to take a more integrated perspective on student learning, by expanding curriculum design beyond choices of textbooks, learning management systems, and assessment methods. They intimate that student learning is a very complex and social process. They elevate the students from recipients of knowledge to collaborators, actors, resources. Put another way, student learning is too valuable for a university to be left in the hands of individual instructors.

The curriculum design process, therefore, must be anchored in the university curriculum, in which the quality strategy (Nygaard & Kristensen, 2010), learning strategy (Biggs, 1996; Ramsden, 1998; Nygaard & Bramming, 2008), e-learning strategy (Nygaard, 2015; Salmon, 2016; Sharpe *et al.*, 2016), evaluation strategy (Nygaard & Belluigi, 2011), branding strategy (Nygaard, 2008) student engagement strategy (Nygaard *et al.*, 2013; Healey *et al.*, 2014), and the strategy for developing student culture (Löfvall & Nygaard, 2013) are all defined and delimited. These shape the university curriculum, and as such must have input from participants throughout the university. And not before the university curriculum has been designed, does it make sense to move to phase 2 and design the academic curriculum.

Phase 2: Design the Academic Curriculum

The second curriculum design phase is devoted to the design of the academic curriculum. This is most often done at the faculty level, because most universities are structured by faculties which each offer a variety of programmes/educational offerings. Note that in some parts of the academic world, what we refer to here as a 'faculty' is also called a 'school', 'college', or 'academic unit'. With the perception of curriculum as academic curriculum, questions ought to include: What characterises the future work life of our graduates? What is the expected future need for the educational offering? Which knowledge is valuable for our graduates? Which skills and transferable skills (Ball, 1986; Bridges, 1993) are valuable for our graduates? What characterises the collective set of competencies our graduates must have to be competitive in the future job market? Which learning objectives do we set for our students? Which learning objectives do our students set for themselves? What is our teaching and learning strategy which supports students in fulfilling their learning objectives?

Asking such questions forces curriculum designers to focus on the educational offering as an integrated entity, not as a collection of courses. As before, they prevent a digression to decisions of textbooks, learning management systems, and assessment methods. They also point to the need for a participation from a broad range of actors, including instructors with expertise in the academic discipline, administrators, and students. After agreement on the academic curriculum, the design process can proceed to the subject-matter curriculum.

Phase 3. Design the Subject-Matter Curriculum

The third curriculum design phase deals with the clustering of teaching and learning activities in a programme according to an underlying philosophy of science. Questions ought to include: Which subject-matter is important for students to master in order to fulfil the ambitions of the academic curriculum? What is the ontology and epistemology of this subject-matter? Which research methods are used within our subject-matter? Which research methods are common across different subjects? How can different subjects be clustered to enable students to learn?

What are the transferable skills which enable students to move from one subject to another during the programme? How do we help students in their transition between subjects?

Asking such questions forces curriculum designers to see subject-matter curriculum from the student's perspective, thereby helping to identify possible routes of learning progression and scaffolding devices. Indeed, Bernstein (1975) distinguished between 'curriculum as a collection' and 'curriculum as integration'. Collection refers to curriculum as a collection of courses and subjects, which are not related, has strong disciplinary boundaries between them, and are taught in different ways. Integration refers to curriculum as a related number of subjects, which are integrated and maybe multidisciplinary, and where the teaching methods are integrated across the disciplines. The perception of curriculum as subject-matter curriculum coincides with this notion of curriculum as integration. Perceiving curriculum as subject-matter curriculum, therefore, is significant, because it discourages curriculum designers from thinking about curricula within the boundaries of existing courses, which have historically served as platforms for content-delivery at universities. The level of reflection on this third curriculum design phase, on the contrary, encourages creative thinking, possibly leading to new ways to 'slice and dice' subject-matter. After this subject-matter curriculum design, the design process can proceed to the course curriculum.

Phase 4: Design the Course Curriculum

The fourth and final curriculum design phase is the design of the course curriculum...or probably more accurately, because we expect several courses to form an educational offering, design of the course curricula. It is important that this design phase is decoupled from departmental resource games and power games. Designing the course curriculum is not about getting the darling of the faculty into a programme. And the focus of the course is not to be the dominant textbook within the academic field. It is about designing a course which is in line with the curriculum designed in the first three curriculum design phases. Return to the university curriculum for inspiration for course curriculum design. What is the brand of the university? What is the teaching and learning strategy? What is the expected culture and identity of students?

Re-consider the academic curriculum and how it can be incorporated in the course. Which knowledge, skills, and abilities will improve the employability of graduates? And re-visit the subject-matter curriculum. Which ontologies, epistemologies, and research methods are required of students? Designing the course curriculum, therefore, is the culmination of the curriculum design process.

At a more pragmatic level, however, the course curriculum includes the content, instructional methods, and assessment methods of a specific course (Eisner, 1965). It is more than simply deciding which textbook to use. In terms of learning, it demands careful consideration of which instructional methods to use. Didactic teaching? Lecturing from a textbook? Problem-based learning (Fogarty, 1998; Dean et al., 2002)? Inquiry-based learning (Healey, 2005)? Case-based learning (Mauf-fette-Leenders et al., 1997; Erskine et al., 1998; Branch et al., 2015)? Research-based learning (Olsen & Pedersen, 2003; Guerin et al., 2015); Project-based learning (DeFillipi, 2001; Meier & Nygaard, 2008). Process-oriented teaching (Vermunt, 1995; Bolhuis, 2003)? Entrepre-neurial activities (Colette, 2013; Davis et al., 2016; Branch et al., 2017). And of course, all three components of the course curriculum (content, instructional methods, and assessment methods) must have constructive alignment (Biggs, 1996), leading to a more holistic and sum-of-its-parts experience for students.

Ten Examples of Curriculum Design

In the previous section, we have we proposed a four-phased curriculum design process, which draws on the four perceptions of curriculum, and which moves learning to the forefront of higher education. We have attempted to demonstrate that the design of course curriculum—the dominant perception of curriculum in higher education—can and ought to draw on the other three perceptions of curriculum, and that in doing so, will improve the student experience.

This book contains ten additional chapters which illustrate curriculum design, and which, more importantly, showcase the power of curriculum design for improving the student experience. These ten examples of curriculum design span the four perceptions of curriculum, and the four phases of our proposed model of curriculum design. As editors, however, we have opted to organise the ten chapters using a different structuring device which draws on two perspectives: 1. learning (how students learn versus what students learn) and 2. curriculum design (how we designed versus what we designed). The consequence is a book with ten chapters which cluster in four sections which correspond to the four quadrants of a 2×2 matrix (See Figure 4.).

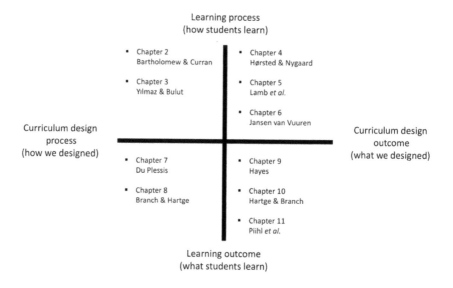

Figure 4: Four viewpoints on learning-centred curriculum design.

Section I: Curriculum Design Process/Learning Process

Section 1 consists of two chapters which detail 'how' curriculum is designed and 'how' students learn. The chapters are detailed case-studies, but simultaneously provide normative suggestions as to how the curriculum design process ought to be structured.

Chapter 2, *Translating Institutional Approaches to Curriculum Design into Practice—A Leadership Perspective,* by Paul Bartholomew & Roisín Curran, takes us to Ulster University in Northern Ireland. With their chapter, they contribute to this book by sharing their experiences of how to enact wholesale enhancement of curriculum design through institutional leadership and empowerment for change at the discipline level.

The chapter addresses learning-centred curriculum design by drawing on research and practice spanning 10 years which led to the development of a nationally available resource 'The Rough Guide to Curriculum Design' which was cited as a reference point within the UK Quality Code. Paul & Roisín wrote their chapter to share their experiences of how to enact wholesale enhancement of curriculum design through institutional leadership and management. The most important lesson in their chapter is that instructors do not come oven-ready to put in place effective learning-centred curriculum design. Coordinated support of instructors is needed to create an environment in which people feel empowered to make curricular changes. Paul and Roisín offer a sequenced recipe so that institutional change of curriculum design can be enacted. They believe their chapter might inspire readers because it shares a framework based on learning-centredness encompassing both design challenges and design principles.

Chapter 3, *From a Teaching-Centred to a Learning-Centred Approach to Curriculum Design: Transforming Teacher Candidates*, by Gülbahar Yılmaz & Sevilay Bulut, takes us to Ankara University in Turkey. With their chapter, they contribute to the book by showing how they have designed the learning-centred undergraduate course *Turkish Grammar: Sentence and Text* which is offered as a part of the Teacher Education Programme at Ankara University in Turkey. Gülbahar & Sevilay wrote this chapter to document their experiences with a learning-centred curriculum design process. They found that the teacher candidates in their undergraduate course were not all good at grammar, which puzzled them, because they had all been taught grammar since early primary school. If they were not good at grammar when they reached their undergraduate education, maybe it was due to the way they have been taught? So, the authors tried to change their own perspective from teaching as delivery to learning as process. The most important lesson in the chapter is that it is possible—with success—to change teacher candidates' perception of teaching and learning, if the curriculum is designed in a way which focuses their attention on the learning process. Gülbahar & Sevilay believe their chapter might inspire readers because they give practical information about how to design, implement, and evaluate a learning-centred course.

Section 2. Learning Process/Curriculum Design Outcome

Section 2 consists of three chapters, which are characterised by their centring on the student learning process, while also showing concrete examples of curriculum design outcome—meaning what they designed to have students' engage in learning activities to improve their learning outcomes.

Chapter 4, *How to Design a Curriculum for Student Learning*, by Anne Hørsted & Claus Nygaard, takes us to Copenhagen Business School and cph:learning in Copenhagen, Denmark. With their chapter, they contribute to the book by suggesting a model of learning-centred curriculum design made up of four interrelated aspects which are important when working with learning-centred curriculum design. The use of the model is shown in three concrete examples of learning-centred curriculum design. Anne & Claus wrote this chapter because they wanted to show how it is possible to make a well-designed learning-centered curriculum which enhances students learning outcome. They show this by presenting three different examples of curriculum design. The most important lesson in their chapter is that developing a curriculum based on what they call 'the process stream' is very different from formulating a syllabus. Curriculum design following the process stream becomes an iterative process of coordination and facilitation, unfolding as students engage in curricular activities and give feedback about their personal learning. The authors believe this will improve the learning outcomes of students.

Chapter 5, *Learning-Centred Educational Development: An Approach That Draws Upon Creative Arts and Philosophies of Emancipation*, by Julian Lamb, Marion Carrier & Jacob Lamb, takes us to Aston University in England. With their chapter, they contribute to the book by showcasing the design, delivery, and impact of an innovative learning-centred professional development programme for newly appointed higher education (HE) teachers at Aston University in the UK. They address learning-centred curriculum design by exploring the relationship between compliance with the Higher Education Academy (HEA) quality benchmarks for teaching (known as the United Kingdom Professional Standards Framework – UKPSF) and the authors' mission to encourage bohemianism (a sense of one's own values) in becoming a teacher in HE. Julian, Marion & Jacob wrote this chapter because they wanted to tell others about the success of their PGCert programme, and also, through researching and writing the chapter, gain a better understanding of why it was successful and how they might build upon its success. The authors believe their chapter inspires readers because it demonstrates that maintaining a seemingly paradoxical (even incompatible) relationship between compliance and bohemianism in educational development can create significant and effective learning-centred environment for the 'training' of early-career HE teachers. The learning environment is likened to an artist's studio in which students are encouraged to study what already exists in their professional practice rather than create simulations of what they ought to be according to the UKSPF. The most important lesson in their chapter is that early-career teachers in HE are best supported by encouraging them to discover, explore, experiment, and commit to their own values, rather than simply adopting the values of the programme teachers or the UKPSF.

Chapter 6, *Improving Learning-Centeredness in a Higher Education Foundation Phase Arts Curriculum*, by Eurika Jansen van Vuuren brings us to University of Mpumalanga in South Africa. With her chapter, she contributes to the book by providing guidelines on designing a more learning-centred curriculum through the contextualisation of learning activities, and through adapting new teaching methods. Her chapter addresses learning-centred curriculum design by adapting the existing curriculum to the learning situation of students, and ensuring that the content is contextualised and works from the known to the unknown to accommodate the African reality. The second important factor she addresses is the way the curriculum is approached by the lecturer, so that the focus moves to the student's learning rather than the lecturer's presentation. Eurika wrote her chapter due to the current South African movement to decolonise the curriculum. She shifted the focus of the curriculum to African cultural knowledge before moving on to global arts. Furthermore, Eurika grappled with methods to assist her students to get actively involved in every aspect of her classes rather than just observing from a distance and disappearing into the woodwork. She felt the need to involve every student despite the class group being so large. The most important lesson in the chapter is that it is possible to manipulate a curriculum to become more learning-centred without considerable changes to the content, and that it is important to start with the known.

Students' ability to learn through discovery must not be underestimated. Let go of the control and allow creativity to prosper! Eurika believes her chapter inspires readers because it shows that working from the foundation of the students' cultural background and knowledge does not mean it is a lesser education, and that it assists in cultivating pride in one's own roots. It shows that even in large groups of students, everyone can be pulled into deep learning and be counted rather than getting lost in the group.

Section 3: Curriculum Design Process/Learning Outcome

The third section of the book consist of two chapters. Both chapters focus on the curriculum design process, and go into detail with the particular outcomes for students following the learning-centred curriculum design process.

Chapter 7, *Designing a Curriculum for Integrating Experiential Learning with Theory During Initial Teacher Education*, by Andries Du Plessis also takes us to University of Mpumalanga in South Africa. With his chapter, he contributes to the book by exploring how school-university partnerships are needed for the experiential learning component in a new Bachelor in Education Foundation Phase (BEd FP) programme. His chapter addresses learning-centred curriculum design by taking the theoretical components of the curriculum into consideration, and by describing the way in which instructors tried to capitalise on the direct relationship which they strive to maintain with the Teaching School and outside partnering schools. Andries wrote the chapter because he wanted to share the experiences which he gained during the implementation of this new Bachelor of Education Foundation Phase degree. The most important lesson in his chapter is that school university partnerships are important for effective initial teacher education because they determine the success of integrating theory and practice. Andries believes his chapter might inspire readers because he reflects upon his personal experiences during the past five years. In doing so, he explores the contexts as well as the numerous challenges which educators are facing in South Africa. He draws upon his interviews with staff, teachers, and students alike, which means that this chapter provides them with a voice. It also contextualises the historical factors at play which affect the quality of education in South Africa. Yet, in many respects others could relate to these challenges given the tensions which exist between schools and higher education institutions.

Chapter 8, *Using the ECTS for Learning-Centred Curriculum Design*, by John Branch & Timothy Hartge, takes us to both the University of Michigan in the U.S.A., and the Luxembourg School of Business in Luxembourg. With their chapter, they contribute to the book by illustrating that the ECTS is itself learning-centred, and that the ECTS can be used to aid learning-centred curriculum design. Their chapter addresses learning-centred curriculum design by demonstrating how the ECTS can be used to help curriculum design. They wrote the chapter to show how they have adopted the ECTS into all of their thinking, and, more importantly, into all of their curriculum designing. The most important lesson in their chapter, they believe, is that ECTS is a constraint on curriculum design which reframes learning as the basic unit of curriculum design, and which, in effect, 'forces' the instructor to reconsider his/her role as a curator of learning activities. John & Tim believe their chapter inspires readers because it demonstrates the usefulness of the ECTS for curriculum design.

Section 4: Curriculum Design Outcome/Learning Outcome

The fourth and final section of the book consists of four chapters. Common for these are that they show the outcome of curriculum design processes, and discuss what students' learn as a result of their learning-centred curriculum design.

Chapter 9, *Introducing the Concept of "A Corresponding Curriculum" to Transform Academic Identity and Practice*, by Sarah Hayes, brings us back to Aston University in England. With her chapter, she contributes to the book by introducing the concept of a corresponding curriculum, dynamically developed by the participants themselves on a master in education (MEd) programme at Aston University in England. Her chapter addresses learning-centred curriculum design by discussing what is created and experienced collectively by students and their teachers, not what is delivered by teachers and received by students. Sarah wrote the chapter, because she wanted to share her ideas about what she has called "a corresponding curriculum". It enables her to discuss what has unfolded as a powerful exchange amongst the students she teaches on a negotiated module, where both learning outcomes and assessment are open to be shaped by each participant. As shown in Sarah's chapter, the sessions are also shaped by the group of students and teachers, as they build collective understandings about their identities, suggest and share individual and mutual experiences and therefore correspond with the curriculum, to collectively develop it. The most important lesson from her chapter is that learning-centredness in the form of a corresponding curriculum has direct effects on both body and mind. Sarah believes her chapter inspires readers, because it challenges a more traditional, modular approach behind which many hidden political agendas might rest...one which leaves no space for theorising about the curriculum.

Chapter 10, *Academic Rigour: Harnessing High-Quality Connections and Classroom Conversations*, by Timothy Hartge & John Branch is a conceptual piece which is not situated in any specific university. With their chapter, they contribute to the book by exploring the impact which high-quality connections can have on the learner, and subsequently on classroom conversations. The most important lesson in their chapter is that the skill to develop high-quality connections can be taught. Tim & John believe that their chapter inspires readers because it demonstrates the importance of, and more importantly, the power of, high-quality connections.

Chapter 11, *Curriculum Design for Enhancing Employability through Learning Experiences with External Stakeholders*, by Jesper Piihl, Anna Marie Dyhr Ulrich & Kristian Philipsen, takes us to the University of Southern Denmark in Denmark. With their chapter, they contribute to the book by offering three metaphors for understanding the role of, and relationship with, external stakeholders, who play an important role in designing and delivering the curriculum. The metaphors are distinguished by their perspective on links to the external environment, on learning, on research-based teaching, and ultimately on student-employability and relevance of curriculum. They wrote this chapter because there is an increasing awareness that higher education must improve graduates' future employment opportunities. However, in the debate amongst researchers on curriculum development, the role of employability and relations to the external society is not always obvious, and is often contested. The most important lesson in their chapter is the metaphor of the perforated curriculum, suggesting that a curriculum should have holes with active and direct interaction with external stakeholders related to the professional arenas the graduates are expected to engage with in their professional lives. The chapter presents a framework which can inspire development of learning experiences, which engages with external stakeholders with gradually increasing levels of complexity. Jesper, Anna Marie & Kristian believe that their chapter inspires readers by developing three metaphors, which discuss how different ideas about how curriculum development links to perspectives on employability and relevance, while still maintaining a foundation in core ideas of research-based teaching and learning.

We hope to inspire you

As shown in our introduction chapter, this book holds many perceptions, perspectives, and conceptualisations of curriculum and curriculum design. As you read the chapters, you will be presented with a number of well-known approaches to learning which play a role in learning-centred curriculum design—from authors like Biggs (1996) 'Constructive Alignment', Dewey (1934) 'Practice-Based Curriculum', and Schön (1987) 'Reflective Practitioner'. You will, however, also meet new and novel ideas and terms, which have evolved from the reflected practice of curriculum design by the authors themselves, who practice as highly engaged instructors with an interest in the scholarship of teaching and learning. You will familiarise yourself with the 'perforated tube', the 'corresponding curriculum', the 'humanistic curriculum', and the 'process stream curriculum', to name a few. The beauty of this book is that it was written by reflective curriculum design practitioners, as they have experienced personal success with their curriculum (re)design processes. The chapters of the book have been written with a "Yes, we did it!" approach. It is our hope that you will be inspired from reading these reflected narratives of learning-centred curriculum design, and jump on the bandwagon yourself. Reading this book and familiarising yourself with the curriculum design steps which were taken by colleagues—which in the end have turned out to benefit students' engagement, students' motivation, students' self-efficacy, students' learning outcomes, and students' employability—will hopefully inspire you to (re)design a more learning-centred curriculum in your university.

About the Authors

Anne Hørsted is Adjunct Professor at the University of Southern Denmark, Senior Consultant at cph:learning in Denmark, and Adjunct Professor at the Institute for Learning in Higher Education. She can be contacted at this e-mail: anne@lihe.info

Claus Nygaard, is Professor and Executive director at the Institute for Learning in Higher Education and Executive Director at cph:learning in Denmark. He can be contacted at this e-mail: info@lihe.info

John Branch is Academic Director of the part-time MBA programmes and Assistant Clinical Instructor of business administration at the Stephen M. Ross School of Business, and Faculty Associate at the Center for Russian, East European & Eurasian Studies, both of the University of Michigan in Ann Arbor, USA. He can be contacted at this e-mail: jdbranch@umich.edu

Bibliography

Ball, C. (1986). *Transferable Personal Skills in Employment: The Contribution of Higher Education*. National Advisory Board for Public Sector Higher Education and University Grants Council, London.

Beauchamp, George A. (1972). Basic Components of a Curriculum Theory. *Curriculum Theory Network*, No. 10, pp. 16–22.

Beauchamp, George A. (1982). Curriculum Theory: Meaning, Development, and Use. *Theory into Practice*, Vol. 21, No. 1, pp. 23–27.

Bernstein B. (1975). *On the Curriculum*. London: Routledge.

Biggs, J. (1996). Enhancing Teaching through Constructive Alignment. *Higher Education*, Vol. 32, No. 3, pp. 347–364.

Bolhuis, S. (2003). Towards process-oriented teaching for self-directed lifelong learning: a multidimensional perspective. *Learning and Instruction*, Vol. 13, No. 3, pp. 327–47.

Branch, J.; P. Bartholomew & C. Nygaard (2015). *Case-Based Learning in Higher Education*. Oxfordshire, UK: Libri Publishing Ltd.

Branch, J.; A. Hørsted & C. Nygaard (2017). *Teaching and Learning Entrepreneurship in Higher Education*. Oxfordshire: Libri Publishing Ltd.

Bridges, D. (1993). Transferable Skills: A Philosophical Perspective. *Studies in Higher Education*, Vol. 18, No. 1, pp. 43–51.

Colette, H. (2013). Entrepreneurship education in HE: are policy makers expecting too much? *Education + Training*, Vol. 55, No. 8/9, pp. 836–848.

Davis, M. H.; J. A. Hall & P. S. Mayer (2016). Developing a new measure of entrepreneurial mindset: reliability, validity, and implications for practitioners. *Consulting Psychology Journal: Practice and Research*, Vol. 68, No. 1, pp. 21–48.

Dean, C. D.; D. Dunaway; S. Ruble & C. Gerhardt (2002). *Implementing Problem-Based Learning in Education*. Birmingham, AL: Samford University Press.

DeFillipi, R. J. (2001). Introduction: Project-based Learning. Reflective Practices and Learning Outcomes. *Management Learning*, Vol. 32, No. 1, pp. 5–10.

Dewey, J. (1934). *Art as Experience*. New York: Putnam.

Eisner, E. (1965). Levels of Curriculum and Curriculum Research". *The Elementary School Journal*, Vol. 66, No. 3, pp. 155–162.

Erskine, J. A.; M. R. Leenders & L. A. Mauffette-Leenders. (1998). Teaching with Cases. Ivey: Richard Ivey School of Business.

Fogarty, R. (Ed.) (1998). Problem-Based Learning & Other Curriculum Models for the Multiple Intelligences Classroom. Arlington Heights: Skylight Training and Publishing.

Goodson, I. F. (1992). On Curriculum Form: Notes Toward a Theory of Curriculum. *Sociology of Education*, Vol. 65, No. 1, pp. 66–75.

Guerin, C.; P. Bartholomew & C. Nygaard (Eds.) (2015). Learning to research - researching to learn. Oxfordshire, UK: Libri Publishing Ltd.

Healey, M. (2005). Linking Research and Teaching: Exploring Disciplinary Spaces and the Role of Inquiry-Based Learning. In R. Barnett (Ed.), *Reshaping the university: new relationships between research, scholarship and teaching*. Maidenhead: McGraw-Hill/Open University Press, pp. 67–78.

Healey, M.; A. Flint & K Harrington (2014). *Engagement Through Partnership: Students as Partners in Learning and Teaching in Higher Education*. Higher Education Academy, UK.

Herrick, V. E. (1965). Strategies of Curriculum Development. In V. E. Herrick & D. W. Anderson (Eds.), *Strategies of Curriculum Development*. Charles E. Merrill Books.

Löfvall, S. & C. Nygaard (2013). Interrelationships between Student Culture, Teaching and Learning in Higher Education. In C. Nygaard; J. Branch & C. Holtham (Eds.), *Learning in Higher Education: Contemporary Standpoints*. Oxfordshire: Libri Publishing Ltd., pp. 127–150.

Lynch, J. A. (1941). A General Theory of Curriculum. *Peabody Journal of Education*, Vol. 18, No. 5, pp. 296–301.

Macdonald, J. B. (1965). Educational Models for Instruction--Introduction. In J. B. Macdonald & R. R. Leeper (Eds.), *Theories of Instruction*. Washington, DC: Association for Supervision and Curriculum Development.

Mauffette-Leenders, L. A.; J. A. Erskine & M. R. Leenders (1997). *Learning with Cases*. Ivey: Richard Ivey School of Business.

Meier, F. & C. Nygaard (2008). Problem Oriented Project Work. In C. Nygaard & C. Holtham (Eds.), *Understanding Learning-Centred Higher Education*. Frederiksberg: Copenhagen Business School Press.

McCutcheon, G. (1982). What in the World Is Curriculum Theory? *Theory into Practice*, Vol. 21, No. 1, pp. 18–22.

Nygaard, C. (2008). *A Learning Strategy as a Possible Vehicle for Branding Universities?* Paper presented at The 30th International EAIR-conference, Frederiksberg, Denmark.

Nygaard, C. (2015). Rudiments of a Strategy for Technology Enhanced University Learning. In C. Nygaard; J. Branch & P. Bartholomew (Eds.), *Technology Enhanced Learning in Higher Education*. Oxfordshire: Libri Publishing Ltd., pp. 31–49.

Nygaard, C. & D. Z. Belluigi (2011). A Proposed Methodology for Contextualised Evaluation in Higher Education. *Assessment & Evaluation in Higher Education*, Vol. 36, No. 6, p. 657–671.

Nygaard, C. & M. Serrano (2010). Students' Identity Construction and Learning. Reasons for developing a learning-centred curriculum in higher education. In L. E. Kattington (Ed.), *Handbook of Curriculum Development*, Nova Publishers.

Nygaard, C. & P. Bramming (2008). Learning-centred Public Management Education. *International Journal of Public Sector Management*, Vol. 21, No. 4, pp. 400–416.

Nygaard, C.; S. Brand; P. Bartholomew & L. Millard (Eds.) (2013). *Student Engagement: Identity, Motivation and Community*. Oxfordshire: Libri Publishing Ltd.

Olsen, P. B. & K. Pedersen (2003). Problemorienteret projektarbejde – en værktøjsbog. (Problem-centred project work – a tool-book). Frederiksberg: Roskilde Universitetsforlag.

Ramsden, P. (1988). *Improving Learning: New Perspectives*. Kogan Page.

Salmon, G. (2005). Flying not Flapping: a Strategic Framework for E-Learning and Pedagogical Innovation in Higher Education Institutions. *Research in Learning Technology*, Vol. 13, No. 3, pp. 201–218.

Schön, D. A. (1987). *Educating the Reflective Practitioner.* San Francisco: Jossey-Bass.

Sharpe, R. G. Benfield & F. Richard (2006). Implementing a University E-Learning Strategy: Levers for Change Within Academic Schools. *Research in Learning Technology,* Vol. 14, No. 2, pp. 135–15.

Tanner, D. (1966). Curriculum Theory: Knowledge and Content. *Review of Educational Research,* Vol. 36, No. 3, pp. 362–372.

Vallance, E. (1982). The Practical Uses of Curriculum Theory. *Theory into Practice,* Vol. 21, No. 1, pp. 4–10.

Vermunt, J. D. (1995). Process-Oriented Instruction in Learning and Thinking Strategies. *European Journal of Psychology of Education,* Vol. 10, pp. 325–349.

Section 1: Curriculum Design Process/Learning Process

Chapter 2
Translating Institutional Approaches to Curriculum Design into Practice – A Leadership Perspective

Paul Bartholomew & Roisín Curran

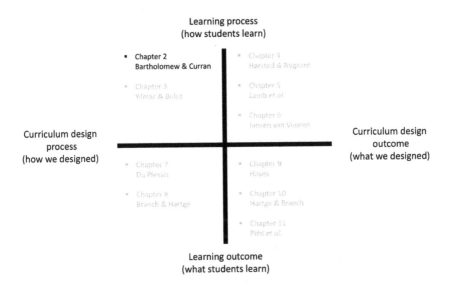

Learning process
(how students learn)

- Chapter 2
Bartholomew & Curran

- Chapter 4
Hørsted & Nygaard

- Chapter 3
Yilmaz & Bulut

- Chapter 5
Lamb et al.

- Chapter 6
Jansen van Vuuren

Curriculum design
process
(how we designed)

Curriculum design
outcome
(what we designed)

- Chapter 7
Du Plessis

- Chapter 9
Hayes

- Chapter 8
Branch & Hartge

- Chapter 10
Hartge & Branch

- Chapter 11
Piihl et al.

Learning outcome
(what students learn)

Introduction

We contribute to this book *Learning-Centred Curriculum Design in Higher Education* by sharing our experiences of how to enact wholesale enhancement of curriculum design through institutional leadership and empowerment for change at the discipline level (Blackmore & Kandiko, 2012). In relation to the central model of the book, we position our chapter in section one – Curriculum Design Process/Learning Process – since we contend that learning-centred curriculum design can be conceived as both a product-facing phenomenon (i.e., activity that is focused on the specification of a study programme) and as a process-facing phenomenon (i.e., activity that is focused on the social and institutional practices that characterise the study programme development process itself). This chapter explores both of these conceptions of curriculum design and shares approaches on how these have been supported at the institutional and discipline/programme level through an infrastructure that sought to support the activity of design and not just the production of documentation for the purpose of securing approval.

The chapter draws on the experience of the authors from their leadership of institutional approaches to curriculum design across three United Kingdom (UK) institutions – with particular reference to sector-wide learning that cascaded from a Jisc (a national agency that supports technology-enhanced learning in higher education) initiative that funded 12 projects across the UK to develop enhanced institutional approaches to curriculum design. These Jisc-funded projects lasted four years and created a body of work that continues to inform curriculum design practice across the sector to this day.

By way of clarifying the authors' context, some reference will be made to UK-specific reference points that aid curriculum design, but it is anticipated that readers from outside the UK will be able to relate such frameworks to their own national contexts and the structures within which they themselves operate. Reading our chapter, you will gain the following:

1. an insight into sector-wide learning – research and resources emanating from the Jisc projects;

2. an understanding of what is meant by "institutional approaches to curriculum design", the concept of "design principles" as they relate to the curriculum design "products" (study programmes), and the concept of "design challenges" as they relate to the team-based activities that underpin the design of study programmes, which is further illustrated by an institutional example of one challenge – designing for better student retention and progression;

3. see how the leadership of curriculum design, at an institutional level, has been enacted within the authors' context.

We have structured our chapter in four sections. In the first section, we explain our own experiences with curriculum design and redesign processes. In the second section, we define the UK sector-wide reference point for quality in curriculum design to provide context. In section three, we provide an overview of the research and resources resulting from one of the Jisc-funded projects, highlighting how these informed the institutional approaches discussed in this chapter. In section four, we outline a sequenced recipe for enacting an institutional approach to curriculum design and translating it into practice.

Section 1: Our Experiences

We, the authors of this chapter, have a great deal of experience in leading on the totality of aspects of curriculum design as an institutional activity. In the two coming subsections, we introduce our experiences in order to enable you to better understand our position and viewpoints on curriculum design processes.

Experiences of Leading Curriculum Design: Paul

Paul began leading on curriculum design at Birmingham City University in 2008 where, as head of curriculum design and academic staff development, he was the lead academic consultant to the Redesign of the Learning Experience (RoLEx) project. This project coordinated and supported the redesign of the entire undergraduate portfolio of the University. This was followed by RoLEx 2, which delivered a similar outcome for postgraduate provision, and RoLEx 3, which had a thematic focus on assessment redesign and the embedding of employability in the curriculum. Also, from 2008, Paul devised and ran one of the institutional approaches to curriculum design projects (Technology-Supported Processes for Agile and Responsive Curricula (T-SPARC)). Following that role, Paul joined Aston University – also in Birmingham, UK – as director of learning innovation and professional practice and spent three years embedding the learning that he had taken from the Jisc-funded projects and using it to inform and enact curriculum design change across all the provision at Aston University. He has recently joined Ulster University as

Pro-Vice-Chancellor (Education) and is once again implementing the approaches he deployed at his last two institutions.

Experiences of Leading Curriculum Design: Roisín

Roisín has been an academic developer at Ulster University since 2004. In this role, she has led teams across the institution in the design and redesign of the curriculum. She advocates curriculum design that moves away from an overemphasis on specific discipline knowledge to more process models of curriculum sequencing that scaffolds the student journey and that promotes a relational-based partnership approach, active learning, peer support, and ways of thinking and practising the discipline. Roisín utilises the successful Ulster Jisc-funded Viewpoints resources (one of the 12 national projects mentioned above), which provides practitioners with a series of simple, user-friendly reflective tools that promote a creative and effective approach to the curriculum design process (Viewpoints Resources, 2013). The project tools allow teams to consider themes such as assessment and feedback, creativity in the curriculum, and learner engagement, and relate these to key points in the learning life cycle. Roisín was project lead for the Ulster team participating in the What works? Student Retention & Success Change Programme that ran between 2013 to 2016 (Thomas *et al.*, 2017). This collaborative action research project, involving 13 institutions, has further extended our knowledge of what works in relation to improving student retention and success. The evidence base from this project is informing the development of curriculum design principles at Ulster in which all programmes will align. Retention and progression – keeping students at university and ensuring that they progress successfully into their second year (and of course beyond) forms a very important metric for HE providers and should be regarded as a critical design challenge for teams planning curricula.

Section 2: The UK Context

Curriculum design does not take place in a vacuum – it is necessarily located within specific institutional (and national) contexts. Within the UK-based HE context of the authors, our account of how curriculum design becomes enacted necessarily includes some explanation of, and articulation with, UK national academic quality frameworks and structures, and the associated infrastructure through which quality is assured and enhanced. Key to this articulation with our national quality framework is to lay out the challenge of securing the engagement of academics with quality infrastructure while they are designing curricula and to so move them to a position whereby they have local "ownership" of the process and outcome of their endeavours. In short, what must be achieved is a perception by study programme development teams that curriculum design (or redesign) is an opportunity rather than just a set of jobs to do "for the university".

What are institutional approaches to curriculum design and what are the university mechanisms for enacting them? Broadly, institutional approaches to curriculum design are those university-level structures that frame, govern, and support the curriculum design activities of an institution's staff.

It is useful to describe institutional approaches to curriculum design under the headings of "policy" and "agency" – both have an influence on the degree to which study programme development teams engage with the "design principles" and "design challenges" briefly introduced above.

Policy

The root policy tool to influence the curriculum design practice of study programme development teams is the programme approval process. In the UK, before a study programme can be delivered it must be first approved by the university's Senate (the top academic committee of the university) – this activity is devolved to some form of "approval panel". The approval panel conducts a peer-review exercise – typically over a full day following thorough scrutiny of the supplied documents that describe the study programme and, crucially for the context of this chapter, the process by which the design of the study programme was enacted. By setting policy, from a senior/executive level, universities can greatly influence the activities that underpin the design of study programmes and the outcomes of that design process.

Agency

Within this chapter, we use the term "agency" to refer to the human infrastructure that empowers people to act and innovate in the service of developing effective study programmes. Such agency can be self-deliverable by encouraging staff to act and innovate on their own behalf and it can also be peer-supported whereby an institution puts in place a system of enabling staff support – often through champions, or staff development personnel.

The Quality Code

UK HE providers have a definitive reference point for the operation of HE provision at the study programme and institutional level, namely the Quality Code (QAA, 2015). Each part and chapter of the Quality Code has been developed by the Quality Assurance Agency (QAA) through an extensive process of consultation with all relevant stakeholders. The Quality Code is arranged into three parts:

+ Part A: covering the setting and maintaining of academic standards;

+ Part B: covering the assurance and enhancement of academic quality;

+ Part C: covering the publishing of information about HE provision to prospective students.

Elements of Part A of this reference point are shared here in order to contextualise UK curriculum design practice and to introduce some of the nomenclature, which is necessarily used within the rest of this chapter.

Part A: Setting and Maintaining Academic Standards

This now formally incorporates, *inter alia*, the following QAA publications as constituent components of this part of the Quality Code:

+ the UK national frameworks for HE qualifications (*The Framework for Higher Education Qualifications in England, Wales and Northern Ireland* and *The Framework for Qualifications of HE Institutions in*

Scotland), that set out the different qualification levels and national expectations of standards of achievement;

✦ Subject benchmark statements, which set out the nature and characteristics of degrees (generally bachelor's with honours) and the outcomes graduates are expected to achieve in specific subject areas.

The Framework for Higher Education Qualifications in England, Wales and Northern Ireland (FHEQ)

The FHEQ (QAA, 2008) defines the amount of credit (quantity of demonstrated learning) and the academic level (quality of learning/challenge). For example, an undergraduate (bachelor's degree) comprises 360 credit points – 120 credits at each of levels 4, 5, and 6, where level 4 is the first year of the degree programme and level 6 is the final year. A master's degree comprises 180 credits at level 7 (normally studied in a single year for a full-time student). Levels 1–3 relate to pre-higher education provision and level 8 relates to doctoral provision. There is flexibility to allow for a proportion of mixing of levels, but that is outside of the scope of this chapter. Traditionally, there has been an expectation that 1 credit equates to 10 learning hours, but the diversity of subject provision means that this is a guiding principle only, used as a tool to guide equivalence between similar programmes. The FHEQ provides one of the primary reference points for the specification of curricula that defines the broad structure of study programmes. This common framework for the quantity and quality of learning that must be demonstrated before an award can be given to a student. These awards are assured through a peer review process that relies on a system of external examiners at the programme (and sub-programme levels) and external assessors/auditors at the institutional level. Broadly, programme (and sub-programme level) external assurance is enacted annually, and institutional external assurance is enacted every five years.

Subject benchmark statements

These are a set of (61) descriptors, each of which gives a high-level reference point that "*defines what can be expected of a graduate in the subject, in terms of what they might know, do and understand at the end of their studies.*" (QAA, 2016:12). Each descriptor is updated periodically as necessary when the subject area changes. By way of offering an indicative example of how a subject benchmark statement is constructed, the one for *accounting* is arranged under the following headings:

+ defining principles;

+ nature and extent of accounting;

+ subject-specific knowledge and skills;

+ cognitive abilities and generic skills;

+ teaching, learning and assessment;

+ benchmark standards.

To illustrate the sort of guidance that is given, a benchmark standard within the *accountancy* subject benchmark statement is thus: "*Threshold graduates will be able to: analyse the operations of a business and perform straightforward financial analyses and projections; and demonstrate a reasonable awareness of the contexts in which accounting data and information is processed and provided within a variety of organisational environments, and the relationships with other systems providing information in organisations.*" (QAA, 2016:12).

There is no guidance in how students should be taught or assessed in order to achieve such an outcome, but the threshold standard defines the expectations of disciplinary competence. The different ways and means that study programme development teams construct curricula to address the standard are what leads to the diversity of programmes across the sector.

In addition to this national reference point for the operation of academic programmes and their design, individual institutions will introduce governing frameworks that guide curriculum design and will require that the study programmes designed by their staff reflect the institutional mission and character and are viable from a financial standpoint. Just as the Quality Code does, these additional (institutional) requirements fundamentally shape the work, and academic practice, of those staff who design curricula – and in this chapter, we try to capture some of the lived experience of enacting curriculum design within this context.

Section 3: Jisc-Funded Projects

One of the main outputs from the Jisc-funded work was the development of the Jisc Design Studio (2013) – work that generated the curriculum lifecycle model (see Figure 1), which describes the sequence of curriculum design, delivery, and redesign and acts as a developmental gateway into a set of resources that support each of the stages.

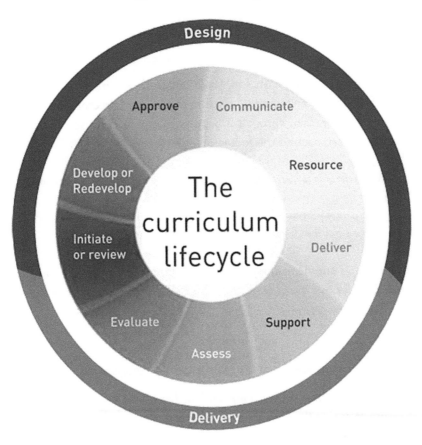

Figure 1: The curriculum lifecycle (Jisc, 2013).

Broadly, this chapter describes and comments on the *"Initiate or review"*, *"Develop or redevelop"*, and the *"Approve"* facets of the lifecycle, although the other facets are implicitly covered too. An interesting requirement of the 12 projects that ran between 2008 and 2012 was that no substantive developmental work could be done for the first year – instead, the project teams were asked to spend a year in review, ascertaining how curriculum design was enacted before considering how to try to make things better. Consequently, each of the funded project teams had to conduct a form of baseline evaluation. For the T-SPARC project (see T-SPARC project website, 2013), which took place at Birmingham City University (BCU), the research took the form of an open exploration of the lived experience (van Manen, 1990) of the way stakeholders in the curriculum design process perceived things to be.

The Lived-Experience of Curriculum Design

Accordingly, interviews with staff were undertaken with a self-selecting sample following an invitation to all programme directors and other stakeholders identified through a process mapping exercise. The interviews were based around the following question:

> *"With reference to your experiences, can you take me through an account of how the curriculum design process – from the decision point to undertake a design process all the way through to the approval event. I'd like to know what that whole workflow is like from your perspective."*

The following supplementary questions were asked to further explore themes if these did not emerge spontaneously from the conversation:

+ *"Who else gets involved in the design and approval process?"*

+ *"When do you interact with them?"*

+ *"How would you say module design fits into programme design?"*

+ *"What systems – either computer based or people based – do you make use of during the curriculum design process?"*

+ *"Who do you think are the stakeholders in the curriculum design process?"*

+ *"What are your thoughts on the documentation that course teams prepare as part of the curriculum design and programme approval process?"*

+ *"Do you have ready access to all of the information you need to undertake the process of curriculum design or to prepare for programme approval?"*

+ *"How well do you think the programme documentation you have taken to approval describes the programme and the rationale behind the design choices that have been made by the course team?"*

The results of this research are worth sharing within this chapter because the findings underpinned not only the institutional approaches to curriculum design enacted at the three UK universities which form the focus here but also led to the development of a nationally available resource "The Rough Guide to Curriculum Design (2014)" which is cited as a reference point within the Quality Code, discussed above, (QAA, 2015).

The video-based interview data generated by this work was seen by two individuals, who undertook thematic analysis directly from the video data and field notes. This analysis led the researchers (one of whom was Paul) to identify a number of themes that characterised how study programme development leads described their lived experience of designing study programmes. For the purposes of this chapter, we have categorised these themes under the headings: External versus Internal and Enabler versus Hindrance (as perceived by participants):

External	Internal
Drivers for design	Compliance
Enabler	**Hindrance**
Coordination	The availability of information
Relationships and mechanisms	Constraints
Stakeholders	Authenticity
The programme director	Specialised language
Holistic and distributed approaches	Audience
Textual representation	
Staff support	
Existing use of technology	
Time and space for design	

Table 1: External vs. internal, enabler vs. hindrance.

External

Drivers for design

Staff reported that drivers for design often originated from workplace settings, whether this was for the design of a new course or for the iteration of an existing one. There was a sense that the starting point was a consideration of the types of skills that might be required by students when they enter post-university employment:

> "What do we want the people to be able to do at the end of the day [...] it is almost like starting at the end, because that's where we want them to be, so how are we going to get them there?"

One interviewee reported that the changing tools available to academics, particularly e-learning tools, may offer new opportunities that could only be fully exploited with a wholesale change in curriculum design:

> "A new delivery mechanism can change a design totally [...] so new technologies in particular can drive the design process."

Another interviewee described how the success of a particular programme may lead to the development of a related course that might address the needs of the emergent market:

> "We were having 400 applications for Music Tech and 30 places and it seemed silly to be turning these students away, so we thought – how can we deliver something that appeals to students who are applying to that but also has its own unique identity."

There was a sense that programme design need not be confined to those opportunities afforded by periodic review; rather, programme design should be seen as an ongoing iterative process. Some interviewees indicated that they utilised the University's minor change mechanism to effectively do just that:

"We would make the most of the minor changes programme, so for me rather than having a course approval and running that course, it was a course approval where we'd already started to plan out how we were going to use the minor changes programme to develop the course further."

Others began to speculate what a future idealised process of curriculum design and approval might look like:

"I would like to see in the future, perhaps the annual review process, being used as a regular mechanism for making, if you like, continual improvements and enhancements to the programme."

Internal

Compliance

Staff at the University were well-versed in what was required of them in terms of documentation at the point of approval, and for the most part they were effective in meeting that expectation. Where this could be problematic was when the documentation itself became the focus of their work rather than the programme design; in such cases, it was felt that a context of tight adherence to documentary requirements might not create the best environment to support innovation in curriculum design:

"We have very clear guidance about what's required in terms of documentation."

"People always wish to be told what is it I have to do to comply with the documentary requirements."

"Because you have a template you have to follow; that, in some way, stifles creativity."

"I do think there is a tendency for people to use tried and tested methods to comply."

Enabler

Coordination

The primary method of coordinating programme design activity often revolved around an initial "away day" event for the programme team. This event was used to identify the "job to be done", to explore and discuss programme philosophy, and to begin the process of sharing the workload. Ongoing coordination was felt to be most effective if done on a face-to-face basis:

> *"You've got to get a lot of the unfinished business and a lot of the baggage out of the way, so you've got to let people have their say [...] before you can move them on."*

> *"If you've got 12 or 14 people, there'll be 12 or 14 different versions of what they think the ideal structure is."*

> *"I do have meetings with the course team, talk to them about what I would like to do. We're a very close team."*

> *"Having people in a room, sitting them down with a piece of paper, was when the decisions got made."*

Relationships vs. mechanisms

"Relationships" were seen to be far more important than effective "mechanisms" in delivering good curriculum design. Prior to making them more relevant through the life of the project, policies and defined processes were not seen to contribute significantly to the curriculum design process. Building relationships – professional and even social – with fellow academics (within a course team and across the institution), senior managers, students, and external examiners were cited as being the most important factor in "getting the job done":

> *"You tend to have people around you who have a very vested interest in the course [...] it really matters to us."*

"Sometimes, having a conversation with somebody makes it much clearer than trying to wade through formal documentation that doesn't necessarily tell you how it actually works."

"That's the way I've approached it, to ask people to use their contacts and to find out what they think, or to pass it on to somebody who they know might answer the questions that we want."

Where good relationships with stakeholders existed, it was thought to be very useful to be able to demonstrate such stakeholder "buy-in" to the curriculum design process to the approval panel.

"I think panels like to see a seamless collaboration between academics and clinicians." (When talking about a healthcare programme)

Stakeholders

Staff identified a wide range of stakeholders (see du Plessis & Piihl *et al.*, in this volume) in the curriculum design process, but there was evidence of a wide variance in the degree to which these stakeholders had the opportunity to input into the curriculum design process:

"I do think that we would benefit from having much more of a team-based approach so we would bring in the marketing staff into that team, as an equal part of that team really."

"Sometimes as academics, we are just slightly one step remote from that because we are not involved in the day-to-day developments – it's a valuable contribution that clinical colleagues, or work-based colleagues can make."

"I think we're just around industry and speaking with industry the whole time."

"Over the institution as a whole I would say that we have tended not to do enough to involve students."

The programme director

The programme director/programme director designate was thought to have a pivotal role in facilitating the curriculum design process and might act as an academic lead and/or administrative support for the rest of the course team. A number of programme directors commented that, on a spectrum running from "programme administrator" to "academic lead", they found they were often involved in administration rather than academic leadership. The programme director is often the person who effectively chooses whether a holistic or distributed approach to design will be taken:

> "*The Programme Leader has probably carried quite a substantial administrative burden and this may have, on occasions, got in the way of academic leadership.*"

> "*The Programme Director's role is to a great extent administration in terms of dealing with programme matters and students.*"

> "*The two other elements, the coordination and the admin, were the bits that you concentrated on the most [...] the academic side of it came third.*"

> "*It feels like more of an administrative role.*"

Holistic and distributed approaches to design

By "holistic" we mean a design approach where the entire programme team have input into the entire programme. By "distributed" we mean a design approach where there is early disaggregation of the programme into modules, which are then designed largely by individuals and then re-collated as a programme at a later stage. Despite this being the most common mode of design, interviewees felt that distributed models were less effective in designing the best possible programmes.

The programme director/programme director designate is very often the person who is empowered to decide whether the programme design process will be "holistic" or "distributed"; they are also the person identified as having responsibility for trying to make a coherent programme from the draft module designs:

"I think there has been a tendency for the team to be convened and then to split up much too early in the process, with people told to go away and design their modules on such-'n-such."

"They will do their own module and it's seen in some isolation, not complete isolation, but some isolation."

"Here, I think what goes on is somebody picks up responsibility for let's say a module and then they give it to a course director who sorts out the document [...] and then there is a preparation meeting before the validation panel, then the validation panel [...] and that's it and then it's taught."

"In the early 90s, modularisation was introduced and seems to me to have led to some of that course team approach being lost – I don't think it necessarily should have led to that [...] I actually think it is modularisation implemented poorly which, rather than modularisation per se, causes that."

Textual representation

Interviewees welcomed the idea of being able to supplement the representation of their programmes at the point of approval with multimedia elements. They were also interested in the potential use of an e-portfolio application for this purpose; particularly its ability to support the reconfiguration of the content for a range of different stakeholder groups. This approach was also thought to offer enhanced opportunities for staff to reflect on their own teaching practice:

"It's so much more powerful to show that sort of evidence to a panel than a few academic words where there'll be some insane debate about whether or not we have 'observation' or 'reflective observation', or 'analysis or 'critical analysis'; and a lengthy twenty-minute academic discussion that has no impact on what follows after they've changed the wordage."

In the final version of the new process that was developed at BCU, we used a single technology for all facets of the curriculum design and approval process. Thus, the evidence shared with those conferring approval was appended to documents and discussions on a bespoke version of Micro-soft SharePoint.

> "*When you sit through the formal review meetings [...] most of those questions tend to come about because of a failure to grasp what we've actually put in the formal documentation.*"

> "*If you can see real examples of those students in practice, doing an assignment, working on project – that's going to be so much more powerful to you because you can see behind the words.*"

> "*I think not only would it convey things it would catalyse things; so in other words – seeing ourselves, seeing what we're doing would make us think harder about what we are really doing in the classroom or wherever it happens to be.*"

> "*When a student thumbs through those paper-based module templates, do you think they really get excited by what they read? [...] but to see a Mahara 'view' of previous students doing things, perhaps tutors giving quality feedback and those sorts of processes – it'll just come alive!*"

What comes out of these data is a clear sense of awareness that those who are conferring approval upon programmes and those who will study them (students) are valid stakeholders in the curriculum design process and that we should construct artefacts that make sense to these audiences too.

Staff support

Staff support has been available to staff in a variety of forms at BCU (and later at Aston too), including the provision of accredited master-level modules to support curriculum design (see Hayes, in this volume).

> "*We sent out questionnaires to all of the academic staff in all of the faculties and asked them what they needed to be able to do their job as course directors, to handle course validations [...] and then we decided to design two new Masters modules based on that information from staff – and those two modules were 'Designing Academic Programmes in H. E.' and 'Enhancing the Quality of Academic Programmes in H. E.'*"

As a consequence of needs identified through this work, Paul led the development of a new MEd programme – MEd Learning and Teaching in Higher Education – comprising thirteen 30-credit modules for staff to choose from. The response to this need for development has cascaded from Paul's immersion in staff's "lived experience" of curriculum design.

Existing use of technology

Some basic electronic systems such as shared drives and e-mail were already being used to facilitate team conversations and collaborative work, and other technologies such as Google Docs and Moodle (BCU's virtual learning environment) had also been tried to facilitate collaboration, but the need for more effective mechanisms that could better embrace the need to involve a wider group of stakeholders was recognised.

Although version control of definitive documentation wasn't seen as a particular problem, this was only the case because the programme director/programme director designate took responsibility for administrating and collating their own definitive archive. It was acknowledged that although this worked, it was inefficient and restricted what might be achievable if collaborative approaches to curriculum design were better supported.

"The use of shared drives is fairly extensive now [...] that's basically to ensure that all of the documents are in one place and that staff can access them easily."

"A lot of it was done by email [...] we didn't really use any other sort of technology."

"I've used Moodle forums this time [...] so that everybody could look at the material and comment on them [...] but unfortunately not many people used the Moodle site and we ended up having a meeting."

"'Track changes' in Microsoft Word is probably the most common way of doing these things [...] we use the Google system a bit."

There was some highlighting of the potential difficulties that can be encountered when trying to collaborate electronically with those in other (external) settings – particularly the health service, where there are very non-porous firewalls.

> "There are massive problems getting access to servers through the Health Service."

The institution also had a track record in developing innovative technology-based solutions for supporting staff as they engage in curriculum design.

> "Module Designer [...] it was a pedagogic planning tool, there was a lot of help and support which is obviously still there now [...] it was quite a rigorous and robust planning tool."

Module Designer was repurposed, with elements of the content being made available through the new curriculum design system that was built to support the new processes. Curriculum management systems (CMS) remain a critical resource to facilitate curriculum design. All three universities have (different) versions of such systems and each are thought to be cumbersome to staff. An effective CMS should be able to host all documentation as it relates to any and all programmes; furthermore, it should be used as a pedagogic planning tool rather than just as a repository for that which has been designed. Accordingly, effectiveness cascades from the extent to which it supports collaboration and manages workflow. Precise specifications for CMSs are beyond the scope of this chapter, but it suffices to say that at the time of writing, in 2017, there is still much work to do across the sector in this area.

Time and space for design

Allowing for and creating effective opportunities for staff to have wide-ranging discussions in relation to curriculum design was deemed an important factor if staff are to take a holistic approach to curriculum design.

> "Staff are under a lot of pressure with their workloads as it is, which makes it exceedingly difficult to get everybody together to spend sufficient time thinking things through."

However, it is possible to rapidly develop programmes and launch them within very short time frames; a capacity to be able to do this on a more routine basis is likely to become more important as universities seek to become more responsive to the needs of their stakeholders.

> *"The very first meeting [...] for this project was on the 30th of October [...] and we were approved and up and running by January."*

Hindrance

The availability of information

Although staff found it quite straightforward to access templates for their documentation, access to other information that might be useful when undertaking curriculum design (progression statistics, external examiners reports, module and programme evaluations, etc.) required a good deal of work to track down.

> *"It's relatively easy to get access to templates [...] it's relatively easy to get access to regulations as well."*

> *"It was certainly very hard to find and it wasn't in one particular place."*

> *"When you are expected to produce a document within quite a short space of time, it's quite problematic having to go around accessing lots of different people and get the information from a number of different sources."*

> *"So, some information that is readily available would be excellent."*

Some staff highlighted the importance of having access to good market analysis information, and one participant (not captured on video) emphasised the need for market information to be made available through a dialogue with marketing staff rather than through access to a one-way information source:

> *"They are requested to perform some market research which would then validate that the idea would be intellectually plausible to a stakeholder*

group and would be commercially viable."

"Some sort of service whereby sense is made of that market information for the academic staff [...] that would be really useful."

Constraints

Many of the programmes at BCU lead to awards that lead to registration with a professional statutory and regulatory body (PSRB). These PSRBs lay down requirements in the form of stated competencies or learning outcomes that form the basis of the design for programmes that seek to offer a route to professional registration:

"In the case of healthcare programmes, they're largely dictated to by the statutory and professional bodies – in terms of what the content should be."

"We're very much tied in with what's required by the professional bodies."

However, it is recognised that the constraints (see Branch & Hartge, in this volume) placed upon designers of programmes by PSRBs should not lead to a situation whereby the "professional agenda" eclipses the responsibility of staff to develop the most effective and engaging programmes:

"If you see yourself as an educator who is helping someone to develop into a practitioner at the end of the day, you might have a more flexible approach to the way that occurs."

Authenticity

The programme documentation was thought to be somewhat inauthentic by most interviewees. They felt that much of the essence of the design choices the team had made and "what it is the students would be doing" on a daily basis was lost within the formal documentation they prepared for the approval panel (their perceived primary audience). However, two interviewees of the seventeen interviewed felt that efforts to try to "capture" the programme in formal documentation allowed for further clarification of thought and ideas:

"Especially with a brand new course that nobody has ever written before, that's never been done before and never been delivered in that way, we could only write down what we thought it was going to be."

"Those documents barely mention what students actually do."

"It's that translation into reality that's the important element."

"Without the padded-out detail, the students would find looking at a module specification almost meaningless in terms of what is actually going to be their learning experience."

"That provides the information that's necessary in order to get an overview of what the course is about."

One respondent pointed out that formal documentation for approval is normally collated or written by a single individual and as such the document becomes framed by their agency:

"It will be my words which will go into that document – which I hope will represent the views of everybody that has had input into it, but if I have a particular phraseology, it will be apparent in the documentation."

Specialised language

Academic language used throughout the curriculum design and programme approval process can limit the effectiveness of employer engagement in this process. This is thought to be especially important since the scoping of the employment "requirements" of a graduate is frequently the first stage in the design process:

"I do think there is a way that we phrase things within the University which requires translation for anybody that's not used to H.E."

"When you're trying to write it in very academic language as well that doesn't necessarily equate to exactly what was said, especially when you are dealing with external people and stakeholders."

Audience

It was felt that the primary audience for programme documentation was the approval panel. Although there was an understanding that programme documentation had a number of audiences (in theory), the crucial nature of satisfying the approval panel meant that documentation was written (almost exclusively) with that audience in mind. This meant that the utility of the documentation for other stakeholders was thought to be lower than it might be. There was a sense that programme documentation was "for the University" rather than for the course team, students, or employers:

> "Historically what has happened in design has been principally governed by deadlines, compliance with process and the set piece occasion is the Approval Panel."

> "Approval is about preparing your documentation."

> "The real design work takes place after the validation."

Additionally, some doubt was raised as to whether the approval panel actually offers scrutiny of the "right things" or offers an opportunity for discussion of things of interest and importance to the programme team:

> "That's the important part that doesn't get spoken about."

> "When it gets to the Validation Panel [...] it appears not to be worthy of any discussion."

Comments that emerged from this theme planted the seed for the most transformational change to the curriculum design and approval processes. At the centre of the project was an infrastructure that sought to support the activity of design and not just the preparation of documentation for the purpose of securing approval.

Section 4: Supporting Two Conceptions of Curriculum Design at Institutional Level

The analysis of the interview data presented above was just a starting point, but much was learnt about the "lived experience" of curriculum design. The outcome of the work allowed for a number of aspirations for institutional approaches to curriculum design approval to be formed; namely, there was a need to:

+ encourage innovation;

+ de-prioritise the production of documentation as the primary curriculum design activity;

+ provide more opportunities for stakeholder engagement;

+ provide better opportunities for influential stakeholder engagement;

+ offer a formative, rather than summative, approach to programme approval;

+ ensure single data entry points where possible (i.e., no duplication);

+ do a better job in relation to version control of documents;

+ provide pedagogic and regulatory support for each stage of the curriculum design process;

+ provide greater transparency between module design and a deconstruction of the silos that can characterise programme design when done by multiple designers.

A full description is outside the scope of this chapter, but a new institutional process and a new technical system were developed according to the needs that were articulated by our stakeholders. These new approaches were enacted at Birmingham City University and have subsequently been enacted at Aston University too. Implementation at Ulster University has just begun.

Curriculum Design as a Constructed Product

As represented in the lived-experience research shared above, there are a set of documents that study programme design teams need to produce before their programmes can be approved for delivery; and although the authors, through their work, have tried to ensure that staff conceive design as an activity that goes beyond the mere production of these documents, there are still some documents to produce. They are:

1. Programme specification;

2. Module specifications;

3. A curriculum map;

4. Student handbook;

5. Assessment briefing documents;

6. Assessment criteria for non-invigilated assessments.

The degree of ubiquity across UK institutions decreases going down the list; in other words, all programmes will have programme specifications, almost all will have module specifications, most will have a curriculum map and a student handbook, but the assessment-facing documents represent additional artefacts to present at the point of approval, and these characterise part of the work the authors have been doing to shape curriculum design processes.

Programme specifications are the formal textual representation of a programme. Primarily, they comprise the name of the programme, the qualification level, the programme duration, the location of study, and the amount of credit awarded. They also describe the aims of the programme, the intended programme-level learning outcomes, and the modules a student must study and pass to achieve the award. Module specifications do a similar job at module level and also offer a summary of how the module is assessed. Curriculum maps are normally in the form of a matrix that show which of the programme level learning outcomes are delivered through which modules. A student handbook includes the above documents with some student-facing narrative to contextualise what can be quite technical documents.

The requirement to submit the assessment briefing and criteria documents for all non-invigilated assessments at the point of approval is an innovation that Paul had enacted at Aston University and is now being enacted at Ulster University. It may seem that this relates to curriculum design as a constructed product – as it leads to the development of an artefact – but the intention behind the requirement is to shape design *process*. To explain this, it is worth reviewing the well-known curriculum design model of "constructive alignment" (Biggs & Tang, 2011) – the alignment part especially. Herein is an easily understood premise that what we teach, how we assess it, and how/what students learn should be connected. However, there is more than one way to enact curriculum alignment, and sequence is critical. Below, we contrast two approaches:

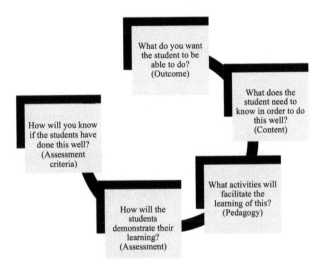

Figure 2: Tutor-centric approach.

As can be seen above in Figure 2, the design approach is to start the module design sequence with considering the intended learning outcomes for the student, and then consider the content we should teach in order for them to learn the "right" things. Then, we consider how we should assess those things, and finally what we will give marks/a high grade for. On the surface, this seems fine, but we would contend this is highly tutor-centric and defines learning as a sequence of events that sees students receiving instruction and then being tested on how well they have received such instruction. There is another way:

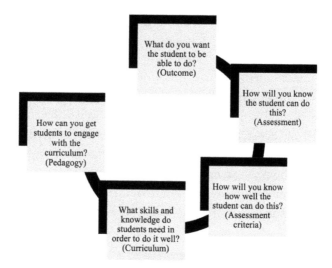

Figure 3: Student-centric approach.

Here, the assessment is designed directly from the learning outcomes, along with the assessment criteria – in this context, the module designer has to decide "what good learning looks like", and through that process it is our experience that they will iterate the learning outcomes until they reflect the learning that the teacher truly expects a successful student should achieve. From this point, what is to be taught and how it is taught cascades from a concretised sense of "what good looks like", and the delivered curriculum will support the student to achieve the very success that has been precisely codified within the assessment criteria.

Since our wish has been to shape curriculum design so that teachers make these considerations early in the design sequence (O'Neill *et al.*, 2014), we require the assessment documents at the point of approval – in that way, it is impossible for assessments to be designed in a post-hoc way "on the back" of teaching.

This principle of using the point of approval to shape the design activity that teachers must do prior to the point of approval has been a crucial consideration in enacting the institutional approaches to curriculum design that we report in this chapter. Additional to the requirements around the supply of assessment documents, the curriculum design guidelines (to be verified at the point of approval) that have been enacted at Aston University and now at Ulster University are:

+ Modules should normally be no smaller than 20 credits in size;

+ A module should not normally have more than four intended learning outcomes;

+ A module should not normally have more than two items of assessment;

+ An assessment should not normally exceed 2000 words (or equivalent) per 10 credits.

These design guidelines are offered as something between a recommended reference point and a requirement. Any study programme design team that wishes to deviate from these need only have their rationale accepted by their peers at the point of approval. The purpose of the design guidelines has been to bear down on over-assessment, thus enhancing the learning experiences of students and improving the working lives of staff.

Curriculum Design as Academic Practice

As the lived-experience research described earlier in this chapter demonstrates, study programme design teams tend to regard "the job to be done" as one of producing documents for the purposes of approval so that they can get on with the "real work of design". This is problematic and wastes the opportunities universities have to optimise provision. As a way of trying to effect better design, the curriculum design practice at the three universities covered in this chapter has been characterised by the development of a number of design challenges. These were codified into the "Rough Guide to Curriculum Design" (2014) and are similar across all three institutions – albeit at Ulster University they are only just being introduced now.

Broadly, the design challenges lay out the considerations/challenges that study programme teams should seek to engage with while they design their programme and constituent modules. The challenges can only be met by taking a team-based approach to design and through the inclusion of a wider range of stakeholders than might otherwise be the case. These stakeholders include students, employers, librarians, ICT specialists, pedagogues, and even administrative staff. The challenges put before staff are:

- ✦ Ensuring market-viability is a preliminary consideration;

- ✦ Designing and evaluating effective induction and transition into higher education;

- ✦ Design for a widening participation agenda;

- ✦ Designing for better retentions and progression;

- ✦ Designing for disability/designing an inclusive curriculum;

- ✦ Designing for stronger student engagement;

- ✦ Designing sustainability into the curriculum;

- ✦ Designing for internationalisation of the curriculum;

- ✦ Designing for the needs of international students;

- ✦ Embedding employability into the curriculum;

- ✦ Embedding employer engagement into the curriculum;

- ✦ Embedding technology-supported learning into the curriculum;

- ✦ Embedding information and digital literacy into the curriculum.

These design challenges are somewhat dynamic and will reflect the current mission of the university within which they are required, supported, and (crucially) "tested" at the point of approval. Rather than offer a comprehensive description of how each of these challenges may be supported within an institution, we offer an indicative account of just one: designing for better progression and retention.

An Exemplar of Institutional Support (Ulster University – Designing for Better Retention and Progression)

As Northern Ireland's civic university, part of our mission is widening participation in higher education. One of the Ulster's key institutional priorities is to improve student retention and success (SRS) in accordance with Ulster's vision to "transform lives, stretch minds, develop skills and raise ambitions" (Ulster University, 2016). Recognising the complexity of improving SRS and wishing to learn from and contribute to sector networks and pedagogies, Ulster applied for and was selected as one of 13 institutions involved in the Paul Hamlyn funded the *What works? Student retention and success change programme* phase 2 (WW2) which ran from 2013 to 2016 (Thomas *et al.*, 2017). To lead WW2, a cross-institutional IWISE (Institutional-Wide approach to Improving Student Engagement) team of 12 members – comprising senior staff, students' union staff, professional services, and academics from seven discipline areas – was established. The IWISE team recognised that focusing on metrics alone places students in a passive role and a "student as consumer" attitude prevails, which the team believe is an impoverished approach to 21st century higher education. Rather, the team involved students from the outset as co-owners of the challenges and issues of SRS and, importantly, as co-designers of the solutions and the enactment of change.

Aim and model of practice (MoP)

The team's overarching aim was to provide transformative, high quality learning experiences through the promotion of meaningful staff-student partnerships that engender a shared responsibility. The team's unique make-up and strategic vision to transform student experiences led to the development of the IWISE MoP to lead sustainable learning and teaching excellence through:

- a whole-institution approach to understanding retention issues, implementing and evaluating interventions, and disseminating and embedding effective evidence-based practice across Ulster and beyond;

- a process of change built on a "students as partners" ethos;

- the changing of learning and teaching culture to value and prioritise success.

Working collaboratively and innovatively

To catalyse the wider institutional roll-out of effective practices, seven discipline areas (accounting, built environment, computing, creative technologies, law, nursing (mental health), and textile art, design, and fashion), were included in WW2 representing four campuses, different pedagogical approaches, learning spaces, and attendance modes across the six faculties. Each of the seven areas incorporated staff and students representing 145 participants (see Figure 4).

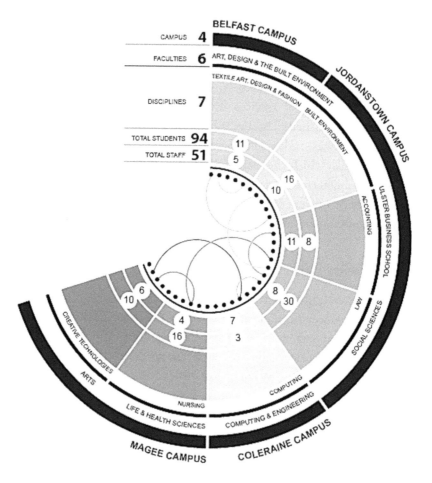

Figure 4: Breakdown of staff and students involved in the change programme.

A key enabler to embedding change involved IWISE facilitating disciplines to understand their local context and SRS challenges, informed by institutional data and research, before interventions were introduced. This allowed staff and students to take ownership, develop capacity for learning and teaching enhancement, and foster wider staff and student engagement. With seven areas, flexibility and creativity was essential, resulting in a diverse range of interventions aimed at increasing *all* students' sense of belonging, engagement, and self-confidence, including *inter alia*:

+ Pre-entry activities and longitudinal induction;

+ Induction with a social focus involving higher-level students;

+ Common themed projects involving different year groups;

+ Academic Mentor System;

+ Peer mentoring activities;

+ "Drop-in, Don't drop-out" campaign;

+ Informal industry-led projects and field trips;

+ Changes to pedagogic approaches – interactive lectures, students as producer, group projects, etc.

Using mixed-methods evaluation as part of the process of change, the IWISE team supported disciplines to undertake evaluation and use the data at local and institutional level to inform a cycle of reflective practice.

Building IWISE leadership capacity

As change was enabled, IWISE developed meaningfully as a team. Students were integral to the process of change. They contributed to the identification of issues and to the implementation and evaluation of interventions. They collated and analysed data and co-presented with staff to reach different audiences. They also acted as mentors, buddies, curriculum designers, and took on leadership roles to help other students. They developed their confidence in pursuing their studies and achieved extra-curricular awards.

This was a step-change towards a more inclusive L&T culture that valued the student voice and recognised the transformative potential of a "students as partners" ethos. Team members' confidence grew and they felt empowered to capture evidence of this impact of partnership and to use this to influence others. As well as enhancing the learning experiences of students and benefiting the wider University through the development of better infrastructure to support SRS, the initiative has supported the career development of the staff involved. Over the last four years, four members of the team have achieved an ILM (Institute of Leadership and Management) Level 5 Certificate in Leadership and Management. Eight members achieved recognition through the UKPSF (United Kingdom

Professional Standards Framework); four achieved promotions to senior posts (pro- vice chancellor, two associate deans (Department of Education), one head of school), and one member achieved their doctorate based on staff-student partnership.

Using workshops and a writing retreat, IWISE used an evidence-based approach to develop 10 case studies of effective practice that have been widely disseminated at Ulster and beyond. This collaborative, peer-supported activity has led to numerous published outputs and the team's contribution to the development of Ulster's guiding resources on how to design-in better approaches to supporting SRS.

Impact

There are a significant number of positive outcomes:

Students	Institution
<ul><li>First-year continuation rates improved</li><li>Increased levels of engagement, belonging and confidence</li><li>Increased success at first attempt</li><li>Increased internal transfers (rather than withdrawal)</li><li>More satisfied students</li><li>Enhanced employability and positive feedback from employers</li></ul>	<ul><li>Improved capacity of staff and students to work together developing enhancement literacy</li><li>Greater understanding and shared responsibility of SRS issues</li><li>Effective practice embedded in other discipline areas</li><li>Pedagogic research outputs and on-going development of curriculum design tools</li><li>Reward and recognition including higher education academy fellowships, L&T awards, and promotion</li></ul>

Table 2: Positive outcomes.

IWISE has a significant record of accomplishment and can evidence a transformative impact on student learning that continues to be sustained through their on-going efforts to lead and embed effective practice institutionally, nationally, and internationally. As such, this particular initiative demonstrates how institutions can and should "make demands" upon their staff to enhance curriculum design practice – but where such demands are made, they are more likely to lead to enhancement where human and policy support structures are put in place.

Conclusion

In conclusion, we offer a senior management perspective on leading institutional approaches to curriculum design and an academic developer's perspective on translating institutional approaches to curriculum design into practice.

I (Paul) have been leading on curriculum design at an institutional level for over 10 years. Over that time, I have formed an opinion of the sorts of things that need to be put in place to make it happen effectively. United States businessman Louis V. Gerstner Jr. is credited with saying *"People don't do what you expect but what you inspect."* There is certainly more than a kernel of truth in that statement when considering institutional approaches to curriculum design. I (Roisín) have been working closely with discipline teams since 2004, facilitating discussions, and developing capacity for new ways of thinking about curriculum design. We have experience of colleagues who are rightly protective of their academic autonomy, but there remains an institutional responsibility for universities to manage their provision and to try to give students the best learning experiences they can and staff the best working experiences they can.

As a consequence, the best way to try to lead curriculum change within an institution is to bring staff with you. There are two main ways to achieve that. Firstly, forget trying to "sell a solution" – people don't want to know. They'll regard it as just another "thing to do", something that will invade their busy lives and get in the way of their personal research and scholarship. Trying to secure "buy-in" to a solution is a waste of time. Instead, we need to get "buy-in" for problems! Academics (and other staff) need to be convinced that there is a problem, one that affects them or appeals to their altruistic natures – they need to come to feel that things need to be better and they need to come to feel that things could be better – if only they had a solution. At that point, the solution (the institutional changes project) is suggested and if the problem has been "bought", the solution will be bought too.

Secondly, the change project must be authentic in its aims and be a genuinely collaborative effort. Academics do not come "oven ready" in relation to enhancing curriculum design practice – it is a specialist academic activity, and mainstream academic staff need to be supported. Academic staff development units, academic quality staff, information specialists, and academic leaders need to be coordinated into a support effort that creates an environment whereby people feel able to make changes to the way they work, are willing to make the changes, and are allowed to make the changes. We think these circumstances have a sequenced recipe and we offer it below:

Institutional Approach	Translating into Practice
Develop an overarching narrative of what needs to change and why – keep it philosophical.	Take into account what is already happening – what is working well?
Get the overarching narrative "signed off" from the highest committees in the institution – this is your green light to start the change process.	Develop the detail with middle managers, those who lead support services and control the policy documents. Make sure they know that they have a contribution to make and they won't be disregarded going forwards.
Start planning what support for staff will be needed – policies, guidelines, toolkits, and workshops – and identify the specific staff who will be contact points to help programme teams when the time comes.	Involve staff – particularly key stakeholders involved in initiating and supporting curriculum change. Utilise existing effective resources and develop these collaboratively.
Develop the detail of what is to be achieved (i.e., write a version of the design principles and the design challenges).	Communicate, communicate, communicate. Keep all stakeholders informed at regular intervals. Invite contribution at all stages.
Write up the detail of the institutional aim and objectives for curriculum design change – design the timeframe (don't be too ambitious – it's probably a three-year time frame to finish the process).	Involve key stakeholders supporting this process (e.g., academic staff development units, academic quality staff, information specialists).

Institutional Approach	Translating into Practice
Ensure that the design principles and challenges will be "checked" at the point of approval/re-approval. Ensure there is an understanding that non-compliant programmes will not be approved unless the study programme design team can demonstrate a solid rationale as to why they have done things differently.	Provide staff development for those involved in approval/re-approval (may involve internal and external approvers). Need joined-up thinking and action to make this work.
Go back to the highest committee and get sign off on the detail.	Run a number of consultation workshops that surface the issues to be addressed – ensure the message is authentically framed around enhancing the learning experiences of students AND improving the working lives of staff.
Identify and target the "low-hanging fruit" – assessment practice will often be straightforward to address, with reductions in assessment marking loads allowing for time to be freed up for other curriculum design work.	Consult with programme teams and support staff. What principles currently inform assessment practice? How can effective practice be further developed and enhanced?
Don't try to force a timetable on people unless absolutely necessary – try to use the natural points of review. If a programme is to be reviewed/reapproved in two years' time – adopt that time frame, that's the target date by which curriculum change must be enacted.	Make the point that they will be doing curriculum change work at that point anyway and this will minimise the extra work.
Don't be afraid to bring forward the re-approval date of programmes that are not performing well, use these as redesign pilots with maximum support.	Reassure programme teams that they will not be on their own – ensure they are allocated a single point of contact for support. You may need to train some staff to become those points of support. Genuinely support study programme teams' needs to deviate from the design principles where appropriate and make it absolutely clear they will be supported where appropriate – professional body requirements for programmes are a case in point.

Table 3: Translating into practice.

If you can achieve those things, our experience is that institutional change of curriculum design can be enacted. It is not very fast – I (Paul) had to do it in a single year before, but that leads to tokenism, and I would not recommend that. Looking at the list above, it may seem like an insurmountable amount of work, but it is about utilising ongoing activity, building capacity, and empowering staff to lead change.

Is it worth the effort? Yes, we believe it is – the universities where the change project has been enacted have seen gains in student satisfaction and retention and progression over the period. These outcomes preserve income from fees and bolster the reputation of the university through student success. And, done with the blessing of the university staff and faculty, it leads to greater work satisfaction.

About the Authors

Professor Paul Bartholomew is Pro-Vice-Chancellor (Education) at Ulster University. He can be contacted at this e-mail: paul.bartholomew@ulster.ac.uk

Dr Roisín Curran is a professional development manager at Ulster University. She can be contacted at this e-mail: r.curran@ulster.ac.uk

Bibliography

Biggs, J. & C. Tang (2011). *Teaching for Quality Learning at University: What the Student Does*, 4th ed. Maidenhead: Open University Press.

Blackmore, P. & C. B. Kandiko (2012). People and Change: Academic Work and Leadership. In P. Blackmore & C. B. Kandiko (Eds.), *Strategic Curriculum Change: Global trends in universities*, Oxon: Routledge, pp. 128–144.

Jisc The Design Studio (2013). Online resource: http://jiscdesignstudio. pbworks.com/w/page/12458422/Welcome%20to%20the%20Design%20 Studio [Accessed on 31 May 2017].

O'Neill, G.; R. Donnelly & M. Fitzmaurice (2014). Supporting programme teams to develop sequencing in higher education curricula, *International Journal for Academic Development*, Vol.19, No.4, pp. 268–280.

QAA (2008). Frameworks for Higher Education Qualifications in England Wales and Northern Ireland. Online resource: http://www.qaa.ac.uk/

publications/information-and-guidance/publication?PubID=2718#. WTFMcxSG87Y [Accessed on 20 May 2017].

QAA (2015). The Quality Code: A Brief Guide. Online resource: http://www.qaa. ac.uk/publications/information-and-guidance/publication?PubID=180#. WTFQIRSG87Y [Accessed on 20 May 2017].

QAA (2016). Subject Benchmark Statement: Accounting. Online resource: http://www.qaa.ac.uk/publications/information-and-guidance/ publication?PubID=3042#.WTFPKxSG87Y [Accessed on 20 May 2017].

QAA (various dates). Subject Benchmark Statements. Online resource: http:// www.qaa.ac.uk/assuring-standards-and-quality/the-quality-code/subject-benchmark-statements [Accessed on 20 May 2017].

T-SPARC project website (2013). Online resource: http://jiscdesignstudio. pbworks.com/w/page/36560187/T-SPARC%20Project [Accessed on 31 May 2017].

The Rough Guide to Curriculum Design (2014). Online resource: http:// jiscdesignstudio.pbworks.com/w/file/77961863/The%20Rough%20 Guide%20to%20Curriculum%20Design%20-%20Generic%20Sector%20 Version%20March%202014.pdf [Accessed on 31 May 2017].

Thomas, L.; M. Hill; J. O'Mahony & M. Yorke (2017). *Supporting student success: strategies for institutional change What Works? Student Retention & Success programme Final Report.* https://www.heacademy.ac.uk/system/files/hub/ download/what_works_2_-_full_report.pdf [Accessed on 31 May 2017].

Ulster University (2016). *Five & fifty: five year strategic plan fiftieth year strategic vision (2016–2034).* https://www.ulster.ac.uk/fiveandfifty [Accessed on 3 October 2016].

van Manen, M. (1990). *Researching the lived experience: human science for an action sensitive pedagogy.* New York: State University of New York Press.

Viewpoints Resources (2013). Curriculum Design Workshop Resources. Online resource: http://wiki.ulster.ac.uk/display/VPR/Home [Accessed on 20 May 2017].

Chapter 3

From a Teaching-Centred to a Learning-Centred Approach to Curriculum Design: Transforming Teacher Candidates

Gülbahar Yılmaz & Sevilay Bulut

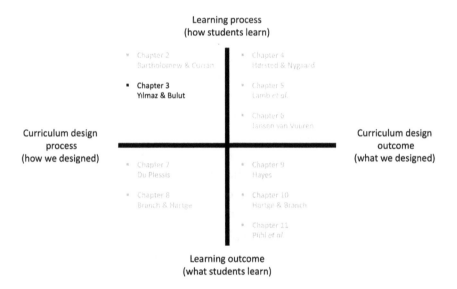

Learning process
(how students learn)

- Chapter 2
  Bartholomew & Curran

- **Chapter 3
  Yılmaz & Bulut**

- Chapter 4
  Hørsted & Nygaard

- Chapter 5
  Lamb et al.

- Chapter 6
  Jansen van Vuuren

Curriculum design
process
(how we designed)

Curriculum design
outcome
(what we designed)

- Chapter 7
  Du Plessis

- Chapter 8
  Branch & Hartge

- Chapter 9
  Hayes

- Chapter 10
  Hartge & Branch

- Chapter 11
  Pühl et al.

Learning outcome
(what students learn)

Introduction

We contribute to this book *Learning-Centred Curriculum Design in Higher Education* by showing how we have designed the learning-centred under-graduate course *"Turkish Grammar: Sentence and Text"* which is offered as a part of the Teacher Education Programme at Ankara University in Turkey. In our case – as we teach at a Teacher Education Programme – students are teacher candidates. They study to become teachers with a professional university degree. We define the learning-centred curriculum as a process rather than a product. By this we mean a curriculum where students' learning process is central to the teaching and learning activities, which enables students to decide what to learn and how to learn, besides reconstructing their personal understandings of their field of study as well as their own personal life based on real-life situations. Our definition is inspired by the thoughts of Dewey (1934:12) as he signified that *"education is not preparation for life, education is life itself."* Therefore, we argue, curriculum should focus on the students' learning needs and their real-life situations so as not to separate the students' life at university from life outside university – the life as a student and the life as a citizen, so to speak, are not to be seen as separated. Being learning-centred also means that the curriculum focusses on *learning* rather than the *subject*. In this sense, a learning-centred curriculum further opens up the opportunity for students to shape their own learning experiences (Brown, 2003). In relation to the central model of the book, we position our chapter in section one – Curriculum Design Process/Learning Process – as we outline the curriculum design process itself while at the same time we focus on the learning process of the student's following our course. Throughout our chapter, we adopt Dewey's (1934:12) words *"education is not preparation for life, education is life itself"* and make them our philosophical stand. In the chapter we, therefore, mainly focus on how faculty can design learning-centred undergraduate courses and how students can learn from experiencing such curricula. Reading our chapter, you will gain the following:

1. insight into some of the current debates on theories of learning in the Turkish higher education context;

2. a vivid example of learning-centred curriculum design in a Teacher Education Programme;

3. an understanding of how a learning-centred undergraduate course can enhance teacher candidates' professional preparation.

We have structured our chapter in three main sections. In the first section, we define the significance of learning-centred curriculum design, and we present the theories of learning widely accepted in the Turkish higher education context. In section two, we explain the development, implementation, and evaluation of the undergraduate course *"Turkish Grammar: Sentence and Text"* and its influence on teacher candidates' professional learning. Finally, in the third section, we outline our lessons learned while working with the learning-centred undergraduate course design, implementation, and evaluation. Suggestions for further improvement are presented at the end of the chapter.

Section I: Learning-Centred Curriculum Design

"The teacher is of course an artist, but being an artist does not mean that he or she can make the profile, can shape the students. What the educator does in teaching is to make it possible for the students to become themselves." (Freire, 1990:181). For us, this is a central quote for shaping our understanding of both the role of the teacher and our understanding of a learning-centred curriculum. The ontology of curriculum leads us to scrutinise the understanding of the patterns behind the logical direction of curricular ideas. In this respect, a quick look at the definitions of curriculum and philosophical underpinnings might be like pathfinders for us in this journey to the centre of the curriculum world. By and large, curriculum has been seen as the content, sequence of courses, and activities, in addition to the experiences and things that students learn during their studies. Oliva (1997:4), for example, defines curriculum as: *"What is taught in school, a set of performance objectives, everything that is planned by the school, a set of materials, a series of experiences undergone by learners in school, what an individual learner experiences as a result of schooling."* On the other hand, some assert that curriculum has as many definitions as there are textbooks on the issue (Gress & Purpel, 1978). Jackson's (1992:10) understanding of curriculum supports this idea: *"What those features mean within the present context is that there is no definition of curriculum that will endure for all time and that it is foolish to search for one, that every definition serves the interest of the person or group putting it forward, and that it is always appropriate to ask what the local consequences of adopting this or that definition might be."*

Indeed, multiple understandings of curriculum exist. Our understanding of curriculum depends on the philosophical backgrounds of the holders of viewpoints. For example, we as authors have an understanding of what we mean when we talk about curriculum, even though multiple realities on curriculum do exist. Our distinctive understanding emerges in the underlying philosophy behind the meaning we ascribe to the concept of curriculum in particular. The meaning of curriculum runs parallel with our conceptualisation of education, knowledge, and nature – in brief, our philosophy of life.

If we think that children come to this world as *blank slates*, we are likely to regard teachers as transmitters of knowledge to fill these *empty vessels* (Freire, 1996). On the other hand, if we conceptualise knowledge as interpersonally created and personally constructed by individual learners themselves, we can describe schools and universities as environments that should be full of real life learning situations. Being the most influential philosopher of the 20th century, Dewey (1934:12) signifies this mission of the schools as follows: *"education is not preparation for life, education is life itself."*

Agreeing on Jackson's idea about the impossibility of a one-size-fits-all definition of curriculum, it is time to decide what we appreciate most in curriculum and instruction, considering the local consequences of it. The philosophical stance we adopt in this chapter is based on the humanistic orientation of curriculum theory. McNeil (1977:1) describes the humanistic orientation of curriculum theory as follows: *"those with a humanistic orientation hold that the curriculum should provide personally satisfying experiences for each individual. The new humanists are self-actualisers, who see curriculum as a liberating process that can meet the need for growth and personal integrity."* We also consider the ideas of Posner (1995:11) as noteworthy when he signifies that *"we have not one but five concurrent curricula to consider"*, drawing attention to the official, the operational, the hidden, the null, and the extra curriculum. However, instead of discussing these typologies of curriculum in more detail, let us handle them throughout the chapter and move on to the next heading that will help us understand where this study stands as learning-centred curriculum from the eyes of humanistic curriculum developers.

Curriculum Design

Curriculum design is crucial for holding the primary consideration in the process of curriculum development. Whereas curriculum development is regarded as an all-involving process, curriculum design stands as the planning of how the components of curriculum are organised. Curriculum design is more varied and complex than curriculum development in determining the ways of the students' learning. By thinking about design, curriculum developers fictionalise the learning environment and place subject or learning in the centre of the educational activities. Therefore, curriculum design can become varied by curriculum developers' educational beliefs or dispositions towards how students learn. It is also diversified by what curriculum seeks to achieve at the end of the teaching and learning process. According to Ornstein & Hunkins (1998), curriculum design is covered under three headings:

1. subject-centred;

2. learner-centred;

3. experience-centred.

However, curriculum developers tend to emphasise subject or discipline-centred approaches instead of learning or experience-centred. One reason for this is the reliance on the importance of what to learn rather than how to learn. Another reason is the tendency to regard curriculum as an official, explicit, or a written document rather than an operational or implicit one.

Subject-centred curriculum design is mainly criticised for foregrounding the subject matter and putting the learning process aside. On the other hand, learning-centred curriculum design opens up an opportunity for learners to shape their learning experiences on their own (Brown, 2003). Particularly after the release of Rousseau's (1712–1778) *Émile* in the 18th century, the focus on the educational environment shifted slowly to the child and his/her learning needs. Along with Rousseau, the ideas of Dewey (1859–1952) on learning through experience and Pestalozzi (1746–1827) on child development encouraged curriculum specialists and teachers to design curriculum emphasising learning. By taking into consideration the paradigm shift towards learner-centred design, it is obvious that learner- and experience-centred curriculum design pave the way for the learning of the children and enrich the teaching and learning process. In this sense, learning-centred curriculum design aims for the attainment of the necessary learning objectives with the help of rich and authentic life situations.

This state of affair in learner-centred curriculum design is generally apparent in K–12 educational settings. However, higher education institutions are less affected from such conceptual changes related to contemporary teaching and learning theories. Most higher education institutions focus on subject-matter teaching, emphasising the need to train the experts of various disciplines. This is the same in Turkey as well as in many other parts of the world. Let us quickly summarise the teaching and learning preferences in the Turkish higher education context, which can lead us to discuss the learning-centred approach, particularly focusing on teacher education institutions.

Learning in Higher Education

Since the foundation of the Republic of Turkey in 1923, there have been significant improvements in school curricula. Particularly the first primary school curriculum of the newly founded republic – the 1924 curriculum – was completely in line with the educational ideas of progressivism and constructivism. John Dewey's visit to Turkey in 1924 influenced the school curricula by introducing such pragmatist conceptions as experiences related to children and life, autonomous learning, and democracy in education. Later curricular changes up until 1968 had the same philosophy of pragmatism and constructivism exclusively in primary school curricula. However, the required objectives and principles of the changing social structures and the necessities of that time were not reflected adequately in the school curricula, particularly after 1968 (İlhan Beyaztaş et al., 2013). Behaviourist learning theory gradually replaced constructivism and it has been the basis of Turkish school curricula since then. In 2004, however, both the result of international tests that Turkey participated in and the trends in learning theories around the world initiated an action to redefine what we understand from learning. Although the curriculum movement of 2005 was initially promoted as being "constructivist" and emphasising the cognitive process in learning, it did not take much time for research to reveal that it was not reflected in school practices in general. Although the curriculum reform movement was constructivist in principle, the practitioners were not prepared and ready to teach constructively, which was supported by numerous research studies in the literature (Bıkmaz, 2006; Akşit, 2007; ERG,

2005). Teachers were not confronted with the constructivist learning theory and learning-centred curriculum development, neither in pre-service nor in-service Teacher Education Programmes. Eventually, this rationale opened a new door for authorities to redefine and reconstruct Teacher Education Programmes in the following years.

The improvements in Teacher Education Programmes in Turkey have long been unable to go beyond the structural changes, and the teaching and learning process has been mostly left to the expertise of the teacher educators. In accordance with higher education law no. 2547, teaching and learning process is left to universities and not explained in detail. Therefore, it is hard to guide the practices of the teacher educators at higher education institutions. In this respect, Turkish higher education curriculum is thought to be less significant than primary and secondary school curricula (Yüksel, 2002). It is also stated in the literature that because teacher educators designate the teaching and learning activities in the classroom, they are influenced by the principles and thoughts of institutions, directors, and students, along with *ethos and culture* (Yüksel, 2002; Stefani, 2009). Therefore, the hidden curriculum, as Yüksel (2002) calls it, although not written and visible, becomes apparent in the peda-gogical decisions of teacher educators during the teaching and learning process. He argues that the hidden curriculum in higher education insti-tutions prevents the dissemination of independent and scientific thinking skills among students (see Hayes, in this volume). It also hinders the active participation of students in problem solving and research discus-sions, which are the basics of exemplary Teacher Education Programmes around the world. However, the Bologna process has brought concep-tual aims to Turkish higher education, emphasising a shift from teacher and content-centred teaching to a learner and learning-centred approach in the European Higher Education Area (see Branch & Hartge, in this volume). However, numerous research has been conducted on teacher education in Turkey, and they have somehow concluded that students are relatively passive in the classroom and that teacher educators are actively lecturing, even in the courses requiring practice such as teaching meth-odology, classroom management, curriculum development, etc.

Although the Teacher Education Programmes are centralised and fixed in Turkey, the teacher educators are given the flexibility and also the responsibility to organise the teaching and learning process. Therefore, it becomes significant for teacher educators to choose among teaching and learning approaches based on their understandings of learning and curriculum theory. Teacher educators' approaches towards learning and teaching have influences on teacher preparation at some significant points. Firstly, it is a widely-known fact that the way teachers approach learning affects the learning approaches of the students. In other words, learning approaches are shaped by the learners' understandings about the teaching and learning environment that they are exposed to (Fry *et al.*, 2009). For instance, teaching activities based on knowledge transfer and teacher-centred approaches cause students to prefer a surface approach to learning instead of a deep one (Trigwell *et al.*, 1999). In this respect, it is not misleading to deduce that a deep approach is likely to be preferred in learning-centred classrooms. Trigwell *et al.* (1999:67) signify this argument with their ideas as follows: *"those teachers who conceive of learning as information accumulation to meet external demands also conceive of teaching as transmitting information to students, and approach their teaching in terms of teacher-focused strategies. On the other hand, those teachers who conceive of learning as developing and changing students' conceptions, conceive of teaching in terms of helping students to develop and change their conceptions and approach their teaching in a student-focused way."*

Secondly, this assertion might be thought to be valid both in teacher education today and in the future classes of prospective teachers. Therefore, the way teacher educators approach learning and teaching will eventually affect the preferences and dispositions of teacher candidates in the near future. Following a research study conducted by Ekinci (2009) in three state universities in Turkey, it was concluded that memorisation and recall-focused teaching and learning activities were extensively used in higher education institutions in Turkey. Therefore, students typically used a strategic learning approach that was generally preferred to score higher in the tests, which led to a surface approach to learning. In short, learning is traditionally interpreted as rote learning and memorisation in higher education in Turkey. As concluded by research studies in the literature, teacher education departments are consequentially in imperilment from technocratic teacher education approaches. However, today, it is widely known that students learn best in collaboration and construct their own ideas by discussing and exchanging ideas with others in the classroom. Considering the ideas of Taylor (2013:42) about learning in higher education as the raison d'être, learning-focused activities *"should explicitly dominate all of our practices for and with students"* in higher education institutions. Barr & Tagg (1995:13) support this paradigm shift as follows: *"In its briefest form, the paradigm that has governed our colleges is this: A college is an institution that exists to provide instruction. Subtly but profoundly we are shifting to a new paradigm: A college is an institution that exists to produce learning. This shift changes everything. It is both needed and wanted .... The very purpose of the Instruction Paradigm is to offer courses. In the Learning Paradigm, on the other hand, a college's purpose is not to transfer knowledge but to create environments and experiences that bring students to discover and construct knowledge for themselves, to make students members of communities of learners that make discoveries and solve problems."*

Section 2: Designing and Implementing a Learning-Centred Undergraduate Course: "Turkish Grammar: Sentence and Text"

In this section, we will explain how we designed the learning-centred undergraduate course *"Turkish Grammar: Sentence and Text"* which is offered as a part of the Teacher Education Programme at Ankara University in Turkey. Through history of teacher education in Turkey, this course has been designed as a subject-centred course. As mentioned earlier, although teacher education curricula in Turkey are centralised and therefore fixed, there is still room for teacher educators to design a course based on their own understandings of curriculum and learning. Particularly with the adaptation to Bologna since 2003, teacher educators have been given an opportunity to design their courses, formulating learning outcomes and choosing evaluation methods. Therefore, we decided to set an example and design the *"Turkish Grammar: Sentence and Text"* course based on learning-centred curriculum design principles. Thereby, we aimed to show the importance of designing a course with learning as outcome. This is contrary to traditional subject-centred courses, where the permanent choice of subject matters has been seen as the most important mean of student learning.

Course Design Process

Forty-four teacher candidates were involved in this undergraduate course. They were sophomores in the Department of Classroom Teacher Education at Ankara University's Faculty of Educational Sciences. They participated in the *"Turkish Grammar: Sentence and Text"* undergraduate course which was organised using the principles of learning-centred curriculum design. In designing a learning-centred course, we developed a set of prevalent and essential principles. These principles of learning-centred curriculum that we employed for the course design can be seen in Figure 1:

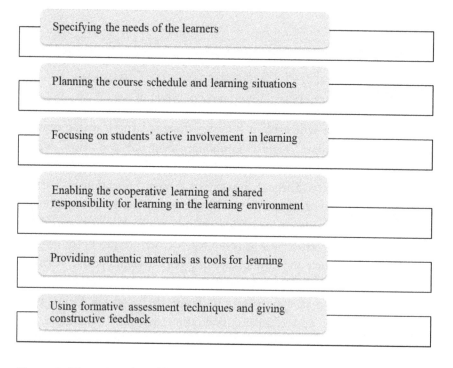

Specifying the needs of the learners

Planning the course schedule and learning situations

Focusing on students' active involvement in learning

Enabling the cooperative learning and shared responsibility for learning in the learning environment

Providing authentic materials as tools for learning

Using formative assessment techniques and giving constructive feedback

Figure 1: The principles of learning-centred curriculum design.

These design principles were both used as the steps of the course design and also as standards for the learning-centred approach in this research study. Although there exists a framework of content for the course speci-fied by the Higher Education Council, the teacher educator preferred to outline the basic content structure of the course according to the target group before specifying the learning needs of the teacher candidates. Learning modules, also referred to as content structure, were formed according to the results of a needs analysis applied during the first week of classes. Content structure was then shared with the teacher candidates and their comments and suggestions were received to finalise the course syllabus. Teacher candidates were asked to specify what they needed in the *"Turkish Grammar: Sentence and Text"* course and what else could be added to the course structure to maximise their learning experiences throughout the course process. Below are the details of the learning modules that were covered each week and a quick look at the course design.

Duration	Learning Modules	Topics	Learning Objectives
1st week	Parts of speech	Nouns, adjectives	Building awareness on topics of nouns and adjectives; Creating text-based learning-centred activities and exercises about nouns and adjectives.
2nd week	Parts of speech	Pronouns	Building awareness on topics of pronouns; Creating text-based learning-centred activities and exercises about pronouns.
3rd week	Lexical bundles	The formation of lexical bundles, types of lexical bundles	Developing awareness on how parts of speech bundle and form bigger lexical structures; Creating text-based learning-centred activities and exercises about lexical bundles.
4th week	Vocabulary	Ways for building children's vocabulary	Creating learning-based activities, exercises and games for vocabulary development of children.

Figure 2: Suggested syllabus of learning-centred undergraduate course.

The result of this needs analysis enabled authors to form the learning modules of the course, as shown in Figure 2. After specifying the learning modules, the course outline was planned, and texts that would be used in guiding teacher candidates in developing language activities were chosen among a variety of Turkish language textbooks.

Reconstruction of Knowledge and Learning Approaches

The above-mentioned Turkish language grammar topics, hereby used as the knowledge base of the course, have already been covered in various depths throughout all year groups, starting from the primary years. After the 2005 curricular reform movement in Turkey, a change in teaching Turkish was introduced: from a deductive and explicit approach to grammar teaching towards an inductive approach and implicitly learning the aspects of the language. The reason for emphasising the implicit learning of grammar was to learn the logic of grammatical structures of the mother tongue instead of teaching the grammatical rules. In this respect, the aim of this course design was to help teacher candidates to reconstruct their knowledge of Turkish language grammar and avoid rote-learning study techniques. To realise this aim, teacher candidates were expected to develop key concepts and ideas on teaching and learning, uncover the misunderstandings, and associate new knowledge with their previous learning structures. Teacher candidates were also expected to change their teaching and learning patterns from a deductive approach to grammar towards an inductive one to support the learning of their students in their future classes (see Lamb et al., in this volume).

Implementation Process

As mentioned earlier, the knowledge base of this course has already been covered in various year groups, from primary through high school education. Therefore, the authors realised that it was time to rethink and redesign the Turkish Grammar: Sentence and Text course, enabling teacher candidates to consider how to teach grammar focusing on the learning of children instead of learning the grammar rules by heart. In the implementation process of the suggested course syllabus, teacher candidates actively participated in the class discussions and created learning activities and exercises. In short, they learned both how to learn and how to teach by doing. At this stage, teacher candidates were faced with real-life learning situations. These situations were basically designing and creating learning activities and exercises with the materials and the texts in hand. In other words, they activated their competencies, skills, and creativity.

Common stages of the teaching and learning process are as follows:

1. *Sharing the text with teacher candidates:* Teacher education curriculum should support teacher candidates not only with a set of content knowledge but also the ways of how to design meaningful learning activities for their future students. In this sense, this course was a systematic effort for programme alignment between teacher education and primary school curricula in Turkey. Texts chosen for the activities were for primary school students and chosen from a variety of resources, including narratives, short stories, memoirs, essays, poems, etc. The materials were varied in order to enable teacher candidates to learn from multiple resources.

2. *Guiding teacher candidates to think about how they can benefit from texts:* Teacher candidates thought of ways to include those texts in their future classes. They answered questions such as: How could this text be used to facilitate learning nouns? How can we enable student learning via this text? What is worth learning in this text? How can we make sure that students learn it?

3. *Micro group discussions about the topic and sub-topics that could be included:* Micro groups comprised of five to six people in total. Teacher candidates worked in small groups to allow a collaborative learning environment and the active participation of all the members. They answered such questions as: What is worth teaching about this topic (e.g., nouns)? What kind of nouns should be included according to age groups? How deep should we go into that topic? What else can we use as learning material besides this literary text?

4. *Writing questions related to the text:* Questions should be prepared to develop students' higher-order thinking skills. In this course,

all groups developed at least two questions about the given text. It was required that the questions were appropriate for the developmental level of the students. Later, they shared the questions with the whole group and discussed the pros and cons of the questions. Some answers to the questions could be found directly in the text, such as: *"How much did the old man pay for the bird?"* On the other hand, some questions were appreciated as promoting thinking skills. Examples from teacher candidate answers are as follows:

+ *"Do we sufficiently understand nature?"*

+ *"Do you think that places without green areas and natural sounds can be seen as nature? (Explanation of teacher candidate: In this question, students are encouraged to think and compare the natural environments. They are also expected to develop their thinking skills by making comments and bringing new perspectives to the discussion)."*

+ *"What does 'living forest' mean?"*

+ *"What would happen if everything on earth was called the same thing?"*

5. *Creating text-based learning activities and exercises:* Teacher candidates developed learning-centred activities in relation to the learning modules specified for each week. Their learning activities were encouraged to be in parallel to the primary school curriculum implemented in Turkey. In the cases where teacher candidates developed more than one learning activity, they almost designed a lesson plan. In their lesson plans, teacher candidates used the discovery learning instead of expository teaching strategy in developing their activities. The impressions and language usage of teacher candidates gradually changed throughout the learning-centred activity design process. In the beginning, they used expressions such as: *"I teach [...], I make students write [...], I make students underline [...]".* This manner of teacher-centred expressions evolved to become collaborative language usage, such as: *"We play [...], We make it clear, we begin with the examples from real-life situations of children [...]."* This is one of the significant changes in teacher candidates'

teaching and learning understandings (see Jansen van Vuuren, in this volume).

6. *Sharing the activities and exercises with the whole group:* The previous step was followed by discussions on how the activities could enhance student learning or what changes could be employed to turn those activities into more powerful tools for learning. Each group had a rapporteur to share the group work with others. Group members' work on the same text was to create activities and exercises about the topic. Thereby, each group member was actively involved in the learning process. They discussed the pros and cons of the developed activities and exercises. During this stage, the teacher educator was gradually less directive. Teacher candidates supplied feedback to each other, which enabled them to productively learn from their peers.

7. *Filing the activities in portfolios:* They collected all the activities and products that they developed during four weeks and collected them in their portfolios.

During the implementation process, the teacher educator's responsibilities were basically to facilitate the micro group discussions and practices, uncover the possible misunderstandings, specify the common mistakes of teacher candidates, and prepare extra activities to correct those mistakes. The teacher educator was the facilitator, particularly during the micro group discussions. Teacher candidates had the chance to ask questions directly to the teacher educator about the assignment that they were involved in. Thereby, the teacher educator was helping candidates to enable learning through the teacher-student interaction and preventing the misunderstandings. In this respect, the teacher educator's role was more focused on guiding, counselling, and moderating of the teaching and learning process than instructing, lecturing, or training.

Extra activities in the implementation process: The teacher educator also aimed to contribute to the professional development of teacher candidates in general. Therefore, various journal articles, columns, and news related to global problems, innovations, and practices regarding education were shared with teacher candidates. With these small activities and discussions in the classroom, the teacher educator tried to get teacher candidates to realise how teaching was related to other fields and how global issues and trends affected it. This was believed to have a positive impact on their conceptions about teaching and learning.

The teacher educator encouraged teacher candidates to become familiar with the current and draft curriculum of the primary school. They were asked to prepare a comparative report between these two curricula. Some of the candidates made comparisons between different components of curricula such as objectives, content, teaching and learning methods, and evaluation. Moreover, the teacher educator aimed to contribute to creating awareness for the aesthetic function of language. Therefore, the teacher educator also encouraged teacher candidates to learn Turkish poems by heart and to sing them in front of the class. Teacher candidates were not evaluated for these extra activities, since the idea behind them was to support their teaching and learning conceptions to lead the way for "learning" instead of "grading" them.

Evaluation Process

The assessment data and feedback supported student learning and informed the teacher educator about the teaching and learning process. Here are some of the techniques used for formative assessment in this course:

+ *One-minute papers:* After some weeks, the teacher educator required teacher candidates to write one-minute papers in order to evaluate the effectiveness of the learning-centred course. Thereby, the teacher educator aimed to get opinions on the design and implementation processes of the course along with what could be added to and left out of the course in order to enhance student learning;

+ *Peer assessment:* Teacher candidates shared their developed activities with the whole group after micro group discussions. Each group had a rapporteur to share the group ideas and work with others. While one group rapporteur was sharing an exercise with the rest of the class, one of the teacher candidates noticed a mistake about noun/verb usage. The teacher educator encouraged her to share his/her objection with others. After discussing the issue, the mistake in the learning process was corrected. In this stage, they had the opportunity to evaluate and comment on each other's work, which enabled peer learning. This also created a less stressful atmosphere for teacher candidates, and they learned to respect each other's opinions and ways to explain their rationale for something that they developed;

+ *Portfolios:* As for the assessment of learning, teacher candidates formed their portfolio files comprised of the activities that they developed over the four weeks. The teacher educator used the portfolios as well as classroom and group contributions of the teacher candidates to evaluate their performance in this course. Therefore, it focused on formative assessment techniques to help the teacher educator to track the learning that took place from the beginning of the course. Portfolios were used to track the teacher candidates' development of learning experiences. Portfolios were effective in evaluating the process and tracking the changes in the understandings of teacher candidates. It was a motivator for teacher candidates to see their products and a reminder for the teacher educator to evaluate the teaching and learning process;

+ *Paper and pencil exam:* It was used for diagnostic purposes and designing extra learning activities for teacher candidates. Therefore, a paper and pencil exam was used to uncover the misunderstandings of teacher candidates.

Changes in the Teacher Educator's Perspective: Sevilay Bulut

I felt excited when I was asked to teach a Turkish grammar course for classroom teacher candidates approximately one and a half years ago at the university where I am working as a researcher. I was also anxious because I had not taught this course before. Later, I specified the course content by looking at the academic textbooks that were written in the field. When it was time to think about the method of instruction, I reviewed my experiences as a learner throughout my educational life and I came up with the only way of teaching that I experienced in my undergraduate school and it was "lecturing". Then I prepared for the topic that

I was presenting each week, taught the grammar topic by using the blackboard, and then walked out of the classroom. In other words, I prepared for my course just as my professors had done during my undergraduate education. At the end of the semester, I was tired of the same routine as a teacher and of the course itself. I realised that the teacher candidates were not feeling happy about the contribution of the course to their professional development. After this enlightenment process, I thought I was at the beginning of my teaching journey, and therefore I could not give up so easily. I felt that I had to find a new way out.

Upon thinking about the possible approaches that could make learning and teaching effective and enjoyable, I remembered my experiences in the course Material Development for ESL classrooms that I had studied as part of my graduate student exchange at the Institute of Education, University of London, about 3 years ago. What made me remember the things that I learned in that course was the way the teacher approached the curriculum design of the course. This curriculum design was learning-centred and required learners to be actively participating in class. Therefore, in the second year when I was asked to teach the Turkish Grammar course again, I had already decided to apply a learning-centred approach in my classroom. Unlike my previous semester, my curriculum design focused on the learning needs of the teacher candidates, and later I designed the course structure to cover their needs throughout the semester. This paradigmatic change in my teaching conception affected my practice in teaching and my understanding about students' learning and the learning process. It was valuable for me to see that this approach motivated the teacher candidates to reflect on how their own teaching and learning can be innate and student-centred. As a teacher educator, I felt close to the teacher candidates when I was involved in their small group discussions. They also started to get to know themselves as prospective teachers by rethinking their role as teachers and the students' role as learners. Towards the end of the semester, teacher candidates were able to ask questions without hesitation. In the end, I was pleased to facilitate a positive learning atmosphere in the classroom with the help of the teacher candidates. Finally, my experience as the teacher of this course provided a personal motivation for me to educate the teachers of tomorrow.

Section 3: Lessons Learned from a Learning-Centred Course Design and Suggestions for Moving Forward

The summary of the lessons learned from the design, implementation, and evaluation processes of a learning-centred undergraduate course in a higher education context in Turkey is presented below. We also present our suggestions for the further improvement of a learning-centred course design process.

Lessons Learned	Suggestions for moving forward
Learning-centred course design is tough.	Teacher candidates may be encouraged to become autonomous learners.
Learning takes time.	The teacher educator should carefully design the process, considering some internal factors.
Teaching is equal to challenging.	The teacher educator should take the role of the constant facilitator.
Evaluation takes time.	An evaluation guide or checklist may be developed for providing feedback systematically.
Similar activities may create a routine.	It could be useful to bring different materials to discuss with teacher candidates.
Teacher candidates are excited about learning how to teach.	The teacher educator should try hard to motivate all teacher candidates to be involved in productive work.

Figure 3: Lessons learned from learning-centred undergraduate course and suggestions for moving forward.

Learning-Centred Course Design is Tough

One of the problems of learning-centred course design, as specified by teacher candidates, was that they were not ready to design learning-centred activities because they thought they were lacking a knowledge base. Although Turkish language grammar had been covered since primary school, teacher candidates still had difficulties in the content area. This finding signified that teacher candidates were not actively involved in the learning process in Turkish language grammar courses during their primary and secondary, as well as high school, education. They mentioned that they learned the grammar rules by heart, since they were preparing for the national standardised tests, but they did not think of learning and applying the grammar in their daily usage. Therefore, we suggest that teacher candidates are encouraged to become self-directed learners so that they can take responsibility for their own learning. In this way, they could begin learning before arriving in the classroom and overcome their deficiencies regarding the content knowledge. Thus, teacher candidates may be much more motivated to create learning-centred activities and be creative in producing some new ideas about the topic they are studying.

Learning Takes Time

In the beginning, this course was designed to last four weeks and included more topics of grammar. However, the teacher educator realised that micro group discussions and whole group presentations lasted longer than anticipated (approximately six weeks). Therefore, the teacher educator had to slow down and allow time for teacher candidates to learn the topics deeply and develop the activities at their own speed. In short, it is concluded that learning absolutely takes time in learning-centred curriculum. This is particularly significant in that learning really takes place even if it takes time. So, teacher educators should carefully design the process considering some internal factors. Teacher educators should not move with a philosophy of *a wide inch and a mile depth* as many traditional course designs do. Rather, the philosophical stance of the teacher educator in the learning-centred design should be *less is more!* As learning takes time, we suggest that content is not so intense but is covered in depth through various learning-based activities.

Teaching is Equal to Challenging

Forty-four teacher candidates took the undergraduate course Turkish Grammar: Sentence and Text. Therefore, it was challenging to involve all the teacher candidates in class discussions and activities. Sometimes, there was so much noise that the teacher educator could hardly hear the ideas of other candidates. In addition, teacher candidates were not familiar with the learning-centred curriculum approach. Therefore, they were resistant to change in the beginning, since they obviously did not know what they were supposed to do and how they were going to accomplish the given tasks. Moreover, teacher candidates' unfamiliarity with learning to learn and learning to teach, as well as research-based learning processes, caused them to slow down in the process of teaching and learning. Teacher candidates were traditionally used to be the passive recipients of knowledge in other courses. They were used to note-taking strategies and passively listening to the lecturers. Therefore, they frequently expressed that the course was so intense that they felt tired of being involved in creative and active work. However, the teacher educator was patient enough to convince teacher candidates to learn more and gave extra time to candidates who were behind in the class. It is necessary to confess that this was sometimes hard with a total of forty-four teacher candidates.

Evaluation Takes Time

The teacher educator allocated most of her time to evaluating teacher candidates' portfolio files. As the class was crowded, it was not always possible to provide constant or regular feedback to all of the teacher candidates. Another difficulty of implying a learning-centred approach to a crowded population was that the teacher educator was feeling tired to listen and guide the teacher candidates during micro group discussions. Moreover, this process took a lot of time, since there was only one responsible teacher educator in the classroom. Therefore, it is advised that more than one teacher educator is assigned for the course or that class sizes are reduced in such courses to strengthen the implementation process of learning-centred curriculum. If it is not possible to arrange two teacher educators for a course, a more realistic and practical advice could be to develop an evaluation guide or checklist for the teacher educator to provide systematic and constant feedback to teacher candidates. To realise this, teacher educators could benefit from an e-portfolio approach and reflect on the work of teacher candidates by using the evaluation guide or checklist.

Similar Activities May Create a Routine

Teacher candidates expressed their ideas about the activities in the course. They were critical that it was becoming routinised when some of the activities, such as creating an exercise based on the text, are applied each week. Therefore, the teacher educator, as mentioned earlier in the design process, involved extra activities and brought new materials into class to discuss the educational innovations, global problems, and practices in education. It is advised to diversify the teaching and learning activities in order not to cause boredom for teacher candidates.

Teacher Candidates Are Excited About Learning How to Teach

The teacher educator realised that candidates were having fun and learning how they would create learning-centred activities in their future classes. It was visible in the one-minute papers that teacher candidates felt excited about being actively involved in the teaching process in a pre-service Teacher Education Programme. One of the teacher candidates expressed her idea as follows: *"I have never thought about how I will teach this topic. So, this course has been an important step for me to begin such a process"*. Although not all of the teacher candidates were excited about learning how to teach, the teacher educator should never give up and should try hard to motivate all teacher candidates to be involved in productive work.

Conclusion

In this chapter, we aimed to develop and implement a learning-centred undergraduate teacher education course and contribute to current debates in learning-centred curriculum design in Turkey. For this purpose, a learning-centred course titled Turkish Grammar: Sentence and Text was developed and implemented by one of the authors of this chapter. The course was expected to enhance teacher candidates' learning as they transform to become teachers. At the end of the course, teacher candidates were expected to be able to design learning-centred activities for their classes in the future. They learned and experienced how it was implemented in an educational context.

With this initiative in teacher education in Turkey, teacher candidates had the chance to experience the learning-centred curriculum design in addition to achieving the learning objectives of the course. At the end of the course, they were able to design learning-centred activities for their classes in the future as they learned and experienced how it was implemented in an educational context. Therefore, it is considered that this research can pave the way for teacher educators to redesign their courses by emphasising the learners and learning instead of merely covering certain topics and leaving the classroom without even considering if learning occurs or not. Although this research was a case of a university, it might serve as a model for teacher educators who are eager to change the way they teach in higher education institutions around the world. Particularly the section of challenges and suggestions could be like a pathfinder in designing the process in similar higher education contexts. Besides, this course design took a leading role in preparing future teachers for the profession. It is also expected to enable teacher candidates to go through permanent learning experiences that can affect their teaching in a positive manner in the future. This is eventually expected to influence teaching and learning environments and teachers' tendency to design learning-centred curriculum in the long run. Barr & Tagg (1995:14) signify this learning paradigm as having such a changing agent role in higher education institutions as follows: "*The Learning Paradigm also opens up the truly inspiring goals that each graduating class learns more than the previous graduating class. In other words, the Learning Paradigm envisions the institution itself as a learner-over time, it continuously learns how to produce more learning with each graduating class, each entering student.*"

Therefore, it is an immediate need of undergraduate teacher education classes in Turkey to have a paradigm shift from a teaching-centred to a learning-centred approach. We regard our action as a small step for the paradigmatic change in the transformation process to learning-centred Teacher Education Programmes in Turkey. Finally, this chapter is expected to enrich the international context of this anthology on learning-centred curriculum design in higher education, since it outlines a country-specific (Turkish) example of learning-centred curriculum design in a teacher education context.

About the Authors

Gülbahar Yılmaz is a research assistant and PhD candidate at the Department of Curriculum and Instruction, Ankara University, Turkey. She can be contacted at this e-mail: gulbaharryilmaz@gmail.com

Sevilay Bulut is a research assistant and PhD candidate at the Department of Turkish Language Education, Ankara University, Turkey. She can be contacted at this e-mail: bulut1087@gmail.com

Bibliography

Akşit, N. (2007). Educational Reform in Turkey. *International Journal of Educational Development,* Vol. 27, No. 1, pp. 129–137.

Barr, R. B. & J. Tagg. (1995). From Teaching to Learning-A New Paradigm for Undergraduate Education. *Change,* Vol. 27, No. 6, pp. 13–30.

Bıkmaz, F. (2006). Yeni İlköğretim Programları ve Öğretmenler [New Elementary Curricula and Teachers]. *Ankara University Journal of Faculty of Educational Sciences,* Vol. 39, No. 1, pp. 97–116.

Brown, K. L. (2003). From Teacher-centered to Learner-centered Curriculum: Improving Learning in Diverse Classrooms. *Education,* Vol. 124, No. 1, pp. 49–54.

Dewey, J. (1934). *Art as Experience.* New York: Putnam.

Ekinci, N. (2009). Üniversite Öğrencilerinin Öğrenme Yaklaşımları [Learning Approaches of University Students]. *Eğitim ve Bilim,* Vol. 34, No.151, pp. 74–88.

ERG (2005). *Yeni öğretim programlarını inceleme ve değerlendirme raporu* [Report on analysing and evaluating the new curriculum]. Eğitim Reformu Girişimi. Sabancı Üniversitesi, Istanbul.

Ornstein, A. C. & F. P. Hunkins. (1998). *Curriculum: Foundations, principles, and issues.* Massachusetts: Allyn & Bacon.

Freire, P. (1996). *Pedagogy of the oppressed (revised).* New York: Continuum.

Fry, H.; S. Ketteridge & S. Marshall (2009). Understanding Student Learning. In H. Fry; S. Ketteridge & S. Marshall (Eds.), *A Handbook for Teaching and Learning in Higher Education: Enhancing Academic Practice.* Routledge, pp. 8–26.

Gress, J. R. & D. E. Purpel (1978). *Curriculum: An introduction to the field.* CA: McCutchan Publishing Corporation.

İlhan Beyaztaş, D.; S. B. Kaptı & N. Senemoğlu (2013). Cumhuriyetten Günümüze İlkokul/İlköğretim Programlarının İncelenmesi [An Analysis of Elementary School Curricula since the Foundation of Republic of Turkey]. *Ankara University Journal of the Faculty of Educational Sciences*, Vol. 46, No. 2, pp. 319–344.

Jackson, P. W. (1992). Conceptions of Curriculum and Curriculum Specialists. In P. W. Jackson (Ed.), *Handbook of Research on Curriculum: A Project of the American Educational Research Association, Part 1*. Macmillan: New York.

McNeil, J. D. (1977). *Curriculum: A comprehensive introduction*. Boston: Little, Brown & Company.

Oliva, P. (1997). *Developing the curriculum*. 4th edition. Longman, pp. 2–40.

Posner, G. G. (1995). *Analyzing the Curriculum*. Second Edition. McGraw-Hill.

Stefani, L. (2009). Planning Teaching and Learning. Curriculum Design and Development. In H. Fry; S. Ketteridge & S. Marshall. (Eds.), *A Handbook for Teaching and Learning in Higher Education: Enhancing Academic Practice*. Routledge, pp. 40–57.

Taylor, J. (2013). What is Student-centredness and is it Enough? *The International Journal of the First Year in Higher Education*, Vol. 4, No. 2, pp. 39–48.

Trigwell, K.; M. Prosser & F. Waterhouse (1999). Relations Between Teachers' Approaches to Teaching and Students' Approaches to Learning. *Higher Education*, Vol. 37, pp. 57–70.

Yüksel, S. (2002). Yükseköğretimde Eğitim-Öğretim Faaliyetleri ve Örtük Program [Teaching and Learning Activities in Higher Education and Hidden Curriculum]. *Uludağ University Journal of the Faculty of Education*, Vol. 15, No. 1, pp. 361–370.

Section 2: Learning process/Curriculum design outcome

Chapter 4

How to design a curriculum for student learning

Anne Hørsted & Claus Nygaard

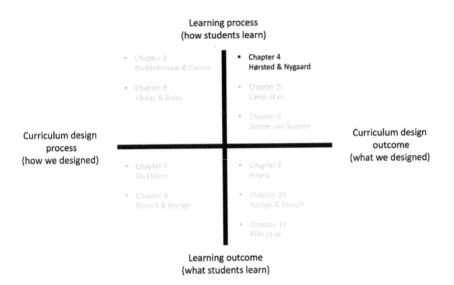

Learning process
(how students learn)

- Chapter 2
  Bartholomew & Curran

- Chapter 3
  Yilmaz & Bulut

Curriculum design
process
(how we designed)

- Chapter 7
  Du Plessis

- Chapter 8
  Branch & Hartge

- Chapter 4
  Hørsted & Nygaard

- Chapter 5
  Lamb et al.

- Chapter 6
  Jansen van Vuuren

Curriculum design
outcome
(what we designed)

- Chapter 9
  Hayes

- Chapter 10
  Hartge & Branch

- Chapter 11
  Pihl et al.

Learning outcome
(what students learn)

Introduction

With our chapter, we contribute to this book *Learning-Centred Curriculum Design in Higher Education*, as we present three examples of curriculum design, which – in our belief – clearly shows how it is possible to inspire and engage students through a well-designed learning-centred curriculum, which enhances students' learning outcomes. The first example is a full semester bachelor course in business economics designed to have students develop a basic understanding of business economy. The second example is an intensive 10-week course (Camp Future) designed to help unemployed university graduates develop an entrepreneurial mindset that will help them land their next job. The third example is a 2-year vocational postgraduate education program designed to improve the leadership skills of 30 top managers in a private company. In relation to the central model of the book, we position our chapter in section two – Learning Process/Curriculum Design Output – because our focus is first and foremost on how students learn. Secondly, we discuss – and show – how curriculum may be designed, when students learn the way they do. Reading this chapter, you should gain at least three insights:

1. the differences between two approaches to curriculum: content stream and process stream;

2. familiarise yourself with a 4-step model for curriculum design centering student learning;

3. insight into three different types of curriculum and how they have been designed to inprove student learning.

Our chapter has two main sections. In section one, we discuss the concept of a learning-centred curriculum. What do we mean by it? And what is to learn from curriculum design theory? In section two, we present the three examples of learning-centred curriculum design.

Section I: Learning-centred Curriculum Design

We open this first main section of our chapter by defining what we mean by learning-centred curriculum design. We do so by presenting a working definition of learning, and we discuss how that definition may have implications for our work with curriculum design. Second, we suggest a model of curriculum design, which presents four interrelated aspects, which are important to consider when working with learning-centred curriculum design. In its most simple form, learning is to link something new with something existing in a way that makes sense (Hermansen, 2005). There are many inspiring definitions of learning. Here are a few. *"Acquiring knowledge and skills and having them readily available from memory so you can make sense of future problems and opportunities."* (Brown et al., 2014:11). *"...the transformative process of taking in information that—when internalized and mixed with what we have experienced—changes what we know and builds on what we do. It's based on input, process, and reflection. It is what changes us."* (Bingham & Conner, 2010:8). *"A change in human disposition or capability that persists over a period of time and is not simply ascribable to processes of growth."* (Gagne, 1985:21). Although inspiring, they are limited in the sense that they somewhat perceive the human being as a mechanical apparatus. It could as well be a machine which took in information, internalised and mixed it with what it already knew, and spat out packages of new knowledge. To us, learning is much more than a statement of human normative behaviour in the act of learning. Inspired by Nygaard & Andersen (2005), Nygaard & Holtham (2008), Nygaard & Bramming (2008), and Nygaard (2015), we define learning with a number of central statements:

1. learning is both an individual and a social process.

2. learning is a process affected by (and a process that affects) the identity of the learner.

3. learning is a process affected by (and a process that affects) the social position of the learner

4. learning is a process affected by (and a process that affects) the learners' embeddedness in social collectivities.

5. learning is a contextual process tied to an order of behaviour that changes over time.

6. learning is the construction and maintenance of meaning.

7. learning is based on experiences whereby learning is different to people.

8. learning involves acquiring new personal knowledge, skills and competencies that can be used to resolve forthcoming challenges in life.

9. learning is the ability to doubt and to question one's own assumptions.

Well, what is learning then? Are these nine statements not just blurring the picture? To us it is difficult to define learning in just one sentence. Learning is both individual and collective. It is private and public. It takes place in time and space. It has inputs and outcomes. It is structure and process. We present these nine statements about learning to show the complexity of learning as concept. And as sources for inspiration and requirements to consider when designing a curriculum which centres learning. When designing a learning-centred curriculum, one has to actively take these thirteen aspects learning into consideration. In main section two, where we present the three examples of learning-centred curriculum design, we will come back to these thirteen aspects of learning.

To be able to link learning to curriculum design, we have to cover the basics of curriculum design too. What is it? Consulting the field of curriculum theory, it is obvious that there is no uniform definition of the term curriculum nor of the term curriculum development. Is there one uniform conclusion in the literature over the past 40 years it is indeed that the key terms are defined in multiple ways and that no authorised definitions exist (Eisner, 1965; Beauchamp, 1972; Rosales-Dordelly & Short, 1985). Based on a desk study of curriculum theory, Nygaard & Bramming (2008) formulated two broad streams of curriculum theory: 1) a content stream, and 2) a process stream. Two streams which may be helpful when understanding curriculum design principles.

	Content stream	Process stream
Curriculum	Syllabus/Guide for teaching.	Learning-centred action plan.
Agency	Teacher-driven activities.	Student-driven activities.
Learning	De-contextual learning.	Contextual learning.
Orientation	Input orientation.	Output orientation.
Evaluation method	Summative.	Formative/developmental.
Main focus points	Curriculum design, syllabus planning, teaching, exams, and evaluation.	Learning design, process facilitation, supervision, and self/peer assessment.

Figure 1: Two broad streams within curriculum theory (based on Nygaard & Bramming, 2008).

Advocates of the content stream of curriculum design hold the view that students learn what teachers do and present. They think of the curriculum as a guide for teaching closely linked to the syllabus. Agency lies with the teacher. It is the teacher who plans, instructs, teaches, evaluates and examines. It is expected of all students that they are able to learn the same in this setting. All students participate in a two-hour session in the lecture theatre, and it is assumed they have all learned to the same level. Learning is thus de-contextualised, as contextual matters are not taken into account. The focus is on what the students have to learn, meaning what teachers need to teach, hence the input is seen as the central element. Often teachers will discuss which book is the best to use for their course. Assuming that all students learn to a certain level by reading a book and being taught by a teacher, the evaluation of student learning can be summative through predesigned tests or assignments. Keywords are curriculum design, syllabus planning, teaching, exams, and evaluation.

Advocates of the process stream of curriculum design hold the view that it is what the students do that is learned, rather than what teachers do and present. They think of the curriculum as a learning-centred action plan closely linked to student activities. Agency lies with the student. It is the student who plans, engages, study, and self-evaluates. It is expected that students are different and thus not able to learn the same in the same way or at the same pace. If a group of students participate in a two-hour session in the lecture theatre, it is assumed they have all learned something different. Learning is contextualised, as contextual matters are taken into account. Who is the student? Where does the student come from? What did the student do before coming to our university? What is the family background of the student? What is the purpose of the student studying? What is the future career choice of the student? The focus is on the student and the students' learning process, and therefore also on the students' learning outcome. Often teachers will discuss which methods is best to use for accelerating learning under the contextual circumstances. Assuming that all students learn in a different way, at a different pace, and to a different level, the evaluation of student learning has to be formative and developmental, engaging the student much more in both learning design and evaluation design. Keywords are learning design, process facilitation, supervision, and self/peer assessment.

Looking back on our nine statements about learning, it should be obvious that they address much more the philosophy behind the process stream of curriculum design. We believe that it is important to work with curriculum design in such a way that student agency and student learning are the most central elements. In figure 2 we present a curriculum design model (Andersen *et al.*, 2003), which holds four interrelated aspects, which we believe will help make the curriculum development process student centred. In order to develop a learning-centred curriculum, it is important that these aspects are aligned.

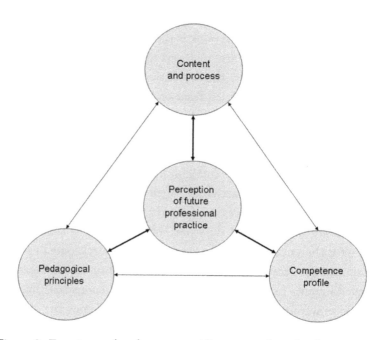

Figure 2: Four interrelated aspects guiding curriculum development (Andersen et al., 2003).

Figure 2 shows four interrelated aspects, which are useful guiding points for curriculum designers when they have to develop a learning-centred curriculum.

Perception of future professional practice

The central aspect of curriculum design is the students' perception of their own future professional practice. It is what the student does that the student learns. Not what the teacher does. As learning is directed towards the future, it is important to understand the students' perception of their future professional practice and link that closely to the development in the job market. What are the career dreams and choices of students? What motivates students to learn? What are the professional identities of students? Where do students see themselves in the years to come? Such questions are important to use as the foundation for curriculum design, because we know that learning is *"…a contextual process tied to particular situations… a process affected by the identity of the learner… a process affected by the social position of the learner… and by the learners' embeddedness in social collectivities."* (Nygaard & Holtham, 2008:13–14). We therefore advise curriculum designers to start the curriculum design process by inviting students to discuss such matters together with external stakeholders (could be members of public sector institutions, members of the private companies, past graduates (alumni organisations), members of advisory board, etc.). A natural step in the curriculum development process would be to conduct focus group interviews with both students and external stakeholders to get input to ways in which the future practice of graduates may be perceived. Teachers, instructors, supervisors, examiners, etc., should be involved too, because students' perception of their future professional practice has to be the backbone of all learning activities in the curriculum. Nygaard & Serrano (2010) conducted a qualitative study at Copenhagen Business School of students' identity construction and learning, where they found that students' learning is closely linked to their identity construction processes. It means that the way in which students see their "future me" has profound implications for their engagement, self-determination and motivation to engage in their studies. Therefore, it is important to use such knowledge when designing the curriculum.

Competence profile

The next important aspect of curriculum design is the competence profile of students. Which competences should students have if they need to fulfil their perceived future professional practice? In the content stream of curriculum design, we discuss which books students need to read to learn a certain threshold. In the process stream of curriculum design, we take into account that students are different, learn different, and has to work in different contexts in the future. That they develop different identities as human beings. And that it is what students' do they learn. Not what the teacher does. The competence profile of students then becomes very diverse. It means that we cannot express the requirements in relative terms, such as level B in math, level A in English, etc. We need to work with methodological competences, theoretical competences, meta-theoretical competences, and contextual competence – all in relation to practice. This may sound abstract, which indeed it is. To determine the competence profile of a student is indeed long-haired, when *"learning is the construction and maintenance of meaning... is a contextual process tied to an order of behaviour that changes over time... is a process affected by (and a process that affects) the identity of the learner..., and a process affected by (and a process that affects) the social position of the learner, and the learners' embeddedness in ongoing social relations."* (Nygaard, 2015:11). Ultimately, students determine what, how, and where to learn, and we need to help them in this process by designing a learning-centred curriculum which has as its (floating) endpoint a competence profile that appeals to students and inspires students to engage in their studies, because they have a perception of their own future professional practice, which is somewhat fulfilled by studying.

Pedagogical principles

The third aspect of the curriculum design model regards the pedagogical principles. Such principles are first and foremost guided by the learning philosophy behind the course and by its competence-profile. By pedagogical principles we mean the activities governing the learning process of students. Self-study, teamwork, project work, assignments, lectures, supervision sessions, research activities, etc. All kinds of activities which are a part of the pedagogical design aiming at helping students engage in meaningful learning activities. Learning-centred pedagogies may be, but are not limited to:

1. case-based learning (Mauffette-Leenders *et al.*, 1998; Erskine *et al.*, 1998; Branch *et al.*, 2015) where students work with analysing and solving a live case or desk case. The case may propose a problem, which has to be solved by students, or students themselves may identify the problem by analysis and then solve it.

2. problem-based learning (Fogarty, 1998; Dean *et al.*, 2003) where students work collaboratively with analysing and solving a problem, which can be given by the teacher or identified by the students.

3. research-based learning (Olsen & Pedersen, 2003; Guerin *et al.*, 2015) where students engage in research activities themselves. Teachers introduce to and involve students in current research practices.

4. project-based learning (DeFillipi, 2001; Meier & Nygaard, 2008) where students engage in larger empirical projects of which they have the main responsibility in relation to analysing and solving problems and bringing the project to its conclusion.

In the three examples of learning-centred curriculum we present in this chapter, the pedagogical principles are guided by the principle of contextual learning. It leads to a pedagogy based on action-reflection-learning.

Content and process

The fourth aspect regards content and process. There is an important point in keeping the content and process as the final aspect. Usually the content-driven curriculum development process starts with defining the content of the course. What academic books should students read? Which assignments do they have to make? And the process is here seen as "where to be" or "what to do". On which days do they go to class? At what times do they hand in assignments? To avoid falling into this de-contextualised trap of instructional behaviour perceiving students as learning machines, we argue that it is important not to discuss content and process *before* one has dealt with the other three aspects. And yet, when choosing content and process, do so with iterative reflections to the other three aspects. Taking this alternative approach, the task is to choose content and processes, which allows for students to strengthen their personal development in line with their perceived future professional practice, and use pedagogical practices that enables them to develop the competencies specified in their competence profile.

Following our introduction of the model showing four interrelated aspects guiding curriculum development (Andersen *et al.*, 2003), we come to the second section of our chapter, where we will show three concrete examples of learning-centred curriculum design.

Section 2: Three examples of learning-centred curriculum design

Example one: Bachelor course on Business Economics

The first example is the curriculum development of a 2½-year course in Business Economic Theory and Analysis (BETA) at a Bachelor's programme in Business Administration and Organisational Communication (COM) at Copenhagen Business School (CBS). This example has been extensively reported in Nygaard *et al.* (2008), where it was also reflected with learning theory. It is not our ambition to replicate the full presentation of the course here. We briefly introduce the course to enable a discussion of learning-centred curriculum design, which is the focus of this chapter.

Curriculum development of the BETA course started almost 1½ years before the course was due to start. The question for us was: how do we best develop a curriculum which integrates theories, methods and practice and which, at the same time, enhances the professional development of students' knowledge, skills and competencies? That led us to formulate five guiding principles for our work:

1. BETA students must take responsibility for and organise a part of their own curriculum;

2. The BETA course curriculum will include current business practices;

3. The BETA course is based on a pedagogy that is orientated towards practice;

4. BETA students must be able to apply theories, work methodically, reflect critically and develop personal and interpersonal competencies;

5. The BETA course will be grounded in ongoing research from the teachers/researchers involved in developing and teaching courses.

These guiding principles were a natural consequence of our belief in contextual learning theories. It made us think of BETA as a course in which students should be enabled to perceive their future professional practice while working with current themes through academic and practical challenges. We developed five modules (one for each of the five half-year semesters of the course). The total workload of BETA was 31 ECTS. ECTS stands for the European Credit Transfer and Accumulation System, which is a student-centred system based on the student workload required to achieve the objectives of a programme. ECTS is devised in such a way that 60 credits measure the workload of a full-time student during an academic year. So, BETA was a relatively important course in terms of time and workload. In the following we will briefly introduce Module 1 (3 ECTS), to enable the further discussion of curriculum design.

When designing BETA, we wanted to avoid being trapped in the traditional content and process of lectures and exercises. We therefore planned BETA with different pedagogical activities on our repertoire. Thus, BETA started with a mini conference. The mini conference ran over two weeks and became the cornerstone of the BETA-course when it came down to integrating theories, methods and practices. The structure of the mini conference is shown in figure 3:

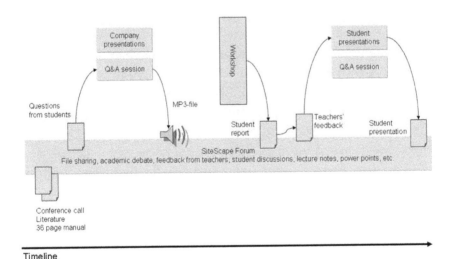

Figure 3: Module one – the mini conference.

We used the learning management system named SiteScape Forum for online communication, file sharing, academic debate, etc., within the group of administrators, teachers and students. We designed a BETA-portal to support a blended learning approach, where our traditional face-to-face interaction during the confrontation hours in the classroom was supplemented by face-to-interface interaction on the learning management system. That enabled us to have synchronous interaction in the classroom and asynchronous interaction in a dedicated online community. Each morning at 5am the system would automatically send an e-mail in digest-format to all students containing headlines and relevant links to all activities. That was a way of continuously placing BETA in the minds of the students and a way to make them develop the habit of visiting the BETA-portal each day.

We started our course in November. During October, we uploaded to the SiteScape Forum a "call for conference" for the mini conference explaining the setup and the goals of the conference as well as the requirements put on students. We also uploaded a 36-page manual explaining in details, how BETA was developed, why it had been developed in this way, what we expected of students, how they may or may not plan their own study process while attending the BETA-course. We also described the learning goals as well as the pedagogy behind BETA. The manual and the conference call was a way to help students see themselves as active participants in the course. We also uploaded the reading list for the course, based on which students have to buy, loan or download the appropriate titles themselves. The preparation for the mini conference called for individual work such as reading, writing, and contributing in debates and discussions on the BETA-portal.

On the first day of the mini conference we had invited the managing directors of two companies to come and present the economic key challenges facing their companies. Their presentations were followed by a Q&A session, where students could interview the managing directors. Before the mini conference began we had required that students did upload their questions for this session to the BETA-portal. This requirement was put on students in order to facilitate their reading of academic literature in which theories on business economics are presented, to read the conference call, to make them visit the homepages of the companies and read the annual reports of the companies. At the end of the first day, the managing directors gave the students a challenge: *"analyse our economic key challenges using the economic theories of your course and write a report and prepare a presentation of your key findings"*. The Q&A

session itself was recorded on MP3 and uploaded on the BETA-portal for the students to use in their forthcoming analysis of the companies and their challenges. Over the next four days, students worked intensively in groups of 5–6 students trying to find ways in which the companies could overcome their economic key challenges. We planned this group work to motivate students to share their knowledge and demonstrate their skills and competencies to each other. But also, to help them perceive their own future professional practice in the light of the professional practices of the managing directors. On day three, we hosted a workshop, which was a full thematic day where students discussed their analysis of the challenges facing the companies with each other and with their teachers, who acted in the role of supervisors and coaches.

Based on the knowledge acquired from reading and discussing the academic literature, students trained their analytical skills when they had to discuss their analysis with each other and with the teachers, and their writing skills when they had to write a 5-page report where they explicitly used the acquired academic terminology to analyse the challenges of companies.

Students uploaded their final reports to the BETA-portal, and would either fail (and have to resubmit) or pass. Teachers evaluated the reports based on the learning requirements of the curriculum, that is if the reports demonstrate a competent use of models and theories, a competent use of research methods, and a competent analysis of empirical practice. The teachers each nominated two reports as the best reports, and from this pool of nominees two winners was chosen. The following week the winning groups had to present their reports in a face-to-face situation with the managing directors and in front of the entire class. The managing directors evaluated the presentations based on the way in which they meet the standard of performance required in their business contexts, and as such whether students are seen as competent outside the academic context. Both teachers' evaluation and the managing directors' evaluation were an important feedback to students, who were in the process of learning how to master a new academic field. Such feedback helps the student create a subjective meaning of a situation based on their past experiences and their expectation of their own future practice.

From the first day of the BETA-course, teachers acted as facilitators of a mini conference, giving the responsibility of content to two managing directors from private companies. It made an important impact on the new bachelor students when the first they meet in the class on business economics is two managing directors asking them to help them solve problems and overcome real life challenges. And the competitive element – winning one of the two slots where you can present your report to the managing directors is a motivating aspect too. We tried to motivate students and facilitate their development of knowledge, skills and competencies throughout the BETA-course by varying the pedagogical tools. Measured on students' workload and learning outcomes it was a huge success to facilitate student learning using such untraditional methods of teaching and learning business economics. The BETA students outperformed students in our traditional courses and they taught themselves theories and methods that were normally aimed at graduate students.

Example two: Camp Future

The second example of a learning-centred curriculum is Camp Future. A 10-week professional course for unemployed university graduates, where they follow a case-based curriculum (Branch *et al.*, 2015) and solve a real-life challenge given by a company. This example too has been extensively reported elsewhere (in Hørsted & Nygaard, 2017), where it was also reflected with learning theory. It is not our ambition to replicate the same full presentation of the course here. Again, we briefly introduce the course to enable a discussion of learning-centred curriculum design, which is the focus of this chapter.

When in 2012 Claus Nygaard developed the concept of Camp Future, he thought that a professional course targeted at unemployed university graduates could help create jobs if the course helped them develop an entrepreneurial mindset. The solution became Camp Future, where participants would be linked to a company to solve a real business-challenge given by the company. During the course, each participant is linked directly to a company. The first six weeks are spent solving the company's' business-challenge. The final four weeks the unemployed graduate continues as an "employee" in the company during a period of internship.

The curriculum is designed as a learning-centred action plan (Bolhuis, 2003; Nygaard & Bramming, 2008). On the very first day of the course, each participant meets with the owner/manager of the case company, who presents the business-challenge to be solved over the coming six weeks. Challenges vary, but are linked to the core aspects of the business. Previous examples are: "Create an export market strategy for introduction of a new product on the German market"; "Make an implementation plan for a new product management system in the organisation"; "Create a social media strategy for our company"; "Develop a brand strategy for our company"; "Develop a CSR strategy for our company"; "Create a concept for employee training through gamification"; "Create an app for customer relation management". Participants need to take personal action from the very first day of the course. They are given full agency in their own learning process. They learn through a process of trial and error. What may work for the company? What don't seem to work? What is possible? What is a dead-end? They engage in their own personal learning process as reflective practitioners (Schön, 1983, 1987) while solving the business-challenge stated by the company. Camp Future thus embeds participants in business contexts where they have to make sense of the business-challenges faced by the companies. Participants learn individually and socially at the same time. And their contextually embedded learning process affects their identity as they transform from unemployed university graduates to worthy "employees" and go through a period of internship, where they make a qualitative difference for the case company. At Camp Future, there is a close link between the learning-centred curriculum and the possible identity projects of participants (Nygaard & Serrano, 2010).

Activities has to be student-driven, because each participant faces a different business-challenge. Pedagogical activities span exploration (e.g., what goes on inside and outside the company), experimentation (i.e., constantly trying out different problem definitions, methods, and solutions), testing (i.e., coming to terms with possible links between problems and solutions). The curriculum of Camp Future is developed with the perception that the participant-group is a heterogeneous group of people who all engage differently in the course. In our view, participants have different experiences and different personal aims for participating in the course. Therefore, we have to centre students' action plan for learning rather than the syllabus itself. It appears that Camp Future has succeeded in developing a culture of deep learners (Marton & Säljö, 1976; Ramsden, 1988), where participants aim to make a qualitative and positive difference for the companies they work for during their studies.

The success of the process-based curriculum is usually evaluated by focusing on aspects like student participation, student reflection, and student learning. At Camp Future, participants are evaluated based on the solution they offer to the company. If a company asks for someone to "create an export market strategy for introduction of a new product on the German market", the participant is evaluated on the content and presentation of that export market strategy plan. This may include an analysis of market conditions, competitor analysis, customer segmentation, logistics analysis, and an implementation plan calling for action. All participants present their work/solution in front of the entire class and representatives from the case company. This is a formative evaluation method focusing on the quality of the solution and the advice given by the participant to the company.

Example three: vocational postgraduate education program

The third example is a two-year vocational postgraduate programme which was developed by Claus Nygaard. Like the previous two examples, this example too has been extensively reported elsewhere (in Nygaard & Irgens, 2011), where it was also reflected with learning theory. Again, it is not our ambition to replicate the same full presentation of the course here. But we briefly introduce the course to enable a discussion of learning-centred curriculum design, which is the focus of this chapter.

This vocational postgraduate education program was designed for 30 managers of the Danish company NKT Flexibles (today renamed to NOV Flexibles) working in the global offshore oil & gas industry. It included the CEO, 6 members of the top management group, and 23 level 2 managers. The overall aim of the programme was to develop the reflexive competencies of the managers in relation to their everyday practice as managers. More specifically, the programme aimed to develop a movement within the organisation from management to leadership. The company wished to see its managers move from spending most of their time as experts addressing technical issues to being active leaders working to nurture a team-based culture for motivational innovation of work practices throughout the entire organisation. Instead of sending individual managers on individual postgraduate courses, the company decided to develop a joint initiative and include all managers at the same time with the obvious benefit of "travelling together on the educational journey" thereby sharing contexts, experiences, and language.

The initial challenge for the curriculum developers was to sell to the company the idea of a vocational postgraduate program based on action-reflection-learning principles. This meant pointing out that the role of faculty would not be to lecture in normative management theories, but to facilitate the personal development of the individual manager to become reflexively aware of the possible consequences of own everyday management practices. It also meant that the curriculum was not to be set in stone, but in order to develop a flexible process of double-loop learning (Argyris & Schön, 1978) in the organisation, it had to be developed based on the aspects of the process stream (Nygaard & Bramming, 2008). To explicate the meaning of the curriculum as a learning-centred action plan, the curriculum developers turned to the notion of Artful Making (Austin & Devin, 2003) with its four stages: 1) release, 2) collaboration, 3) ensemble, and 4) play.

Managers on the vocational postgraduate programme should be *released* in the sense that they should be allowed to work explicitly with their own challenges in the light of their own role in the organisation. Managers should be encouraged to act first on their own and then *collaborate* in network groups to solve immediate challenges. Further on, based on the processes of shared reflections, they should be motivated to work as an *ensemble* using the same theoretical language as a reference point for analysing and understanding the collective managerial challenges. Ultimately that should lead to situations of *play* where theory and practice melted together in new informed everyday leadership practice.

Contrary to other situations we have been in when developing vocational postgraduate programmes, in this particular case getting to a joint understanding of the point of the programme was refreshingly easy. The CEO and the Human Resources manager both had a desire to go further with their management group. Earlier the company had spent time and money on loosely coupled initiatives for individual managers, and they had also worked with suppliers of traditional courses, which had not been closely linked to the personal development of managers. Company management contributed many inspiring ideas about the programme, so working from the principles of artful making was not considered to be a problem. On the contrary, it was considered to be the formula that would help engage and develop not only the individual managers but the organisation as a whole.

Active leadership – the programme

Since the aim of the programme was to facilitate a change from management to leadership, it was quickly decided that its brand name should be "Active Leadership". A brand name was seen as important in order to gradually build a brand community within the company during the programme. In this way, participating managers would continuously perceive, enact and perform their new roles as reflexive leaders. The aim was to develop the managers as „autonomous ethnographers" (Picard et al., 2011) who have the ability to investigate, analyse and reflect on their own leadership practice using the theoretical input as new lenses to study and understand own leadership practice.

The development of the themes and modules of Active Leadership became an iterative process between faculty and responsible participants from the company. The number of modules and their form were conceptually decided upon and it was agreed that the content would be decided upon throughout the programme as it took form. The programme ended having six modules, where participants would meet for 2 days each module.

From our experience with learning-centred education (Nygaard & Holtham, 2008; Nygaard et al., 2008) we knew that a main key to success would be active participation. We wished to change the roles of both participants and teachers. The participants should change from customers to partners, and the teacher should change from academic expert to facilitating coach. We also knew from our experience with learning outcomes (Nygaard et al., 2009) that another important key to success in improving participants' learning outcomes would be to link actively academic content with their everyday practice. And we knew from our experience with creativity in teaching (Nygaard et al., 2010) that a pedagogical model was needed, which engaged participants in many different ways, using different methods for preparation, work and reflection.

Therefore, we developed an online platform for communication between participants and between participants and teachers. Each participant had access to a private room for communication with teachers and supervisors and a public room for communication with fellow participants as well as teachers and supervisors. The reason for giving them a private room was that some of their challenges as leaders in the company had to do with their colleagues and subordinates. It was felt that if this analysis was open to all it could prevent participants from engaging in rich case descriptions and reflections. We also thought it would be unethical to discuss perceptions of problematic colleagues and subordinates in public. The online platform also had folders for each module, for literature, assignments, web surveys, minutes, and additional resources created as the programme took form.

Each of the modules required active preparation by participants. They had to read 150+ pages of academic literature representing various perspectives on the theme and they had to complete a web survey about their everyday practice and their understanding of the theories for each module. They also had to write a two-page assignment about their personal challenges as leaders and link these to the overall theme of the current module. In this way, the teachers obtained rich and detailed insights into the everyday practice and the academic knowledge of each participant. It allowed the teachers to focus their attention on the areas where participants needed most help in moving forward. Doing so, the teachers were able to move from didactic lecturing of academic content to inquiry-based facilitation of group processes that focused on the challenges experienced by participants. During the five two-day modules, participants were divided into two groups of 15 to facilitate in-depth discussions and engage in case-work which reflected as closely as possible the everyday leadership practice of the participants. Each of the first five modules was therefore delivered twice. As a means to further develop network between participants the two groups were mixed from module to module. It meant that you could be in one group of 15 people at module 1, and a different group of 15 people at module 2, and so on. Upon completion of the five modules participants had to engage in activities that required them to reflect upon their learning outcomes and how these linked to their current leadership practice. They wrote a two-page assignment where they had to describe challenging cases they had experienced in the past and then analyse them with the new theoretical models they had just learned during the module. The rationale would be: 1) what would I usually have done? 2) After following this module, what do I now see as alternative possibilities for action? 3) How would I act in a similar situation today? 4) What would the possible consequences be for my employees, and for myself as a manager?

Each written assignment for reflection would be examined by the responsible teachers, and these submissions could be failed if they did not actively apply the new theoretical models in their reflections. This of course happened during the programme, so a certain level of reflection was required. Each participant was also required to take part in a minimum of two network group meetings following each of the modules. Here four or five colleagues met to discuss their personal outcome of preparing, participating, and reflecting. The rationale would be: what did I learn at the previous module? How can I use that in my everyday leadership practice? What do I commit myself to do alternatively in my leadership in the immediate future?

As participants met in network groups after each module, they had to write minutes of their meeting and upload them to the online community. The teachers would then read and comment on the outcome of the network groups and each participant would receive follow-up questions in their private room in regard to their personal commitment. Such questions could be: "at the network meeting two months ago you told your colleagues that you would work more actively with the motivation of the group of lead engineers in your department. What have you done? What was the outcome?"

The sixth module was dedicated to participants writing a personal Action Learning Project. It was initiated after the first module, and during the programme, participants would work on their action learning project as their understanding of own leadership practice developed. The project itself was handed in and given a grade after module six.

What we learned from the Active Leadership programme was that if you centre your vocational postgraduate education around the participants' own perception of their future professional practice, and plan your pedagogies such that you enable participants to further analyse and understand the problems and challenges they are facing in their everyday management practices, you acquire both engaged and deep learning participants.

Conclusion

In this brief chapter, we have aimed to show how a change in our perception of the curriculum from a content stream to a process stream has helped the responsible faculty to perceive teaching and learning differently in three very different cases: 1) a bachelor programme in Business

Economics at a business school; 2) a professional course for unemployed university graduates delivered by a private consultancy company; 3) a vocational postgraduate programme delivered by the executive training unit at a business school.

It appears from studying the theory on curriculum that there may be two broad streams at play in curriculum development. 1) the content stream, and 2) the process stream. The content stream is most of all a linear process aimed to develop the curriculum as a syllabus/guide for teaching. Linear in the sense that all aspects of curriculum are designed and put in place before the student start on the programme. The process stream is mostly a non-linear process aimed to develop the curriculum as a learning centred action plan. It has to be non-linear, because students are different, they learn different, and they have different ambitions and different perceptions of future professional practice in which they will use what they learn.

Developing a curriculum based on the process stream is therefore very different from formulating a syllabus. Curriculum development becomes an iterative process of coordination and facilitation, unfolding as students engage in the curricular activities and give feedback about their personal learning. In this chapter, we therefore suggested that a useful model for curriculum development would be the model showing *Four interrelated aspects guiding curriculum development* (Andersen et al., 2003). We hope that the three examples of curriculum development shown in the chapter, will inspire readers to play with this model (figure 2), and also try to work according to the philosophy of the process stream seeing curriculum as a learning-centred action plan. It is our belief that this will improve the learning outcomes of students.

About the Authors

Anne Hørsted is adjunct professor at the University of Southern Denmark, senior consultant at cph:learning in Denmark, and adjunct professor at the Institute for Learning in Higher Education. She can be contacted at this e-mail: anne@lihe.info

Claus Nygaard, professor, PhD, is executive director at the Institute for Learning in Higher Education and executive director at cph:learning in Denmark. He can be contacted at this e-mail: info@lihe.info

Bibliography

Andersen, I.; L. Lillebro; J. Ravn; J. Tofteskov & C. Nygaard (2003). *A Learning Strategy for Copenhagen Business School. Learning-Centred Curriculum Development in Practice.* Frederiksberg: CBS Learning Lab.

Argyris, C. & D. Schön (1978). *Organizational Learning.* Reading, MA: Addison-Wesley.

Austin, R. & L. Devin (2003). *Artful Making: What managers needs to know about how artists work.* New Jersey: Financial Times Prentice Hall.

Beauchamp, G. A. (1972). Basic Components of Curriculum Theory. *Curriculum Theory Network*, No. 10, pp. 16–22.

Bingham, T. & M. Conner (2010). *The New Social Learning.* American Society for Training and Development.

Bolhuis, S. (2003). Towards process-oriented teaching for self-directed lifelong learning: a multidimensional perspective. *Learning and Instruction*, Vol. 13, No. 3, pp. 327–47.

Branch, J.; P. Bartholomew & C. Nygaard (2015). *Case-Based Learning in Higher Education.* Oxfordshire, UK: Libri Publishing Ltd.

Brown, P. C.; H. L. Roediger III; M. A. McDaniel (2014). *Make It Stick: The Science of Successful Learning.* New York: Belknap Press.

Dean, C. D.; D. Dunaway; S. Ruble & C. Gerhardt (2003). *Implementing Problem-Based Learning in Education.* Birmingham, AL: Samford University Press.

DeFillipi, R. J. (2001). Introduction: Project-based Learning. Reflective Practices and Learning Outcomes. *Management Learning*, Vol. 32, No. 1, pp. 5–10.

Eisner, E. (1965). Levels of Curriculum and Curriculum Research. *The Elementary School Journal*, Vol. 66, No. 3, pp. 155–162.

Erskine, J. A.; M. R. Leenders & L. A. Mauffette-Leenders. (1998). *Teaching with Cases.* Ivey: Richard Ivey School of Business.

Fogarty, R. (Ed.) (1998). *Problem-Based Learning and other Curriculum Methods for the Multiple Intelligences Classroom.* Arlington Heights: Skylight Training and Publishing.

Gagne, R. (1985). *The Conditions of Learning.* New York: Holt, Rinehart & Winston.

Guerin, C.; P. Bartholomew & C. Nygaard (Eds.) (2015). *Learning to Research - Researching to Learn.* Oxfordshire, UK: Libri Publishing Ltd.

Hermansen, M. (2005). *Relearning.* Copenhagen: Danish University of Education Press/Copenhagen Business School Press.

Hørsted, A. & C. Nygaard (2017). Teaching Unemployed University Graduates to think like Entrepreneurs. In J. Branch; A. Hørsted & C. Nygaard (2017),

Teaching and Learning Entrepreneurship in Higher Education. Oxfordshire: Libri Publishing Ltd.

Marton, F. & R. Säljö (1976) On qualitative differences in Learning – Outcome and process. *British journal of Educational Psychology*, Vol. 46, No. 1, pp. 4–11.

Mauffette-Leenders, L. A.; J. A. Erskine & M. R. Leenders (1997). *Learning with Cases.* Ivey: Richard Ivey School of Business.

Mauffette-Leenders, L. A.; J. A. Erskine & M. R. Leenders (1998). *Teaching with Cases.* Ivey: Richard Ivey School of Business.

Meier, F. & C. Nygaard (2008). Problem Oriented Project Work. In C. Nygaard & C. Holtham (Eds.), *Understanding Learning-Centred Higher Education.* Frederiksberg: Copenhagen Business School Press.

Nygaard, C. (2015). Rudiments of a Strategy for Technology Enhanced University Learning. In C. Nygaard; J. Branch & P. Bartholomew (Eds.), *Technology Enhanced Learning in Higher Education.* Oxfordshire, UK: Libri Publishing Ltd, pp. 109–128.

Nygaard, C. & I. Andersen (2005). Contextual Learning in Higher Education. In R. G. Milter; V. S. Perotti & M. S. R. Segers (Eds.), *Educational Innovation in Economics and Business IX. Breaking Boundaries for Global Learning.* Springer Verlag.

Nygaard, C. & P. Bramming (2008). Learning-centred Public Management Education. *International Journal of Public Sector Management*, Vol. 21, No. 4, pp. 400–416.

Nygaard, C.; N. Courtney & C. Holtham (2010). *Teaching Creativity – Creativity in Teaching.* Oxfordshire: Libri Publishing Ltd.

Nygaard, C.; T. Højlt & M. Hermansen (2008). Learning-Based Curriculum Development. *Higher Education*, Vol. 55, No. 1, pp. 30–55.

Nygaard, C. & C. Holtham (2008). The Need for Learning-Centred Higher Education. In C. Nygaard & C. Holtham (Eds.), *Understanding Learning Centred Higher Education.* Frederiksberg, CBS Press, pp. 11–29.

Nygaard, C.; C. Holtham & N. Courtney (2009). *Improving Students' Learning Outcomes.* Frederiksberg: Copenhagen Business School Press.

Nygaard, C. & E. Irgens (2011). Artful Making in Vocational Postgraduate Education. In C. Nygaard; N. Courtney & L. Frick (Eds.), *Postgraduate Education – Form and Function.* Oxfordshire, UK: Libri Publishing Ltd.

Nygaard, C. & M. Serrano (2010). Students' Identity Construction and Learning. Reasons for developing a learning-centred curriculum in higher education. In L. E. Kattington (Ed.), *Handbook of Curriculum Development*, Nova Publishers, pp. 233–254.

Picard, M.; R. Warner & L. Velautham (2011). Enabling Postgraduate Students to Become Autonomous Ethnographers of their Disciplines. In C. Nygaard,

N. Courtney & L. Frick (Eds.), *Postgraduate Education – Form and Function.* Oxfordshire: Libri Publishing Ltd., pp. 149–166.

Ramsden, P. (1988). *Improving Learning: new perspectives.* Kogan Page.

Rosales-Dordelly, C. & E. C. Short (1985). *Curriculum Professors' Specialized Knowledge.* University Press of America.

Schön, D. A. (1983). *The Reflective Practitioner.* New York: Basic Books.

Schön, D. A. (1987). *Educating the Reflective Practitioner.* San Francisco: Jossey-Bass.

Chapter 5

Learning-Centred Educational Development: An Approach That Draws upon Creative Arts and Philosophies of Emancipation

Julian Lamb, Marion Carrier & Jacob Lamb

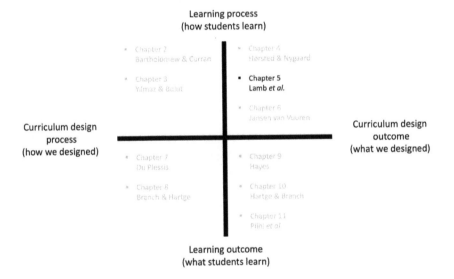

Introduction

We contribute to this book *Learning-Centred Curriculum Design in Higher Education* by showcasing the design, delivery, and impact of an innovative learning-centred professional development programme for newly appointed university teachers studying to receive a postgraduate certificate (PGCert) at Aston University in the UK. In so doing, we reveal an innovative link between curriculum design and student learning that is inspired by creative arts and philosophies of emancipation. In relation to the central model of the book, we position our chapter in section two – Learning Process/Curriculum Design Output – because our primary focus is on how students learn, and in light of this we discuss and explore how a learning-centred curriculum for early-career university teachers can be designed to be a transformative experience rather than simply "staff training".

In writing this chapter, we recognise an almost unavoidable conflation of the terms "learning-centred" and "student-centred", and we strive to navigate the subtle cross-cuts, parallels, and differences between these terms. As such, where we use the term "learning-centred", it points to our notion that the teacher is concerned, primarily, with understanding how students learn in a given setting and with designing a curriculum to engage with this. Where we use the term "student-centred", we point to our particular view of student learning that is grounded in a constructivist epistemology.

Throughout our chapter, we use the term "teacher" rather than the term "lecturer" that is commonly used in higher education; this is because we find the use of the term lecturer problematic in a number of ways. From one perspective, the term lecturer can infer some kind of primacy in the use of a lecture theatre and the didactic pedagogy that is associated tacitly with such space. From another perspective, the title of lecturer can bestow exclusivity, power, and status in higher education to those with this job title. In Aston's taught programme (explored in this chapter) we have taken great strides, and some risk, to widen participation to include other staff members, such as those in careers, library services, IT, chaplaincy and so forth, who are deeply engaged in teaching but may not have the same institutional recognition for doing so within the UK HE sector.

We also use the term "participant" for those who are enrolled as students on the PGCert. The use of the term participant acknowledges the fact that our "students" are teaching colleagues who are usually highly qualified in their field and, furthermore, are frequently as old and life-experienced as those who teach the programme. The term participant also points to our learning-focused pedagogy: Students come to our programme to participate in their learning rather than be passive recipients of the knowledge.

In our chapter, we define learning-centred curriculum design as deeply humanistic and we focus on the agency of participants to enhance their own practice through self-reflection and co-creation of knowledge, rather than obediently assimilating the views of teacher-experts or corporate standpoints. We concur with Hodge (2010) that the humanistic approach to education stems from an ancient tradition of learning that reaches as far back as Socrates, who compelled students "to know themselves" (see Yilmaz and Bulut, in this volume, for another example of humanistic teacher education). The impact of our learning-centred/student-centred approach is measured in the accounts of personal and professional transformation given by those who have participated in the Aston Postgraduate Certificate in Higher Education (PGCert) since 2014. Reading this chapter, you will gain the following insights:

1. that a Higher Education Academy (HEA) accredited PGCert need not be delivered in the manner of "training, compliance and audit". Instead, it can be designed as a student-centred emancipatory project that offers significant rewards in terms of students' personal and professional transformation;

2. that there is risk in delivering a student-centred PGCert, and this needs to be recognised and managed in both the design and delivery phases;

3. that the impact that our learning-centred programme has had over the last three years.

We have structured our chapter in three sections to reflect these three different perspectives. In the first section, we account for the reasons why we adopted our approach to the design of the Aston PGCert. In the second section, we explore the PGCert as curriculum model from the perspective of faculty and students. In the final section, we provide guidance for others who may be considering a similar approach to the professional development of early career teachers in HE.

Section I: Designing and Delivering the Aston PGCert

The structure of our chapter draws upon the work of Wright-Brown (2011), who argues that there are five essential dimensions in teaching, and we feel that it is helpful to reveal our viewpoint at this early stage. These five essential dimensions are:

+ responsibility of learning;

+ the balance of power;

+ the function of content;

+ the role of the teacher;

+ purpose and process of assessment.

We argue that our curriculum is designed to *balance power* towards the student and encourage *responsibility for their learning*. Our approach, however, differs to Weimar's (2012) view that teachers do too many learning tasks for students and therefore it is a matter of workload-redistribution to make teaching more resource-efficient. Instead, we believe it is a matter of relinquishing power (Crumly, 2014) so that learning is authentic, reflective, and collaborative (Curtin, 2017). This stance reveals our passionate critique and rejection of those who seek to re-enforce the dominant ideology that "proper teaching" occurs when the teacher "holds all the cards" and where students are taught what to know. Towards the end of this chapter there is a seemingly ironic twist in this stance, and we reconsider the extent to which we have actually relinquished power.

We argue that the *function of content* on the PGCert is only to serve as a temporary scaffold that helps students initiate collaborative conversation and debate. It is important to dismantle our scaffolding after it is used and encourage students to build their own frameworks of knowledge and practice.

We believe that the *role of the teacher* on the PGCert is to provide a creative studio for learning and teaching where anything can happen. And, drawing on Gormley's (2016) concept of art-experimentation, we argue that the classroom is a catalyst for people to look at what is already "here" in their practice (see Jansen van Vuuren, in this volume, for another perspective on arts in HE).

Our view of learning is not primarily concerned with imagining "new" contexts, case studies, or simulations. Instead, it is focused primarily on leading participants to a fuller, deeper, richer understanding of their practice and its setting as it presents itself in the here-and-now. In this respect, we see our role as counsellors in the students' journey and, in particular, draw upon the work of Rogers (1976) to shape our view of self-disclosure and unconditional positive regard.

Finally, we see that the *purpose of assessment* is to act as a counter-balance to ensure that the focus and output of work on the PGCert is drawn back to a core mission, which is the development and enhancement of our participant's professional practice as HE teachers and for them to embrace the United Kingdom Professional Standards Framework (UKPSF).

PGCert Design

The PGCert is a taught educational development programme for early career teachers and is accredited with the UK's Higher Education Academy (HEA); successful completion of the programme provides professional recognition for participants as Fellows of the HEA (FHEA). The HEA is the UK's main professional body for teachers in HE, and fellowship of the HEA bestows a measure of readiness and competence to teach in a university setting.

The provision of an HEA-accredited PGCert programme is common across the UK HE sector. Such programmes are frequently delivered in the context of "staff development" in which early career HE teachers are trained, and then assessed, in relation to their personal assimilation of the UKPSF 2011. The UKPSF is a comprehensive set of professional standards for those involved in teaching and supporting learning in HE across a wide range of teaching and support roles and environments. The standards are expressed in the Dimensions of Professional Practice, which are summarised as:

+ areas of activity undertaken by teachers and support staff;

+ core knowledge needed to carry out those activities at the appropriate level;

+ professional values that individuals performing these activities should exemplify.

Areas of Activity	Core Knowledge	Professional Values
A1 Design and plan learning activities and/or programmes of study	K1 The subject material	V1 Respect individual learners and diverse learning communities
A2 Teach and/or support learning	K2 Appropriate methods for teaching, learning, and assessing in the subject area and at the level of the academic programme	V2 Promote participation in HE and equality of opportunity for learners
A3 Assess and give feedback to learners	K3 How students learn, both generally and within their subject/disciplinary area(s)	V3 Use evidence-informed approaches and the outcomes from research, scholarship and continuing professional development
A4 Develop effective learning environments and approaches to student support and guidance	K4 The use and value of appropriate learning technologies	V4 Acknowledge the wider context in which HE operates, recognising the implications for professional practice
A5 Engage in continuing professional development in subjects/disciplines and their pedagogy, incorporating research, scholarship and the evaluation of professional practices	K5 Methods for evaluating the effectiveness of teaching	V1 Respect individual learners and diverse learning communities
	K6 The implications of quality assurance and quality enhancement for academic and professional practice with a particular focus on teaching	

Table 1: UKPSF Dimensions (adapted from www.heacademy.ac.uk, 2017).

Successful completion of an HEA-accredited programme is intended to provide a degree of quality assurance that the trained individual has been audited for compliance with the UKPSF and deemed competent to teach in an HE setting.

Aston University has delivered an HEA-accredited PGCert since 2008, and by 2013 this programme was due for review, redesign, and re-approval. Feedback from participants on the outgoing programme revealed a clear view that it was overly theoretical and lacked linkages to practice. Participants reported that this was reflected in the manner of assessment and also the manner in which it was taught. The heart of the review is illustrated tersely by one former participant's view that: *"The PGCPP is a bolt-on to the work I have to do here; it adds nothing to my job other than extra work in my already busy diary"* (PGCPP participant 2012–2013).

In the Spring of 2014, our view was that the Aston PGCPP (a forerunner to the "new" PGCert programme) required a fundamentally new approach that engaged with the ways students learn and added value to participants' professional practice as teachers in HE. Through implementing Aston's programme design and approval process, we employed an iterative progression that engaged the views of those across the university and resulted in a three-module PGCert structure. The final programme demonstrated clear mapping to the UKPSF and also created a cognitive journey for participants towards their "readiness" to teach in HE (see Branch & Hartge, in this volume, for a view on how the HEA design-constraints could be seen as a design stimulus).

Module sequence	1st Module (20 credits)	2nd Module (20 credits)	3rd Module (20 credits)
Module subject	Underpinning philosophy & practice	Design & assessment	Research in practice
Module aim	Critical reflection on personal teaching identity	Gaining key design skills, knowledge, and vocabulary	Coaching to embrace change and innovation in teaching
Module title	"Evolving your Teaching Practice"	"Becoming a Designer of Academic Programmes"	"Becoming a Research-Led Innovator in Higher Education"

Module sequence	1st Module (20 credits)	2nd Module (20 credits)	3rd Module (20 credits)
Mapping to UKPSF		A1	
	A2		
	A3	A3	
		A4	
	A5		A5
	K1		
	K2	K2	
	K3		
	K4	K4	
	K5		K5
		K6	
	V1		
	V2	V2	
			V3
		V4	

Table 2: Mapping contents of the new Aston PGCert programme against UKPSF.

Central to the design process was our explicit "teaching philosophy". This philosophy was written in conjunction with key stakeholders at the university (e.g., teachers, managers, students, support services) and acted as a mission statement that declared our collaborative intention to deliver a constructionist learning-centred programme. At the launch of the programme it was used to explain our intentions to participants and has served as a powerful mission statement to clarify our intentions when required.

"Our teaching is designed from the perspective that learning is a social activity, best undertaken within a multi-disciplinary community. We see

learning as a product of discussion and debate. Using conceptual modules and theoretical perspectives of learning and teaching to underpin debate we intend to be provocative and so enhance critical reflection upon tacit assumptions about professionalism and 'power' within higher education. We uphold diversity of identities and approaches to teaching within an anti-oppressive and anti-discriminatory context. We support the development of creative academic practice and innovation."

Section 2: Impact of the PGCert – Voices from Practice

PGCert Delivery: A Teacher's Perspective – Julian Lamb

Writing this chapter in the early months of 2017, we are a third of the way through the third year of PGCert delivery and have a clear vantage point to compile a retrospective analysis of the programme's delivery. First, I consider the balance of power and responsibility of learning in the context of our facilitative approach to teaching on the PGCert. Whilst we agree with Johnson-Bailey & Cervero (1997), who identify "facilitation" as the hallmark of learning-centred adult education with all its concerns for neutrality, it is important to recognise that our teaching identity is much more than that of a passive facilitator. At key points in the programme, our teaching also incorporates the role of "provocateur", and our published teaching philosophy is explicit about this: *"we intend to be provocative and so enhance critical reflection upon tacit assumptions about professionalism and 'power' within higher education"*. Provocative intervention has two main aims: first, to draw participants to a constructionist view of knowledge and learning in the context of understanding what a teacher "does", and then to coach students towards a deeper critique of their practice.

On the first PGCert module, we steer our participants towards a constructionist approach to learning, and we make no apologies for this to our participants. We guide our participants into a structured conversation about the epistemological stances that could be adopted in the context of teacher training and proceed from natural science to constructionism, stopping at risky pseudo-science along the way. This is a crucial moment in our PGCert, because, as Harvey (2007) points out, programmes that aim to engender autonomy and self-direction run the risk of misalignment for those participants who view good teaching as the provision of facts, data, and theory. There is certainly risk for our PGCert in this respect, because participants are drawn from a wide range of disciplines from arts and humanities to science and engineering.

It would be fair to say that the balance of power is indeed towards the teacher in this aspect of the programme. We want students to take a constructionist view of their development as a teacher and discourage them from anything that looks like a positivistic stance. There are a number of philosophical reasons why we discourage positivism on the PGCert, but the main reason is that it risks turning "good teaching" into a matter of assimilating a set of expert-driven rules and procedures, restricting the scope and range of possibilities that a participant might discover for themselves as effective in their own setting. By encouraging students to take a constructionist approach, the balance of power shifts back to the student and they are encouraged to develop their own context-situated views regarding effective teaching in their discipline.

Of course, it is vital that we inform participants about our intention in relation to the balance of power on the PGCert, and we do this through establishing the notion of "contract" at both public and individualised levels. At a public level, our explicit statement of teaching philosophy stands as a contractual "invitation to treat"; it tells applicants about our view of knowledge, our approach to teaching, and sets the expectation that students will not be passive recipients of knowledge but will be active in the co-creation of knowledge. The teaching philosophy is used as an explicit point of reference in any interaction with a prospective applicant to raise awareness regarding our approach to teaching on the programme. From an individualised perspective, we establish a contract that is akin to Berne's (1966) view of counselling, in which two parties come together and agree what can be done; reaching an agreement about "what can be done" is the sole objective of the first full day of activities on the PGCert.

Over a period of six hours of classroom contact time on day one, the teaching plan proceeds as follows:

Activity	Title	Underpinning concept	Task	Outcome
1	The answer is 42; now what is the question?	Douglas Adams (1985) Karl Popper (2007)	Mapping the boundaries between different knowledge domains: science, pseudo-science, social construc- tionism, and faith	Understanding the nature, source, and limits of different knowledge domains
2	Sketching a view of the HE teaching landscape	Paulo Freire (1970)	Locating educational development on a conceptual map of teaching models	Establishing that educational devel- opment resides in the domain of constructionism
3	Sharing a meal	Randhir Singh (2017)	Restaurant lunch with teachers and participants; eating around large table to get to know each other	Evolving a safe, shared commu- nity of practice
4	Formative incidents	Carl Rogers (1976)	Reflecting upon markers of teaching quality	Developing a model of develop- ment towards "enhanced" teaching
5	Action Learning Set	Eric Berne (1966)	Discussing what can be done	Agreeing a contract of "what can be done"
6	Engaging with the UKPSF		Participant's UKPSF gap-analysis	Identifying the areas of UKPSF that require development

Table 3: Teaching plan for day one, module 1 of the PGCert.

One significant criticism of the former PGCert (known as the PGCPP) was that the content was too theoretical, and, moreover, that theory was treated as something removed and absolute. One participant stated that:

> "In the end it [the outgoing PGCert] was a course on theories of education: interesting enough but of little relevance to my job. The final assessment was to get us to write a journal paper about some aspects of my job as a lecturer. Easily done for me but I didn't really get a sense of it being anything more a second-rate literature review task." (PGCPP participant 2012–2013).

We claim that content takes a backseat on our PGCert. In our view, the module's content serves as no more than a temporary scaffold to enhance discussions amongst participants on the PGCert. Our published teaching philosophy is explicit about this: "We see learning as a product of discussion and debate. Using conceptual modules and theoretical perspectives of learning and teaching to underpin debate."

Activity	Title	Underpinning concept	Task	Outcome
1	The importance of being reflective	Kolb, Schön	Relocating abstract concepts (theory) away from the "top of the bill" in teaching, to the supporting act.	Understanding the role that theory plays as a temporary scaffold to making sense of experience.
2	Mapping the teaching landscape	Vaughan-Williams (a musician educationalist)	Using the metaphor of a map in relation to theory to establish a view on learning and teaching practice issues.	Learning how to select and use theoretical concepts from a wide range of disciplines as a temporary scaffold of discussion.
3	Removing the scaffold	Mortiboys (2007)	Developing students' context-specific models of practice	Learning to create theoretical positions from the student's own setting rather than imposing theory on their own setting

Table 4: Teaching plan for day two, module 1 of the PGCert.

As the lead teacher on the PGCert, I see my role as being to produce an environment that is akin to a creative studio for learning and teaching. Drawing on Gormley's (2016) concept of art-experimentation, I view the classroom as a catalyst for people to look at what is already "here" in their practice. My view of learning is not primarily concerned with simulations or fantasy teaching scenarios, it is primarily focused on leading participants to a fuller, deeper, richer understanding of their practice setting as it presents itself in the here and now.

In many ways, I see clear parallels between my role as the PGCert teacher and the role of an art teacher. In recent years, views about how to teach of art have shifted away from technique-driven instruction to idea-driven creation. In the same way, I see myself as a teacher in the "art of teaching" and I do not instruct PGCert students to work in a single medium or technique, but instead I compel them to explore ideas, events, and situations through multiple resources and strategies (Art–21, 2017).

My pedagogy is inspired by contemporary installation artist Dion (2008) who reveals that his methodology is to bring a "suitcase of ideas and history" to a place and then tries to insert himself into a specific social setting. He does not claim to know exactly what it is like to be in that place, but he can offer a new view to those who live there. This is exactly what I do as a PGCert teacher: I bring a suitcase of ideas and histories and insert myself into my students' professional setting as early career teachers in HE. The ideas in my PGCert suitcase are theories and concepts that I might choose to pull out in order to scaffold a discussion, and the histories are my own personal anecdotes that are offered in the spirit of Rogerian self-disclosure. I do not claim to know *exactly* what it is like to be in my students' professional settings, but I can offer viewpoints through which they might find enhancement of their practice (see Hayes, in this volume, for a similar approach to teaching). There are three underpinning ideas that are important to me in the classroom-as-studio:

+ positive regard for students;

+ self-disclosure (by teachers and students);

+ non-directive teaching.

Positive regard stems from our most basic view that learning can only occur where the student feels unconditional acceptance and regard by the teacher; and the PGCert is fundamentally intended to be a place of nurture. The diametric opposite of our stance is illustrated in the movie "Whiplash", where the music teacher creates a classroom that is dominated by intense competition for acceptance, and learning is viewed as an outcome of exclusion and anxiety. The movie is recommended viewing for PGCert participants and is used as a common set of ideas to discuss approaches to teaching (usually over lunch). To illustrate the power of this resource, the following edited extract from the film script:

> "Terence Fletcher (music teacher): I don't think people understood what it was I was doing. I wasn't there to conduct. Any moron can wave his arms and keep people in tempo. I was there to push people beyond what's expected of them. I told you that story about how Charlie Parker became Charlie Parker, right? Parker's a young kid, pretty good on the sax. Gets up to play at a cutting session, and he fucks it up. And Jones nearly decapitates him for it throwing a symbol at him. And he's laughed off stage. So, imagine if Jones had just said, 'Well, that's okay, Charlie. That was all right. Good job.' And then Charlie thinks to himself, 'Well, shit, I did do a pretty good job.' End of story. No Bird. That, to me, is an absolute tragedy. But that's just what the world wants now. People wonder why jazz is dying." (Sayre Chazelle, D. 2015).

The film provides a common point of reference to disclose and explain our fundamental view of our teaching on the PGCert, and we declare that it is the diametric opposite of Fletcher's approach. It also enables us to start a conversation about our own formative events in becoming a teacher. Drawing on our own histories, we see self-disclosure as an essential teaching strategy. On a simple level, the ability to tell "war stories" provides a means to find a footing to engagement in a discussion and debate, but the real impact comes from an enhancement of the therapeutic bond between student and teacher. From one perspective, the teacher's self-disclosure can help to normalise a student's fears and apprehension about an issue – it empowers a student to realise that the teacher has "walked in their shoes" and can genuinely empathise. Care needs to be taken, however, to observe appropriate barriers, and in particular, it is important to consider our own motivation for self-disclosing (Goldfried, 2003); the focus must be on how self-disclosure can enhance the learning of the student, not the teacher.

Non-directive teaching has been described in many different ways, but drawing upon the experience of Roger's own student, I view it as an approach to teaching in which *"there is no finality in the process; issues are left unresolved; problems raised in class are always in a state of flux, on-going; nothing is ever summarized"* (Tanenbaum, 1959:53). Whilst this approach might seem contrary to everything that could be described as good instruction, my intention is to leave possibilities, opportunities, and space for change open to students: Anything learned on the PGCert can and should be open for revision in the students' practice setting, leading to evolution and growth in both personal and professional development.

Activity	Title	Underpinning concept	Task	Outcome
1	Exploring viewpoints: reflecting on practice	Kolb, Schön	Film scenarios: Whiplash, Good Will Hunting, Dead Poets Society	Recognising the impact of a teacher's identity
2	Exploring relationships	Berne, Myers-Briggs	Personality and conflict in the classroom	Managing difference and the "games" we play
3	Engaging with the UKPSF	UKPSF	Gap analysis: creating a personal development plan	Drawing the PGCert back to the enhancement of participants' teaching practice

Table 5: Teaching plan for day three, module 1 of the PGCert.

Whilst my Rogerian-inspired approach to learning is held to be both effective and emancipatory, I am alive to the criticisms. Cissna & Anderson (1990) review the literature and find that a Rogerian approach to teaching can create a lack of clear-cut goals and priorities and can lead to self-interested indulgence in the classroom amongst students. I can see how this could occur, but on the PGCert, we have two main counterbalances to this risk: the UKPSF and our assessment. Throughout the programme, each activity is mapped to the UKPSF so that students are continually drawn back to reflect upon their personal engagement with the framework. For example, at the end of day one, the final session directs students to consider how that day has prepared them to engage with the UKPSF. This gives a strong degree of orientation for the goals and priorities of their work on the programme. This is further enhanced by the assessment on each module, which requires reflection upon and engagement with the UKPSF in order to pass. Above all, our role as teacher is also to ensure that participants on the PGCert have engaged with the UKPSF, and assessment provides the opportunity for students to demonstrate that they have done so in relation to UKPSF descriptor 2: Fellowship of the HEA.

PGCert Impact: A Student's Perspective – Marion Carrier

I attended the PGCert from January to December 2016. Coming from a chemical engineering background, the orientation of the class was a surprise, and in many ways a welcome change. I feel at some point in our learning journey there is need for change and progress, whether it is as a student or a professional. This is often sparked by something that could be seen as a breach in the "contract" between your teacher/supervisor/manager and yourself; I was open to possibilities, but I had expected a formal teacher training programme, and that is not what I received. What I received was a full personal and professional reappraisal of my identity as a teacher. The first module was unsettling and confusing. I was out of my comfort zone; it was intimidating but also made me curious. It jolted me out of the taken-for-granted views I had about what teachers do and how they do it.

The substructure to the success of the PGCert is that it is designed to engage with how people learn. Coming from a natural science background, I expected formal delivery of knowledge in lectures and reading lists. The expectation being that we should familiarise ourselves and adopt this knowledge and seek ways to inject it into our own teaching. I did not realise it at the time, but this "banking concept" of education (Freire, 1970) was the only approach to learning I had expected. In the first module, I was exposed to a wide range of different possibilities for learning, and I mapped these to a spectrum of epistemological positions.

I came to realise that in some areas of science the banking approach is the one to use; but learning "how" to teach it is not, and the PGCert teachers gently and kindly brought us to see that learning on the PGCert comes from looking at ourselves and the socially-constructed world we create with our colleagues and students (Berger & Luckmann, 1968).

Looking back to my early days on the PGCert, I have created three of my own sketches to convey my experience. Julian always described the PGCert as an artist's studio, so I have taken this to include actual expressions of art, not just metaphorical expressions, to convey my experiences in this chapter. Here, the drawings have been used as a starting point of my testimony. They embed states of emotions that I wanted to capture and share with people. The roughness of charcoals and pastels will hopefully provide some space for free interpretation as well.

In the first two days of the PGCert, I stepped outside of my comfort zone. These challenging learning situations are delicate and could be difficult to overcome; they could lead to the loss of curiosity, enthusiasm, and confidence. This gradual declining wellbeing is here in my illustration of a human body with both hands over its head as the representation of a tortured soul (Figure 1). What was this PGCert about? Surely, they should tell us how to be a good teacher. It bothered me. But I quickly understood that it *had* to be that way; it was all part of the PGCert pedagogy. It was carefully orchestrated and intended to be intrusive, unsettling, and challenging in order to bring us out of the histories of our own backgrounds and our experiences of being taught.

*Figure 1: "The tortured soul – the impact of module 1 of the PGCert".
(Original charcoal drawing by Marion Carrier, inspired by a photograph by
Dirk Mentrop).*

The feeling of confusion was caressed away from any real damage in
two ways: by invoking the self-disclosure principle and a deep respect
of anonymity. The PGCert highlighted the importance of building trust
and safety to explore what we might not otherwise talk about. Lydia,
another PGCert student, shares that:

> *"So, the PGCert was a place of 'love and acceptance' because we did not
> perceive each other as competition .... OK, I am not turning into a hippie
> person, because I am not. Work is not for kisses and cuddles, which are
> way overestimated anyway. This is absolutely insane to think, but people
> cannot help themselves .... After 8 years spent teaching in HE, I could
> only make a couple of friends. People keep their 'guard up' but there is no
> reason for it. If we think about 10 candidates for a job, it's like comparing
> apples, pears, plums, oranges, etc. There is absolutely no reason we should
> be shit to each other. The PGCert was a place of 'love and acceptance';
> where we could say what we think and know colleagues for the first time."*

Relationship as a vector of a rich experience was the most important aspect of the PGCert. It allowed a revision of my views and expectations of teaching and grew an arena, in that anything could be discussed and new ideas developed about the purpose of teaching and the way in which it can be enhanced.

As I continued on the programme, my experience as a participant on the PGCert is represented by my drawing "The forest" (Figure 2), which has long been associated with life and fertility, and seen in this educational context as a great source of inspiration. A woodcutter fells the old trees and nurtures the areas with new growth. Young trees should not be kept upright by props and stakes, but should be left to push against the wind and strive upwards with strong roots. The PGCert felled the preconceptions and then nurtured the growth of new, more authentic views about our identities as teachers. However, these views had to stand the pressure of discussion, debate, and even challenge, just as a young tree has to grow strong roots to remain upright.

Figure 2: "The forest". A representation of the growth of community and trust following the early disruption. (Original pastel drawing by Marion Carrier).

Undertaking an educational development programme is seen as a way to improve our professional conditions. The Aston PGCert is designed to convey participants in transformative learning through a cognitive process within a safe environment, and an important part is becoming bohemian – finding one's self in the cloudiness of all the pressures to conform in our work. Mike, another participant on the PGCert, reveals:

> "Aston University's 'bohemian branded' PGCert is a uniquely transformative experience. It has helped me add professionality to my educational idealism and led me to discover a halcyon path of integral teaching."

It is indisputable that this programme was designed to help participants explore their identity in a reflective and reflexive manner and that it offers a unique opportunity for coaching participants towards enhanced authenticity; that is, living a bohemian life. The pronunciation of the concept "authenticity" is recurrent in order to allow students to convey their own vision of truthfulness. Some of the participants referred to a gain in confidence; Ewan felt that the PGCert helped him: "*to go with my instinct and do things a little differently. It helped me see the value in stepping away from the norm.*" Lydia went further and revealed that "*This type of authenticity usually gets me into trouble.*"

The safety of the PGCert allows us to take risks and step away from conformity. Transformation is at the heart our experience on the PGCert. This journey of transformation has been crystallised in my final drawing entitled: "The levitating human" (Figure 3), which is directly inspired by the work of Gormley. The British sculptor has devoted his life to capture the essence of being a human on Earth and materialises the human body for the sake of being and pertaining to the earth. In a parallel objective, the PGCert aims to capture the human with teaching. It is a transformative journey where individuals engage with their emotional honesty as teachers.

Figure 3: "The levitating human". Human levitation to illustrate how participants become free of the constraints of tradition. (Original charcoal drawing by Marion Carrier).

The learning and teaching landscape drawn by the teachers had the function of promoting collaborative work through debates, conversations, and activities. By sharing their teaching experiences and reflections on their actions, the participants came to this unavoidable conclusion that teaching practices do not have to look like those of everyone else in order to be valuable and worthwhile. Michael told me that:

> *"The liberation felt on realising that we were not all misshaped pegs needing to conform to a strict set of rules was exhilarating. In fact, diversity, use of our own strengths and identity was actively encouraged."*

In working with this multidisciplinary audience, the PGCert teachers have turned this programme into a fantastic collaborative therapy. The participants find genuine empathy, support, and direction from others and are therefore able to unleash their talent. Becky reports that:

"I learnt that it is okay, actually more than okay, that I might not appear like a 'typical academic', especially being based in a creative and very human-centred field, it makes sense that I relate to those I teach."

A lot has been said of the transformative and therapeutic impact of the PGCert, and this is based on the PGCert teacher's understanding of how people learn. Of course, this wasn't just a therapy session; the PGCert is intended to enhance our professional practice as teachers and to also bring an embracement of the UKPSF to our development. It is interesting that the UKPSF was never forced upon us, but it was used in discussions as a set of "good ideas" to consider. It helped to use it as a set of "good principles" in teaching: Who can argue that the UKPSF dimensions of "knowing our subject", "how students learn", and "upholding diversity" are bad things? It was more a pledge of allegiance to ideas that enhance the lives of our students. Patrycja reports that:

"The PGCert at Aston was an interesting experience: A unique link between formal standardised knowledge, on one side, and then more open approach and exercise/discussion based implementation. It really helped me to evaluate my teaching style, reflect on things I could improve, and encouraged me to experiment with it."

The PGCert was also forward-looking and prepared us for all future possibilities. It gave us a set of long-term tools that can be used, shaped, and adjusted. This was made possible by the way it was so embedded in how we learn; and this was not just how we learn on the programme but how we learn after the programme and deal with the constant change and flux of our profession. Mike tells us that:

"The [PGCert] idea is spot on and will prepare future academics for this changing environment and equip them for what is going to be an interesting few years, especially with the aspect of Brexit as well, where SMEs, corporations and universities are going to have to be more local and global!"

For many PGCert students, the prospect of the course coming to an end was disheartening. It felt like a long summer holiday that comes to an end. However, that had already been considered, and we were given more chances to stay in the family through more studies on the PGDip and MEd (see Hayes, in this volume) and Teachers' Anonymous. Teachers' Anonymous takes the idea of the PGCert one step further: There is no syllabus, no learning outcomes, no enrolment, no records, and absolute confidentiality to talk about our lives in teaching and feel safe to express our frustrations and joys in the company of others who are treading the same path.

PGCert Legacy: An Undergraduate's Perspective – Jacob Lamb

During the spring of 2016, I volunteered to assist in the maths tutoring at Aston University's Learning Development Centre. It was an interesting experience. Not only did it give me an insight into the life of Aston students, but it also brought me alongside Aston teaching staff – I had a foot in two camps. This was an excellent primer to understand both the challenges of *teaching* and of *learning* in HE.

It has been very interesting to learn about the Aston PGCert, and, frankly, I am intrigued by the way teacher training is conducted. I assumed that university teachers received some sort of training and that this would be all about good PowerPoints and planning the syllabus. But now that I am fully immersed in life as an undergraduate, I can appreciate why the bohemian approach to the PGCert is so important. I have experienced a wide variety of teaching experiences and, above all, the most effective ones are those that really get into the mind of a student and use methods that best suit the way they learn. A nicely designed PowerPoint slideshow is worthless if the lecturer does not understand how students learn.

A really good illustration is in the way Zander (2008) teaches. Zander is a musicologist who teaches classical music appreciation to children who are probably more interested in thrash metal. Explaining his approach to teaching in a TED talk, he uses an anecdote:

> "Probably a lot of you know the story of the two salesmen who went down to Africa in the 1900s. They were sent down to find if there was any opportunity for selling shoes, and they wrote telegrams back to Manchester. And one of them wrote, 'Situation hopeless. Stop. They don't wear shoes.' And the other one wrote, 'Glorious opportunity. They don't have any shoes yet."

Zander, like the artist Dion, then proceeds to unpack a metaphorical suitcase of anecdotes and theatrical skills to bring his audience to grasp how he teaches classical music to disengaged children. He only conveys three conceptual ideas in his one-hour talk, and these ideas could be explained in ten minutes. The other fifty minutes are used to draw the audience into some sort of synchronised zone of "learning awareness" that makes them receptive to new ideas and, importantly, to be able to retain these ideas afterwards.

There are two reasons why I use the illustration of Zander in this chapter. First, I want to make the point, from my undergraduate perspective, that those lecturers who are the most effective in the lecture room or laboratory are the ones who ask the question: *"how can I get into the heads of my students and make this fun"*. Now, I do not mean fun as in trivial or low-level, but fun in terms of understanding that students learn best when they are in the best conditions for learning. Whilst I recognise that this is an obvious comment, it is remarkable how few lecturers give any thought to this; most appear to be intent on delivering *their* content and assuming that students are responsible for creating their own learning conditions. Those students who cannot or do not create their own effective learning conditions are assumed to be either poor students or not up to the task. This is illustrated by the sort of comment you might hear a lecturer pronounce at the end of a class: *"Come and ask for help if you need it; if you don't ask for help you are invisible to me and there is nothing I can do."* Whilst this might seem to be a reasonable thing for a teacher to say, I argue that it is not. This statement underlines that the lecturer has no interest and/or understanding of how students learn.

The second point is that the PGCert uses the same approach as Zander to engage with the curiosity of its participants. Speaking with several people who have recently taken the Aston PGCert, it is clear that whilst they experience some sort of personal and professional transformation, they also have a great deal of fun. They open up and absorb the subject because they are relaxed, respected, and are having fun.

Here is a "heads-up" to the teachers on the PGCert: You make a big point to say that it is not a training course, but I am afraid to say that it is. You are training them to have fun, to understand that student learning occurs best when students are at ease, feel respected, and have a right to be an individual learner. You teach the PGCert like this, and these HE teachers-in-training do the same with their own students. It is a form of training or instruction because you train them that the most important principle for being an effective teacher is to make a personal and intellectual connection with your students, and in so doing enhance the learning conditions.

Section 3: Guiding Thoughts for Other Curriculum Designers

This chapter discusses the pedagogy, design, delivery, and impact of the Aston PGCert. Our purpose is to showcase an approach to educational staff development that is both learning-centred and humanistic. We believe our experiment in education has been a success, and drawing on the voices of our PGCert students, it has been a powerful, immersive personal, and professional experience that has engaged with the ways in which students learn. Drawing on an undergraduate's viewpoint, it appears that success has much more to do with our careful nurturing of the "conditions for learning" on the PGCert than it has to do with the syllabus or any transfer of knowledge. Ironically, despite our early protestations that we do not train participants on the PGCert, it appears that the programme is something of a training scheme: We spend a year "training" participants to take the conditions for learning, and hence a learning-centred approach, as central to their own teaching practice.

Whilst the PGCert has been a success, it has also been a risky project. There is risk that a learning-centred approach might be misunderstood or even sabotaged. As an illustration, during a high-level meeting sometime after the launch of the new PGCert, a senior member of staff snorted, "*The content of the PGCert has little intrinsic value.*" Naturally, this was intended to be disparaging and would fit well with Luoma-aho's (2015) concept of a "hate-holder" (in contrast to a stakeholder) in programme design, but somehow this comment struck a note. Of course, there was a backstory to this person's disparaging view, but we have appropriated her comment and now use it at the start of every PGCert induction session as a narrative hook that draws participants to understand our learning-centred approach. We start by recounting the 19th century folk law origin of the word "snob" in HE. It is said that the letters S.N.O.B (which stand for "Sine Nobilitate", i.e., without nobility) were placed after the names of undergraduates who did not come from aristocratic families. This was done in order to mark them out as somehow "different" and not part of the norm (De Botton, 2007). The use of the word "snob" was later re-appropriated by social reformers to publically "out" those with conceited attitudes. In a similar vein, we have appropriated the comment *"The content on the PGCert has little intrinsic value"* and find it to be a powerful resource to explain that theory and content stand a distant second to participants *own* theorising and experience.

There is also a risk that some participants will struggle with the learner-centred focus of the PGCert and the first module in particular, which asks participants to embrace a social constructionist approach to teaching. From Marion's account in this chapter, it is clear that the first module can create confusion and anxiety for participants. Of course, this is part of the pedagogy; we intend for participants to feel confused and uncomfortable so that they take notice that this is not just another course in the theory of education. As the session proceeds, we take great care to engage each participant in personal conversation and establish the extent to which they have been able to orientate themselves to the challenge. If we find participants who are struggling to orientate, we offer additional tutorial support.

Towards the end of the PGCert programme, there is a further risk that participants will feel a sense of loss or abandonment when their year-long immersion in a close learning community comes to an end. We believe that it is important to attend to the rituals of closure: the final meal, the final session, the final goodbye. However, we also provide a route of progression to a postgraduate diploma (PGDip) and a master of education (MEd) for those who wish to continue the learning journey; and it is important to note that the PGDip and the MEd are also free at the point of delivery to those who work at Aston University (see Hayes, in this volume). For some participants, however, something more informal is desired. In view of this, we have created Teachers' Anonymous (TA), where on a monthly basis we meet and talk in a context of safety, security, and mutual support. There are no records of who attends TA or what is said, and there is a firm rule that nothing is discussed outside the TA sessions unless there is explicit permission to do so.

Finally, we offer some guidance for others who are considering a deeply learning-centred approach to educational development. First, do not water down the approach. Make your stance clear and unequivocal. Do not be put off by those in HE who might attempt to undermine the approach – engage with the hate-holders, make it political, and remember that: *"All evolution in thought and conduct must first appear as heresy and misconduct."* (Shaw, 1924:126).

Second, for an HEA-accredited programme, do not underestimate the importance of the UKPSF and assessment. The UKPSF provides an effective counterbalance to ensure that transformation on the PGCert is focused on the participant's professional practice, and assessment acts as the vehicle by which this transformation can be documented and evaluated.

About the Authors

Dr. Julian Lamb leads the HEA-accredited PGCert Learning and Teaching in Higher Education at Aston University. He can be contacted at this e-mail: j.lamb1@aston.ac.uk

Dr. Marion Carrier is a research fellow at the European Bioenergy Research Institute (EBRI), Aston University. She can be contacted at this e-mail: m.carrier@aston.ac.uk

Jacob Lamb is an undergraduate studying physics at Imperial College London. He can be contacted at this e-mail address: Jacob.lamb16@imperial.ac.uk

Bibliography

Berger, P. & T. Luckmann (1968). *The Social Construction of Reality*. New York: City Anchor.

Berne, E. (1966). *Games People Play: The Basic Hand Book of Transactional Analysis*, New York: Ballantine Books.

Cissna, K. & R. Anderson (1990). The contributions of Carl R. Rogers to a philosophical praxis of dialogue. *Western Journal of Speech Communication*, No. 54, pp. 125–147.

Crumly, C. (2014). *Pedagogies for Student-Centered Learning: Online and On-Ground* Fortress Press.

Curtin, J. (2017). *The importance of integrating authentic, reflective and collaborative learning experiences when designing for student-centred learning.* Curtin University, Perth, Western Australia 6102.

Dion, M. (2008). *Art 21 short film – Mark Dion.* Online Resource: https://art21.org/watch/exclusive/mark-dion-methodology-short/ [Accessed on 2 May 2017].

Freire, P. (1970). *Pedagogy of the Oppressed*, New York: Herder & Herder.

Goldfried, M. R. (2003). Therapist self-disclosure in cognitive-behavior therapy. *Journal of Clinical Psychology*, Vol. 59, No. 5, pp. 555–568.

Gormley, A. (2000). *Anthony Gormley*, Phaidon Press, London.

Gormley, A. (2017). *Antony Gormley: Sculpted space, within and without.* Online Resource: Ted.com. https://www.youtube.com/watch?v=vJ66jv8ICjc [Accessed on 2 February 2017].

HEA (2011). *United Kingdom Professional Standards Framework (UKPSF).* Higher Education Academy.

Hodge, S. (2010). *Occasional Papers on Learning and Teaching at UniSA – Paper 3 Student-centred learning in higher education and adult education.* Online Resource: http://w3.unisa.edu.au/academicdevelopment/what/documents/2010/Hodge.pdf [Accessed on 23 March 2017].

Johnson-Bailey, J. & R. M. Cervero (1997). *Crossing borders, breaking boundaries: Research in the education of adults: Beyond facilitation in adult education: power dynamics in teaching and learning practices.* 27th Annual SCUTREA conference proceedings 1997.

Kolb, D. (1984). *Experiential Learning as the Science of Learning and Development.* Englewood Cliffs, NJ: Prentice Hall.

Luoma-aho, V. (2015). Understanding Stakeholder Engagement: Faith-holders, Hateholders & Fakeholders. *Research Journal of the Institute for Public Relations*, Vol. 2, No. 1.

Mortiboys, A. (2005). *Teaching with Emotional Intelligence: A Step-by-Step Guide for Higher and Further Education Professionals*, London: Routledge.

Popper, K. (2007). *The Logic of Scientific Discovery*, London: Routledge Classics.

Rogers, C. (1967). *A Therapist's View of Psychotherapy – On Becoming a Person.* London: Constable & Company.

Rogers (2004). *On Becoming a Person.* London: Robinson.

Sayre Chazelle, D. (2015). *Whiplash.* Online Resource: https://www.youtube.com/watch?v=S6vTI5g198E, [Accessed on 29 May 2017].

Schön, D. (1984). *The Reflective Practitioner: How Professionals Think in Action.* London: Basic Books.

Shaw, G. B. (1924). *Saint Joan: a chronicle play in 6 scenes and an epilogue.* London: Constable.

Singh. R. H. (2017). *Brummy Sikh Honoured with Pride of Birmingham Award*, http://www.theasiantoday.com/index.php/2017/04/12/brummy-sikh-honoured-Pride-birmingham-award/ [Accessed on 2 February 2017].

Tanenbaum, S. (1959). Carl R. Rogers and Non-Directive Teaching, *Journal of Educational Leadership, Association for Supervision and Curriculum Development*, pp. 296–328.

Weimar, M. (2012). *Five Characteristics of Learner-Centered Teaching*. Online Resource: http://www.facultyfocus.com/articles/effective-teaching-strategies/five-characteristics-of-learner-centered-teaching/ [Accessed on 2 April 2017].

Wright-Brown, G. (2011). Student-Centered Learning in Higher Education. *International Journal of Teaching and Learning in Higher Education*, Vol. 23, No. 3, pp. 93–94.

Zander, M. (2008). *The transformative power of classical music*. Online Resource: https://www.ted.com/talks/benjamin_zander_on_music_and_passion [Accessed on 7 February 2017].

Chapter 6

Improving Learning-Centeredness in a Higher Education Foundation Phase Arts Curriculum

Eurika Jansen van Vuuren

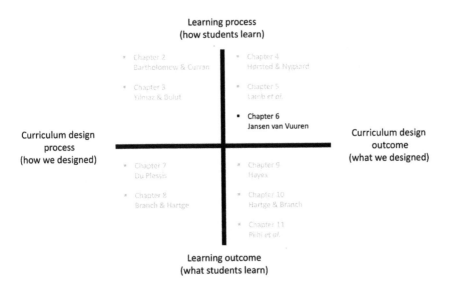

Learning process
(how students learn)

- Chapter 2
  Bartholomew & Curran

- Chapter 4
  Horsted & Nygaard

- Chapter 3
  Yilmaz & Bulut

- Chapter 5
  Laleb et al.

- Chapter 6
  Jansen van Vuuren

Curriculum design process
(how we designed)

Curriculum design outcome
(what we designed)

- Chapter 7
  Du Plessis

- Chapter 9
  Hayes

- Chapter 8
  Branch & Hartge

- Chapter 10
  Hartge & Branch

- Chapter 11
  Riihi et al.

Learning outcome
(what students learn)

Introduction

I contribute to this book *Learning-Centred Curriculum Design in Higher Education* by providing guidelines on designing a more learning-centred curriculum through the contextualisation of learning activities and through adapting new teaching methods. My focus is specifically on the arts (drama, music, and visual arts) curriculum for generalist Bachelor of Education (BEd) foundation phase pre-service teachers. This course is aimed at teachers working professionally with children aged five to nine. Dance (creative movement), which is a valuable part of the arts, was excluded from this chapter due to it not being offered as a part of the arts module but rather as a section under physical education, where there is more time available. In relation to the central model of the book, I position my chapter in section two – Learning Process/Curriculum Design Output – because my focus is, firstly, on how students learn and, secondly, on what I designed to ensure a contextualised and learning-centred curriculum. I argue that the curriculum should be designed as a learning-centred action plan because student learning is individually contextualised. This is something I will come back to in much more detail.

I define a learning-centred curriculum as one where deep learning takes place through active student involvement followed by reflection, abstract conceptualisation through theory, and then a return to the initial activity with renewed knowledge (Mayer, 2004; Fry, 1979). Conditions for deep learning start with "an intention to understand the material being studied." (Gordon, 2002:484). Once students have the "intention to understand", one can progress and move onto developing Hermida's (2014) higher-order cognitive skills (analysing, synthesising, problem solving), which will ensure retention of knowledge that can then in turn be utilised in new learning situations.

I focus on student learning in the arts module, where new skills have to be obtained and retained in a time-restricted programme. Unlike the content matter of many other subjects, the arts cannot easily be acquired through reading and learning. An effective learning-centred curriculum has to be in place to ensure that practical work is followed by reflection (lecturer and students) and abstract conceptualisation before returning to further teaching to ensure that students go through a process of deep learning to build confidence for future teaching.

Lecturers in the arts have a dual task: they not only teach theoretical knowledge that students can also acquire on their own through reading, they have the added task of teaching artistic skills in various art forms. These artistic skills, such as playing a musical instrument or mastering a paint or drama technique, are traditionally acquired over many years of practise, yet in the BEd curriculum for the foundation phase it must be taught in a few weeks.

I share insights gained from the literature regarding curriculum development, contextualisation, and learning-centred teaching methods. I also provide the framework I used for developing an arts curriculum for BEd foundation phase teachers (grade R to 4) and indicate how learning-centeredness and contextualisation was approached. As a segment of contextualisation, I touch on the meaning of decolonisation in an arts curriculum in an attempt to address the issues currently plaguing higher education in South Africa, where students are calling for a move towards an African-centred curriculum rather than focusing on global education. Furthermore, I discuss the way I adapted my teaching methods to be more learning-centred. By comparing some sections of the newly adapted curriculum with the original curriculum, I provide a glimpse into the subtle changes that sometimes need to be made to improve learning. The main challenges in the arts curriculum for BEd foundation phase students that motivated the reworking of the curriculum are discussed. These challenges are predominantly caused by students' lack of prior knowledge, untrained role models, unsuitable teaching spaces, time limitations in the curriculum, and contextual inappropriateness. Reading this chapter, you should gain at least three insights:

1. the framework needed for a contextualised arts curriculum;

2. how to integrate teaching methods that promote learning-centeredness;

3. a comparison of the previous curriculum to the new contextualised, learning-centred curriculum.

I have structured the chapter in three sections. In section one, I give a background to the events and challenges that led to the redesign of the BEd Foundation Phase curriculum at the University of Mpumalanga, where I am employed. In section two, I present suitable frameworks exploring learning, learning-centeredness, and contextualisation. In section three, I provide insight into how the changes were made through addressing the challenges and restructuring the curriculum to meet the needs of being learning-centred and contextualised.

Section 1: Challenges

As a newly appointed arts lecturer at a newly established university, I was tasked with the development of a curriculum for the BEd Foundation Phase arts module. Having had many years of experience as a teacher in the arts at school level as well as in the position of subject advisor where I trained in-service teachers, I felt honoured to be given the task and confident that I had a good understanding from different perspectives of what is required in an arts module to ensure that new teachers are suitably equipped for their task. The students in our university are all African and mostly come from rural areas where the majority of teachers still use traditional teacher-centred methodology and rote learning. Despite the university curriculum being designed to be more learning-centred and the majority of lecturers using learning-centred approaches, the students often fall back on traditional teaching methods in their own micro-teaching situations, especially when they are confronted with a challenge in the classroom. I realised that I had to reflect on, and adjust my own teaching methods in order to assist these education students to experience alternative teaching methods. By being more exposed to constructivist methods, they would have the courage and be empowered to break free from the teacher-centred teaching approach cycle that is prevalent in the majority of South African schools.

The general challenges facing arts curricula in BEd Foundation Phase programmes in many parts of the world, and which were considered when drawing up the arts curriculum, include:

1. students' lack of sufficient prior knowledge;

2. the arts modelling pre-service educators were observing – or not seeing at all;

3. time constraints in offering the subject;

4. contextual inappropriateness;

5. unsuitable teaching spaces.

These challenges can be grouped into three main categories, as displayed in Figure 1:

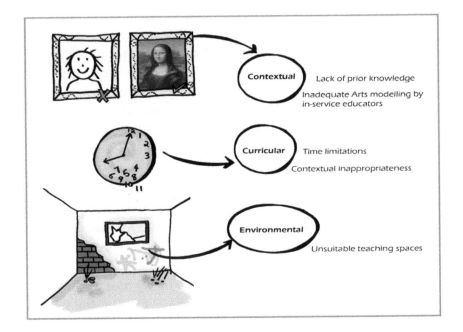

Figure 1: Challenges in the BEd Foundation Phase programme.

In the following subsections, I will unpack the challenges experienced in the programme.

Contextual Challenges

Lack of prior knowledge

All the students at the University of Mpumalanga are of African descent, and black South Africans are lauded worldwide for their cultural arts skills, which are mostly integrated and have a social dimension. This phenomenon where the arts do not stand alone but are part of an intertwined whole of dancing, singing, and drama is referred to as the "Ngoma" principle (Kiel, 2006). Being a South African and having experienced the African arts throughout my life had led me to believe that my students would have a good foundation of cultural arts to build upon. The contradicting lack of arts knowledge I found amongst the students was unexpected. My high expectations were curbed by the reality of students who have started losing their indigenous cultural knowledge due to a variety of factors, including moving away from a traditional lifestyle where children grow up dancing and singing along with their parents around the campfire and listening to master storytellers. Whilst some students can still do traditional dancing and singing, visual art and craft skills such as weaving, pottery, patterning, and beading are not so easily found in communities any longer. Foundation phase teachers in South Africa are trained as generalist teachers, and unlike their counterparts in the intermediate phase university courses, they do not have areas of specialisation. Consequently, arts specialists are seldom found in the foundation phase unless they had private arts tuition whilst at school. This lack of arts knowledge poses a challenge, since it forms an important part of teaching in any foundation phase classroom – not only for teaching the arts in its own right or for use in integrated teaching, but also as part of the holistic development of the child. Very few African children in rural areas are fortunate enough to be exposed to formal arts training due to the scarcity of funds, suitably qualified arts teachers, and the remoteness from city centres where courses are sometimes sponsored by large companies and international aid.

For the arts in schools not to lose its integrity, it is essential that all these previously disadvantaged students are given the necessary skills to, firstly, regain their pride in their traditional arts and, secondly, also pass the arts module at a reasonably high level in order to provide them with the confidence needed to break the negative cycle of arts poverty in schools. Due to this changed and still-changing social and cultural landscape, the curriculum I had originally designed for culturally rich African students with a reasonable level of prior knowledge did not ensure real learning, since it was too far removed from their limited background in the arts. Although this chapter is focused on African students in particular, due to the context where the research took place, arts lecturers in the rest of the world concur about pre-service education students generally arriving from school with very limited arts knowledge. These students then have to be taught a large number of practical arts skills, didactical knowledge, and arts philosophies to have a suitable knowledge to be able to teach confidently and effectively in the foundation phase.

Inadequate arts modelling by in-service educators

Another negative impacting factor on arts learning is the "apartheid" legacy, which did not develop teachers appropriately in the arts in teacher training programmes. With many of these teachers still in the system, good practice arts modelling is limited and the cycle of arts poverty is perpetuated. When visiting foundation phase schools in many parts of South Africa, it is found that limited arts are taught – let alone integrated arts – except for the occasional song. Teachers regard colouring-in as art and include a large amount of it in class, whereas colouring in does not promote creativity and leads to carbon copy pictures with no creativity being displayed around the class. Many teachers avoid teaching the arts because of their own limited training and exposure. The situation in turn leads to pre-service education students not being exposed to best practice arts lesson presentations when they visit schools. In addition, the learners in these classes, once they reach universities, have limited formal arts skills. This cycle of arts illiteracy must be broken for the arts to regain its rightful place in education. Although teacher modelling does not in itself necessarily lead to deep learning, it provides a "case" that can be reflected on and used to develop analytical problem-solving skills, which are essential for deep learning.

Environmental Challenges

Unsuitable teaching spaces

Adding to the arts lecturer's woes are the buildings sometimes occupied by the universities which were not designed with the needs of educator training in mind. Lecture halls are built in the typical pitched-floor style, allowing few options for group work or practical work. It is thus not the ideal situation to show good teaching practice to students and often causes lecturers to revert to traditional lecturing instead of being at the forefront of innovative teaching methods. The remainder of venues on the campus where I teach either have fixed tables (science lab format) or are not large enough to house an entire group (100–108) of students. These inadequate learning spaces impact negatively on learning-centred teaching.

Curricular Challenges

Time limitations

Probably the most debilitating factor in BEd Foundation Phase programmes must be the limited time afforded in the curriculum to arts training. Many arts courses comprise of only one semester, where students must be taken from zero to arts hero. It is almost impossible to learn, as well as obtain retention of especially music skills, in such a limited time span. The content of school subjects that are taught in foundation phase teacher education programmes can mostly be attained through reading, observing, and learning, unlike the arts, where skills must be practised for a considerable time to ensure retention and to develop confidence. Due to the briefness of the arts module, students move from the cognitive phase to the associative phase of motor learning when doing practical work but do not have the opportunity to get to the autonomous phase where they have suitable skills and confidence (Fitts, 1967). At the university where I teach, drama, visual art, and crafts, as well as music skills, must be attained in one module comprising of 14 lectures of 90 minutes each. At least two of these lectures can be subtracted for revision purposes, and in the current troubled higher education in South Africa where students strike to force the government to provide free higher education and to decolonise the curriculum, some lectures are lost due to student unrest. Each lecture is augmented by a tutorial session later in the week where work already covered is revised and practical work linked to the theory is done. This time allocation is totally unrealistic for a subject where a variety of skills need to be learnt, developed, and practiced.

Contextual inappropriateness

The original curriculum I designed, covered all the content and didactic aspects as required by the Department of Basic Education in the curriculum and assessment policy (CAPS, 2011). I was confident that my students, armed with this knowledge, were going to make a difference in ensuring quality teaching of the arts in foundation phase schools. After two years as an arts lecturer at this university, I made the disheartening discovery that having an arts curriculum with well-balanced content and with all the globally accepted theories and philosophies does not always suffice to ensure that pre-service educators are suitably empowered to teach arts with confidence. The carefully researched curriculum that I designed was not producing the outcomes I envisaged and desired. Moreover, the teaching approach I was using was not always ensuring deep learning. This lack of proper arts learning was especially evident when observing micro-teaching where students were avoiding any arts activities that went beyond singing or colouring in a picture. I realised that a more contextually grounded curriculum with an altered teaching approach was essential to ensure deep learning that would in turn yield retention of skills and knowledge. Higher education in South Africa has been in turmoil, with calls for "Rhodes must fall", fees must fall, and the decolonisation of curricula. This movement began at the University of Cape Town on 9 March 2015, where students rioted and demanded the removal of the statue of Cecil John Rhodes to highlight racism in South African universities and to decolonise education. Rhodes was believed to have promoted the extension of British rule throughout the world and students wanted his statue to be removed, despite the scholarships from which South African students were still benefitting. The student unrest has academics revisiting curricula and grappling with the notion of "decolonisation". I am of the opinion that "decolonisation" in the arts domain should rather be referred to as "contextualisation", since acculturation has merged arts in Africa to an extent where taking away colonial influences will mean killing popular African genres like "gospel" music, which came to the continent with missionaries from the West. A balanced curriculum approach leading from African philosophies rather than the current Western approach will give students a more understandable point of departure, which will in turn provide a better foundation from where deep learning can take place. Many students use a surface learning approach and just want to meet the minimum requirements to pass, partially due to having to learn material that is not part of their heritage whilst not even having the knowledge of their own arts traditions.

Section 2: Framework for a Contextualised Arts Curriculum

When contemplating the adaptations required to produce a more learning-centred curriculum, I had to do it in a way that would simultaneously meet the needs of the Department of Higher Education and Training (DHET), address arts-specific learning, learning-centeredness in general, and deal with contextualisation. In addition, the challenges experienced in arts training had to be considered to ensure that the curriculum would be fitting.

Learning

When studying the National Qualifications Framework Act of 2008 (DHET, 2015: 9), five types of learning are required in the South African curriculum for educators. These learning types are:

1. disciplinary learning;

2. pedagogical learning;

3. practical learning;

4. fundamental learning;

5. situational learning.

These learning types are associated with the "acquisition, integration and application of knowledge for teaching purposes" and are graphically presented in Figure 2.

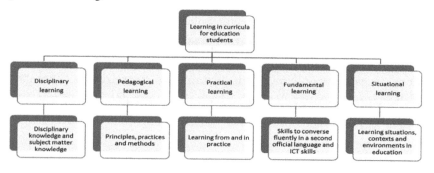

Figure 2: Learning in South African curricula for education students.

This array of learning competencies that are required in the curriculum are also mentioned in work by Marsh (2007), who defines curriculum as the total learning experiences (disciplinary, pedagogical, practical, and fundamental) that are given to students at a variety of places (situational) for them to attain skills and knowledge. When looking at this definition in the context of pre-service teacher education, this would then include the two main components of the curriculum: theory and practice. Taking into consideration the different types of learning required by the DHET, it is also important to decide how to harness the different learning processes to make sense in an arts context. When focusing on the arts, pedagogical approaches to learning are somewhat different. Arts-specific learning is required to be successful in the retention of specifically practical skills. When planning an arts curriculum, it is necessary to heed educational theorists such as Dewey (1938), who was one of the first to strongly believe that people learn by doing and that all genuine education is achieved through experience. Students are not clean slates that can be shaped into perfect teachers, they arrive at university with experience of their own schooling – the 12-year apprenticeship in teaching (Lortie, 1975). Many students think they have all the experience and knowledge to teach because they have seen and lived it for so many years. In the South African context, many students' apprenticeship exposure to an underprivileged education needs to be remodelled with best practice exposure in order to enable South Africa to move away from the label of being one of the countries with the worst education in the world (Spaull, 2013). Although the "doing" in the arts is important, theory is also essential (Kolb, 2014) to rectify students' sometimes warped images of education and to ensure they have a solid understanding of teaching. Gravett (2012:6) strengthens this notion and alludes to the fact that pre-service students *"are not in a position to identify concerns if they do not have theoretical lenses or at least declarative knowledge with which to note concerns. If you do not know you cannot see."* Without theoretical lenses, students will not have the ability to discern between a lesser education and best practice education.

Learning-Centeredness

In an effort to put theory and practice onto the same stage as important players in the arts curriculum, it is essential to ensure that it is done in a way that ensures deep learning. In my opinion, even the best learning-centred curriculum will not produce the desired outcomes if the different facets of the curriculum are not managed and controlled effectively. I concur with Nygaard & Kristensen (2009:6), who provide a cyclical "map" in their definition of curriculum in order to ensure a successful outcome. They define a curriculum as a learning-centred action plan where learning takes place as an action-reflection learning process and where theory and practice are interlinked through a case-based pedagogy. This definition emphasises the learning in the curriculum, which should be fluid and adapt as it deepens through reflection and action. The learning is based on created situations (cases) that simulate real-life scenarios and which are then observed and analysed. I have replaced Nygaard & Kristensen's (2009) notion of "case-based" pedagogy in his learning-centred curriculum with "practical arts" since the same principles that are used to analyse and learn and develop when studying a case can be used in the arts curriculum when practical work is done, reflected upon, linked to theory, and then continued in a cyclical manner. This "learning-centred action plan" meets the needs of the pre-service education sector, where theory and practice sometimes sing on two different stages and are not composed into one harmonious song. Figure 3 provides a graphic representation of the thinking of Nygaard & Kristensen (2009) regarding the structure of a learning-centred curriculum infused with my own notion of a learning-centred arts curriculum. The cycle of arts education must start with the action – doing an activity and then followed up with reflection and learning (which should include theory) before going into more action.

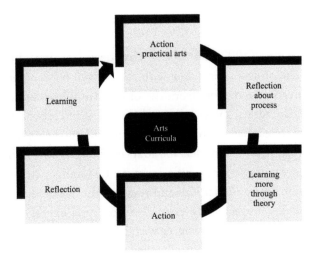

Figure 3: Learning-centred arts curriculum.

Although theory is an important part of learning the arts, it must not necessarily be the point of departure. Elliott's (1990:153) words ring very true and support the notion of doing practice before theory when it talks about learning music: "*Music, then, is essentially a fourfold phenomenon: it involves a doer, a doing, something done, and a context in which the doing is done.*" Learning to *do* the arts rather than just learning *about* the arts is essential for equipping foundation phase teachers – they must first *do* and then learn why. Just like Elliott (1990), music theorist Carl Orff said, "*Experience first, then intellectualize*" (Alberta Chapter, 2017, n.p.). Orff was supported by Shinichi Suzuki (International Suzuki Association, 2017, n.p.) who also advocated the practical approach. Suzuki made the simple observation that all Japanese children can speak Japanese, so all children can then learn to play a musical instrument in the same way that they first learn language. In line with these thoughts, I propose that a good arts curriculum should have a certain amount of practical experience before delving into theory. Theory will then strengthen the understanding of a skill that you have already acquired and give insight into the processes that led to attaining the skill, which in turn will equip you to pass the skill on to your learners (see Branch & Hartge, in this volume).

Contextualising an Arts Programme

I interpret Gordon's (2002:484) notion that deep learning comes from *"active integration of new information with old, or with information derived from other sources"*, like moving from the old (cultural heritage and prior knowledge) and integrating it with the new (Western and other arts philosophies). This implies that a contextualised curriculum can enhance deep learning. There are various models for adapting or designing curricula to make them more suitable for specific contexts. Le Grange (2016:9) refers to decolonisation of the curriculum and suggests the use of four Rs: *"relational accountability, respectful representation, reciprocal appropriation, and rights and regulation."* Although I agree with his notions of decolonisation, I would rather refer to a "contextually adapted" curriculum with a focus on the revival of indigenous arts than a "decolonised" curriculum with regard to this study. Le Grange (2016:9) describes relational accountability as the idea that curriculum must be connected and accountable to all relations – human and "more-than-human" relations, which I interpret as respect for religion and cultural beliefs. Respectful representation is reached when a curriculum has space for the voices and knowledge of its indigenous people. "Reciprocal appropriation" shows the mutual benefit of communities and universities in knowledge production. "Rights and regulation" refer to acknowledgement of ownership of some knowledge as belonging to indigenous people all over the world. In adapting a curriculum to become learning-centred and contextualised, I kept the learning types in mind to ensure DHET compliance, but I focused on learning-centeredness and contextualisation, as represented in Table 1.

Learning-centeredness	Contextualisation
+ Learning-centred action plan: action-reflection learning process and where theory and practice are interlinked through a case-based pedagogy + Active student involvement	+ Relational accountability + Respectful representation + Reciprocal appropriation + Rights and regulation + Actively integrating new information with old information

Table 1: Facets incorporated into the adapted curriculum.

Section 3: Towards Making the Changes

When making changes to the curriculum, I had to refrain from focusing on the contextual elements that are beyond my control – in-service teacher role models and prior knowledge of students – and focus on elements that could be changed in the actual arts curriculum to make a positive difference. Making the difference in the lecture hall should eventually impact the situation in the classroom by providing adequately trained teacher role models and, ultimately, learners with arts knowledge. Creative thinking and alternative strategies had to be employed to assist with securing more time and finding suitable teaching spaces for the arts. To ensure a learning-centred curriculum, changes were mostly made in presentation methods and points of departure.

Environmental Changes

Finding a suitable teaching venue

During previous years, I taught music in a lecture hall with tiered seating. This was not conducive to proper learning and was also time consuming, since the instruments (percussion) had to be moved around the class to allow every student to get some instrumental experience. The ideal situation is to have a room where instruments can be laid out on tables and students move from one table to the next to get to a new instrument. Since it was not possible to teach guitar in the lecture halls, I had to resort to an unused classroom that could house 35–40 students and their guitars at once. The groups receive 30-minute tuition sessions each, and although this is not the ideal situation, it has been workable and has assisted in teaching in a more learning-centred manner. There is also limited space available for members of other groups to join in with percussion and marimba playing.

Curricular Changes

Securing more time

Trying to find extra time in an already overflowing arts curriculum was one of the most challenging tasks. The allocated 14 lectures (90 minutes each) and their tutorials hardly ever materialise due to factors previously discussed. Unlike in other modules where tutors replace the lecturer during tutorial time, the arts lecturer has to be present during tutorials due to practical skills that have to be taught to a cohort of students (100–108) with limited skills in most art forms. This doubles the load of the arts lecturer. To find more teaching time, some sections of the curriculum that were dealt with separately before had to be synthesised and taught in an integrated teaching style. This style encompassed teaching content along with didactics. This process made more time for practical work, where the real learning occurs in the arts. Guitar practical takes place from week one to week eight – during tutorial time. In addition, all students attend two guitar practice sessions with tutors every week. As from week eight, the guitar practices are only done in students' free time due to the tutorials then being used for drama or art practical.

Adapting the curriculum to become more learning-centred

Lecturers in arts education cannot effectively teach if they use only traditional lecturing. Along with singing the theory, they also have to model best practice teaching in all the art forms. One of the main adjustments that had to be made to the curriculum was incorporating more learning-centred methods and moving away from the previous mostly lectured format interspersed with practical work. The tables that follow below only include some of the topics of the curriculum to illustrate how the teaching was transformed to become more learning-centred (see Yılmaz & Bulut, in this volume). Furthermore, the inclusion of the two main frameworks used in the new curriculum – learning-centeredness and contextualisation – are indicated and displayed below each topic. Table 2 addresses the general background section of the arts curriculum.

Curriculum topic	Teaching method before 2016	Teaching method since 2016
Integrated arts teaching	• Students read articles about integrated arts teaching. • Articles are discussed and summarised during lectures.	• Students watch videos of arts-integrated lessons. • Students answer questions regarding integration methods. • Students prepare group lesson plan for arts-integrated teaching. • Lesson plans are swapped between groups and peer assessed. • Entire class meets to reflect and discuss outcomes with the lecturer.

Learning-centeredness:

Students watch an authentic classroom situation, reflect on procedures and methods, and then design their own lesson plan using the newly obtained knowledge about arts-integrated teaching. The lesson plan is then peer assessed and outcomes are discussed.

Contextualisation:

No specific contextualisation.

African arts philosophy	• This was not covered previously.	• In groups, students read different articles regarding African arts philosophies. • Students give report back on most important facets, using A1 flip chart sheets. • A1 sheets are displayed on lecture hall walls. • Groups compile their own African arts philosophy using information from the articles and combining it with their own ideas. • Groups present their philosophies using a PowerPoint presentation and submit for assessment.

Curriculum topic	Teaching method before 2016	Teaching method since 2016
Learning-centeredness: Students read, analyse to report back, share, and develop their own philosophy and present it. All students are involved in developing and sharing of an African arts philosophy and have to produce a new product. Contextualisation: Developing an African-specific arts philosophy based on writings of African arts scholars.		
Curriculum and assessment policy statement (CAPS) for foundation phase	• The school curriculum (CAPS) topics were given to students. • The BEd curriculum content is presented to see how it is aligned.	• Students are divided into three groups (drama, music, and visual art) and summarise school curriculum content for grade R to 3 in each art form. • Lecturer presents the students with the existing BEd curriculum for arts which they then compare with the one they have compiled. • Students get 15 minutes for evaluation of the existing curriculum and to suggest changes for contextualisation of the BEd curriculum without diminishing it in order to enhance their own learning. • A class discussion takes place.
Learning-centeredness: Active student involvement where students have to balance practice and theory in order to create a new product. Reflection happens to compare curricula and make suggestions for improvement and contextualisation. Students become part of the process of curriculum development and feel part of the learning process. Contextualisation: Respectful representation can be accomplished when students have the opportunity to suggest material that would be beneficial to their own contextualised learning.		

Curriculum topic	Teaching method before 2016	Teaching method since 2016
Lesson planning in the arts	• Students were given a lesson example done on the correct template, and then the lecturer explained to them how it was done and what the thinking was behind each section.	• Students are given the headings of the sections of the lesson template and have to order them logically. (Competition – the team who is first to complete the task correctly, wins). • They are then given a broken-down arts lesson plan and have to fit it into the correct sections – this is done outside on the grass or a flat surface so that everyone stands around it and can give an input. • The lecturer moves between groups to assist if needed (also done in competition form where the winners are the first to finish with the correct layout). • Each student designs an integrated arts lesson plan and submits online for assessment. • Lecturer assesses and does full review. • Students resubmit the improved lesson plan.

Learning-centeredness:

Students use existing theoretical knowledge to assemble a lesson plan. When partaking in a competition, students become more involved. They then construct their own lesson plan, keeping the theory in mind. The lecturer assesses the lesson plan, reviews it, and makes suggestions. The student effects improvements. All students are involved and cannot disappear into the group.

Contextualisation:

No formal contextualisation.

Table 2: General introduction to arts curriculum.

Table 3 has the music section of the curriculum as the focus.

Curriculum topic	Teaching method before 2016	Teaching method since 2016
Western music education theories vs. African music education theories: Resemblances and differences	• African music philosophies were not covered previously.	• Students sit in pairs and find and compile African music education methods that they have been exposed to personally or from the Internet through the use of their mobile phones. • They hand these methods in on A4 sheets to appointed study leaders, who summarise the information on flip chart sheets and display it on the board. • The lecturer introduces Western music education theories on PowerPoint. • The class discusses differences and resemblances between African and Western music education philosophies and decide which Western theory is best aligned to the African music education theories. • Lecturer shows video clips of different music education methods in action and students have to identify the teaching philosophy involved using either the Western or the African philosophies.
Learning-centeredness: Students find information in pairs and do not have the opportunity to get easily sidetracked. They have to compare to find similarities and differences and have to be able to identify the different teaching methods. Moving from cultural practices (the known) to Western education methods (partially unknown). Contextualisation: The accent is placed on African music education methods and using indigenous knowledge to move to global knowledge. This assists students in regaining pride in their own cultural heritage and taking ownership of it.		

Percussion: Bought and handmade	• Students are taught the names of different percussion instruments. • Students are taught how to write a percussion score (using Western notation rhythms) and also play the instruments in class. • Students make three percussion instruments and write their own percussion score for these instruments. 	• Students are asked to assist in naming traditional African percussion instruments and their sounds shown on PowerPoint. • They share information on how, by whom, and where these instruments are used. • Students are shown Western percussion instruments – on a presentation or, where available, the real instrument. • Comparisons are made between Western and African instruments, focusing on sound and construction. • Instruments are classified using the Hornbostel-Sachs method. • Students construct percussion instrument kits with 10 instruments using recycled materials and submit it for assessment. • Students are shown how to prepare a percussion score (using their own notational symbols) for ensemble playing and write group scores of no longer than two minutes using the percussion instruments they made and including body percussion and beatboxing. • Ensemble is recorded and submitted for assessment along with written score. • Videos are viewed and peer assessed in groups. • Each assessment must be accompanied by a written report reflecting on the allocated marks.

Learning-centeredness:

Learning starts by the sharing of indigenous knowledge, which gives students a foundation for understanding Western instruments. By making their own instruments and developing a notational system, students have to do research, reflect on possibilities, and show creativity and skill. When exposed to this type of practical work, there is a high level of involvement.

Contextualisation:

Indigenous instruments are used as a point of departure before continuing to Western percussion. Knowing that music resources are limited in schools, students have to make 10 percussion instruments to ensure that they have a "starter kit" when starting their teaching careers. I moved away from staff notation and used colour notation and examples of symbols that can be used instead of staff notation.

Guitar

- Students were divided into four groups, and 20–25 students and their instruments were squeezed into a very small room for lessons.
- One tutor with limited guitar skills was appointed to assist but could not move between the students due to lack of space.
- Students learnt to play three major chords (D, A, and G), which enables them to play accompaniment for a large variety of children's songs.
- Final practical guitar assessment took place after the six-week guitar training period.

- A larger room was obtained where up to 40 students and their instruments could be housed.
- There is enough space for four tutors to move amongst the students and assist with chord placement and strumming, whilst the lecturer leads the lesson by playing, singing along, and also instructing the use of dynamic and tempo changes.
- Students who are awaiting their turn to play now have the opportunity to join in by playing the other instruments (e.g., marimbas and percussion).
- Students learn to play three major chords (D, A, and G), which enables them to play accompaniment for a large variety of children's songs.
- In addition, they have to prepare a song from their own culture for their assessment. They are provided with guitar books with repertoire and teaching ideas and contexts for each song.
- Although the formal guitar training period has remained six weeks, they now continue with lessons with the tutors until almost the end of the semester and have approximately 10 weeks to polish their skills for assessment.
- The extra time will ensure that students have a better chance of retention.

Learning-centeredness:

Smaller groups ensure better teaching and remedial work. The social component of having students from other groups joining in has heightened levels of enjoyment and class attendance. The cycle of practical playing, followed by reflection and in turn by remedial work where necessary, certainly ensures deeper learning. The retention of playing skills has improved and more students are joining the music groups in other year levels to continue with their playing.

Contextualisation:

The addition of songs from each student's own culture.

Table 3: Music curriculum.

One of the remaining concerns in the learning-centeredness of the music curriculum remains the retention of guitar skills. Due to this curriculum only being in place since 2016, it is not yet possible to report on retention. However, a marked improvement could be seen in skill levels in the final assessment.

Table 4 gives a glimpse into the activities covered in the drama curriculum.

Curriculum topics	Teaching method before 2016	Teaching method since 2016
Elements of drama	• A traditional approach was used where I was teaching elements of drama through the use of PPT and by referring to well-known TV programmes and theatre productions as examples.	• Students watch three videos of typical African productions (I would prefer taking students to theatrical events, but we are very isolated). • We recap the elements of drama (which they also learn in home language and second language) and I teach them how to critique a production for a newspaper column. • They work in pairs to write a critique in table form using all the elements of drama in the first column and then give their opinion of the success or failure of the play in each respect. • We then have a panel discussion to select the winning production.

Learning-centeredness:

Students who have previously just sat and stared in lectures are now involved in practical analysis in pairs. Being in such a small group ensures maximum participation.

Contextualisation:

African productions are used for analysis and ensure that students are exposed to work from their own cultures rather than only Western productions.

African drama genres	• Newly added.	• Students are grouped according to cultures and have to list the drama genres found in their own cultures along with a definition. • The class assistant then helps with the compilation. • Knowledgeable students in the class then share their knowledge about the different genres indicated in the groups. • Students are shown short videos from YouTube and have to place them in the correct genre.

Learning-centeredness:

This section of the work was made more learning-centred by allowing the students to find the genres rather than presenting them with the genres. They become very involved when watching videos and enjoy deciding on the genres.

Contextualisation:

Using African genres of drama as a point of departure assists students in having a foundation for comparison with global genres and also assists with the appreciation of their own cultural productions.

Drama technique – mime, storytelling, praise singing, poetry, role play, choral verse	• Students were given a summary of each drama technique on PowerPoint and then did short group activities to practice each of the techniques.	• The lecturer presents drama technique by teaching it to the students in the same way that the students have to teach it to their learners. • After each technique, lecturer and students reflect about the didactical method used and also talk about ways to include it in everyday teaching. • An emphasis has been placed on storytelling because it is an integral part of traditional African cultural arts. • Praise singing, another traditional African art form, has been added to the array of techniques.

Learning-centeredness:

All drama work is done practically with the lecturer demonstrating techniques and all students then being given topics for impromptu performances in group format. All students who attend are directly involved in "doing", which ensures better retention of knowledge.

Contextualisation:

The emphasis on storytelling and praise singing has added an African dimension to the curriculum.

Script writing and technique for puppet theatre (hand puppets)	• Newly added.	• Students are shown how to use puppets in teaching and volunteers are given a chance to be puppeteers using a story provided by the lecturer. • Students critique presentation. • Students then write a three-minute script in their groups that is suitable for foundation phase and based on a topic taken from the CAPS document. • Students practise and perform in front of peers for assessment.

Learning-centeredness:

Students are involved through the entire process and also have to create a show incorporating elements required by the curriculum (CAPS) before being assessed for their production.

Contextualisation:

Puppetry is not a traditional cultural activity in South Africa but was included due to its immense value in sharing knowledge where young children are involved.

Table 4: Drama curriculum.

Table 5 gives a summary of the most important material in the visual art and crafts section of the curriculum and how the curriculum was adapted.

Curriculum topics	Teaching method before 2016	Teaching method since 2016
Elements and principles of art	• Students were taught the elements and principles of art through watching a PowerPoint presentation where the elements were taught. • The group as a whole then had to recognise the elements in paintings and pictures that the lecturer took to class.	• Students are taught about the principles and elements of art using a PowerPoint presentation and then accompany the lecturer on a campus tour where a variety of paintings and murals are analysed to illustrate the use of the elements and principles. • Each student chooses an artwork by an African artist and has the opportunity to analyse it and write a review using elements and principles of art as a point of departure.
Learning-centeredness: Although students are taught as a group, they then go into individual analysis of art to write a review. All students are involved in their own project. Contextualisation: Artwork on campus is used for analysis rather than work on the worldwide web. Some of the campus artwork falls into African art genres (e.g., patterns). Furthermore, the works of African artists specifically are reviewed instead of random artwork provided by the lecturer.		

Art genres	• Students were taught the different art genres by looking at a PowerPoint presentation. • The focus was on typical Western art.	• Students are taught the different art genres by looking at a PowerPoint presentation with a large number of examples. • A variety of pictures of different art genres made by African artists are given to the groups and they have to sort the pictures according to genres. The lecturer gives clues where there are difficulties. • Different groups are given different genres and must draw up characteristics for each genre as observed in their examples. • Students then have to go around the campus in their groups, photograph artwork, categorise it according to genre, and compile a PowerPoint presentation for the next art lecture.

Learning-centeredness:

Once again, students are actively involved in categorising and writing characteristics for the different genres instead of it being given to them to learn. By going on an art treasure hunt around the campus and compiling a PowerPoint presentation, they consolidate their learning of art genres.

Contextualisation:

Most pictures supplied to groups, as well as the art on campus, cover African art and craft genres.

South African artists	• Newly added.	• Students have to choose an artist from a list of South African artists compiled by the lecturer and in groups do a PowerPoint presentation on the history, genre, and style of the artist. The work done by each student must be indicated on the submission. An assessment rubric is provided to guide students.

Learning-centeredness:

The entire exercise is done by students after receiving guidelines and a rubric from the lecturer. Students learn through research.

Contextualisation:

The presentation is focused on South African artists rather than global artists and can include any genre.

Table 5: Visual art and crafts curriculum.

Conclusion

To be truly learning-centred in the African context where it concerns university curricula means more than adhering to the learning requirements of the DHET or having the appropriate content to be able to teach what is required in a school curriculum. Firstly, the curriculum content must be structured in a way that enables students to move from indigenous cultural knowledge and practices towards global cultural knowledge so that they have a foundation for learning. This in itself is not easy, since students have to be taught about their cultural heritage because it cannot be assumed that they know their cultural heritage. Due to colonisation, acculturation, and globalisation, many students in South Africa have negated their own cultural arts and given more value to global arts which they have seen being elevated in the media.

Secondly, a positive difference in South African education will only be brought about when lecturers model teaching methods that support deep learning to ensure that newly qualified educators are sufficiently prepared for their task of teaching the arts.

Due to the programme being newly adapted and adjusted, it is not yet possible to measure outcomes. However, students will be monitored during micro-teaching and work-integrated learning to see if they effectively and confidently increase the use of the arts now that the focus has been moved to more contextually appropriate practical work with more reflection, student-led activities, and prolonged practice to ensure retention.

Early observations are that student attendance has improved and that the constructivist approach with more practical work and reflection is bringing about change in the deeper understanding and learning of content in the arts module. Videoed snippets from practical classes show increased enjoyment and participation. It is hoped that the implementation of more practical work and the approach of practical first, followed by reflection and visiting theory before returning to the practical will assist in turning around the hesitancy experienced by the previous cohorts when it comes to using the arts in their own right and as part of integrated arts teaching. The teaching method where lecturers model the way students eventually need to teach their learners has assisted with covering didactics simultaneously with content and has been important in utilising the restricted time efficiently.

For the arts to thrive, it is essential to move from cognitive, through associative, and into the autonomous phase, where "doing" the arts becomes automatic and natural. If more time can be awarded to the arts in the BEd Foundation Phase curriculum and the learning-centred approach be upheld, the arts will regain its rightful place in education, ensuring augmented learning outcomes and renewed creativity in a country where a large proportion of education, as stated by many, has become an embarrassment.

About the Author

Eurika Jansen van Vuuren is a senior lecturer at the University of Mpumalanga. She can be contacted at this e-mail: eurika.jvvuuren@ump.ac.za

Bibliography

Alberta Chapter (2017). Online resource: http://www.albertaorff.ca/about.html. [Accessed on 22 February 2017].

Department of Basic Education and Higher Education and Training (2011). *Integrated Strategic Planning Framework for Teacher Education and Development in South Africa.* South Africa: Pretoria.

Department of Higher Education and training (DHET) (2015). National Qualifications Framework Act 67_2008 *Revised Policy for Teacher Education Qualifications.* Government Printing Works.

Dewey, J. (1938). *The theory of inquiry.* New York: Holt, Rinehart & Winston.

Elliott, D. J. (1990). Music as culture: Toward a multicultural concept of arts education. *Journal of aesthetic education,* Vol. 24, No. 1, pp. 147–166.

Fitts, P. M. & M. I. Posner (1967). *Human performance.* Oxford: Brooks/Cole.

Fry, R. & D. Kolb (1979). Experiential learning theory and learning experiences in liberal arts education. *New directions for experiential learning,* Vol. 6, pp. 79–92.

Gordon, C. & R. Debus (2002). Developing deep learning approaches and personal teaching efficacy within a pre-service teacher education context. *British Journal of Educational Psychology,* Vol. 72, No. 4, pp. 483–511.

Gravett, S. (2012). Crossing the "theory-practice divide": Learning to be (come) a teacher. *South African Journal of Childhood Education,* Vol. 2, No. 2, pp. 1–14.

Hermida, J. (2014). *Facilitating deep learning: pathways to success for university and college teachers.* CRC Press.

International Suzuki Association. (2017). Online resource: http:// internationalsuzuki.org/shinichisuzuki.htm [Accessed on 22 February 2017].

Kiel, H. & T. W. Anundsen (2006). Is there a Swahili way of teaching music? *Centering on African practice in musical arts education,* Cape Town: African minds, pp. 61–74.

Kolb, D. A. (2014). *Experiential learning: Experience as the source of learning and development.* FT press.

Le Grange, L. (2016). Decolonising the university curriculum: leading article. *South African Journal of Higher Education,* Vol. 30, No. 2, pp. 1–12.

Lortie, D. (1975). *Schoolteacher: A Sociological Study.* London: University of Chicago Press.

Marsh, C. J. & G. Willis (2007). *Curriculum: Alternative approaches, ongoing issues.* Upper Saddle River, New Jersey: Pearson Education, Inc.

Mayer, R. E. (2004). Should there be a three-strikes rule against pure discovery learning? *American psychologist,* Vol. 59, No. 1, pp. 14–19.

Nygaard, C. & B. Kristensen (2009). *Improving Students' Learning Outcomes-Curriculum and practices at CBS.* OECD.

Spaull, N. (2013). *South Africa's education crisis: The quality of education in South Africa 1994–2011.* Johannesburg: Centre for Development and Enterprise.

Section 3: Curriculum Design Process/Learning Outcome

Chapter 7
Designing a Curriculum for Integrating Experiential Learning with Theory during Initial Teacher Education

Andries Du Plessis

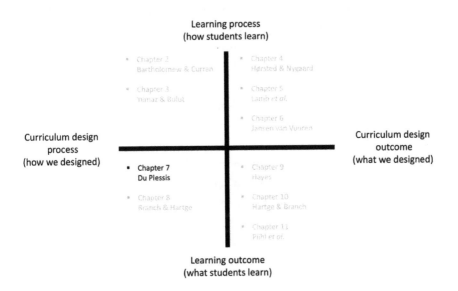

Learning process
(how students learn)

* Chapter 2
Bartholomew & Curran

* Chapter 4
Hørsted & Nygaard

* Chapter 3
Yanaz & Bulut

* Chapter 5
Lamb et al.

* Chapter 6
Jansen van Vuuren

Curriculum design
process
(how we designed)

* Chapter 7
Du Plessis

* Chapter 9
Hayes

Curriculum design
outcome
(what we designed)

* Chapter 8
Branch & Hartge

* Chapter 10
Hartge & Branch

* Chapter 11
Piihl et al.

Learning outcome
(what students learn)

Introduction

I contribute to this book *Learning-Centred Curriculum Design in Higher Education* by exploring how school-university partnerships are needed for the experiential learning component in a Bachelor in Education Foundation Phase (BEd FP) programme. In our case, we use both a teaching school (TS) – which is still in the making – and a number of so-called outside partnering schools. The use of two types of partnering schools has implications for curriculum design and programme delivery which affect students' learning experiences. In relation to the central model of the book, I position my chapter in section three – Curriculum Design Process/Learning Outcome – because I focus predominantly on how we designed the curriculum given the constraint that we must involve schools-as-partners. This means that during curriculum design we are limited by a set of constraints (see Hartge & Branch, in this volume). Also, as explored by Piihl (in this volume), involving partners opens the curriculum in a way that can be likened to a perforated tube. I draw attention to the multi-faceted nature of the concept "curriculum". The definitions and approaches centre around two main streams: content and process. Following Hørsted and Nygaard (in this volume), I subscribe to the latter. Moreover, I present Stenhouse's (1975:4) definition of curriculum: *"A curriculum is an attempt to communicate the essential principles and features of an educational proposal in such a form that it is open to critical scrutiny and capable of effective translation into practice."* Furthermore, Tabak's (1962:421) widely accepted interpretation of "curriculum design" is considered relevant to the process view I hold of curriculum: *"Curriculum design is a statement which identifies the elements of the curriculum, states what their relationships are to each other and indicates the principles of organization and the requirements of that organization for the administrative conditions under which it is to operate. A design, of course, needs to be supported with and to make explicit a curriculum theory which establishes the sources to consider and the principles to apply."*

It is necessary to contextualise developments in education generally and initial teacher education specifically. By the turn of the 20th century, a wave of educational reforms occurred at international level affecting initial teacher education. In South Africa, changes were particularly profound following our first democratic elections in 1994. Faced with the legacy of the apartheid system, curriculum reforms, among other changes, had to help ensure a greater degree of relevance, quality, and accessibility. Efforts were also made to increase the number of qualified teachers.

By 2011, policymakers had re-envisioned the role of schools in initial teacher education. Later in this chapter, I explain how the type of partnership influences the nature of the engagement. In turn, this determines what we can expect to achieve in terms of students' (experiential) learning. Clear outcomes are required, which need to be worked at constantly by the partners for the benefit of all involved (Gibson et al., 2002). Insights derived from reading this chapter include:

1. curriculum design principles following a learning-centred approach, which takes into account the two different types of partnering schools;

2. processes and systems to manage various sets of relationships among the main role players of a school-university partnership;

3. management approaches to ensure organisational learning among diverse partners in school-university partnerships.

I have structured the chapter into three sections. In the first section, I introduce the concept of experiential learning and contextualise it. In the second section, a detailed explanation of the type of partnership with schools is given, namely a teaching school (an intense practicum component) and outside partnering schools (a work-integrated learning component). In the third section, I describe the lessons learned thus far which include attention to curriculum design and review of the practical aspects related to school-university partnerships.

Section I: The Practice

A new discourse became necessary in the wake of large-scale reforms in South Africa after the first democratic elections of 1994. The sweeping changes that followed were directed at normalising society by addressing the vast inequalities caused by the apartheid system. Education – above all else – was to be a cornerstone for transformation in the "new" South Africa (Reddy *et al.*, 2008). From 2000, a new discourse with its focus on "whole school development" was widely propagated. This came in the wake of the publication of a set of seven roles for South African educators. Initially published in *Norms and Standards for Educators* (Government Gazette, 2000), the seven roles were later reiterated in *Minimum Requirements for Teacher Education* (Government Gazette, 2011). These roles include:

+ subject matter expert;

+ learning mediator;

+ assessor;

+ interpreter of curriculum and designer of learning material;

+ classroom manager and administrator;

+ lifelong learner and researcher;

+ pastoral caregiver for community engagement.

A Contextualised Curriculum

The reorganisation of the South African education system also necessitated changes to teacher education marred before 1994 by institutionalised inequalities (Rusznyak, 2015; Welch, 2002). The strategies of the new democratically-elected government mirrored some of the changes abroad. New policies and arrangements affected education at all levels, including initial teacher education programmes. In-service teacher development programmes were also initiated to help with (re) skilling. Overall, education is considered a matter of national importance. This view prevails under the current government and is in accordance with that of other successful nations (Fataar, 2003; Osman & Casella, 2007). A range of changes, such as the introduction of a new qualifications framework, followed. In particular, a number of pertinent questions were raised about how best to approach teacher education in South Africa (Edwards & Mutton, 2007; Osman & Casella, 2007; Welch, 2002). One outcome of this was that initial teacher education became the concern of universities instead of provincially based teacher training colleges (Reddy et al., 2008).

This interrogation has become part of an ongoing debate since 1994 given increased concerns about the quality of school-based education in a post-apartheid South Africa. In recent years, policy changes have been questioned following inefficiencies that have become more pronounced. Through criticism of school performance, one of the areas that has come under scrutiny is initial teacher education. There is consensus that teaching and teacher education are complex, perhaps more so in South Africa given our history and the dire need for large-scale professionalization. As a result, careful planning is necessary during curriculum design to help ensure that the underlying principles governing approaches to initial teacher education are adhered to (Rusznyak, 2015). What is at stake here is a revival of the South African education system and efforts to increase its quality. This, together with efforts to achieve a socially just society, help explain the call for drastic improvements.

As explored in this chapter, I focus on efforts to train student teachers. We follow the University of Johannesburg's (UJ) Bachelor of Education in the Foundation Phase (BEd FP) programme. UJ was instrumental in the establishment of the Siyabuswa campus on behalf of the newly established University of Mpumalanga.

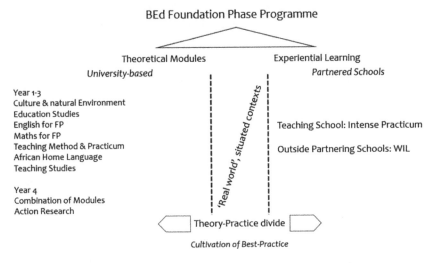

Figure 1: School-university partnerships in an initial teacher education programme.

The programme involves the use of a teaching school (TS) alongside public schools. The latter have traditionally served as partners for the so-called practicum to institutions that offer initial teacher education programmes. The TS concept is a departure from the traditional model and, as I explain later in this chapter, the use of a TS allows for an intense practicum programme similar to the Finnish model. In our case, Mareleng Primary School has been earmarked for development as a TS. It is, however, necessary to emphasise that rural schools, including Mareleng Primary School, suffer from a range of problems that are not uncommon to former black schools, especially those in rural areas of the country. Such realities have a range of consequences for curriculum design and programme delivery.

Experiential Learning: An Intense Practicum and Work-Integrated Learning

One important aspect of initial teacher education is experiential learning, which has a long-standing history and goes by different names (Blunden, 2000; Cohen *et al.*, 2013; Reddy *et al.*, 2008). Changes in approaches to university-based education and calls for greater employability have resulted in a revision of how to approach experiential learning. In recent years, work-integrated learning (WIL) has become a pronounced requirement for many university programmes, not only for teacher education programmes. A number of models for WIL exist in terms of their structure and application (Gibson *et al.*, 2002). WIL is distinguished from other forms of experiential learning, although some educationists use the terms interchangeably. Atkinson (2016:2) describes WIL as follows: *"Work-integrated learning at university is learning that comprises a range of programs and activities in which the theory of the learning is intentionally integrated with the practice of work through a specifically designed curriculum, pedagogic practices and student engagement."*

This necessitates clarity in terms of the theoretical premises on which the WIL component is based, given the *"complex mechanics underpinning learning from experience"* (Gibson *et al.*, 2002:2). However, debates about experiential learning and initial teacher education are not new. They centre mostly around the contribution that in-service teachers and schools can, and ought to, make to the holistic development of pre-service student teachers' education (Carney, 2003; Chitpin, 2011; Cochran-Smith, 1991; Darling-Hammond, 1994; Jenkins, 2014). Reference is usually made to Dewey's views on experiential learning traced back to the 1900s (Allen & Wright, 2014). Similar to other professions, such as medicine, health, the legal profession, engineering, business studies, or even accounting, it behoves the teaching profession to expose student teachers to real classrooms and actual school environments (Abeysekera, 2006; Burton & Greher, 2007; Darling-Hammond, 2006).

School University Partnerships: Internationally and in South Africa

Both learning *from* practice and learning *in* practice are used to prepare future teachers for the demands of their working environments (Gravett, 2012). Universities are required by policy directives to draw upon the knowledge and skills embodied by in-service teachers. In following a process view of curriculum design, such a design constraint also means that students can be regarded as *"active participants in their own professional growth [and] knowledge constructors"* (Mule, 2006:205). Such is the importance given to the role of schools as partners in training that, in some countries, schools – and not universities – play a prominent role during initial teacher education. The UK offers an example (Grudnoff, 2011). In the USA, so-called professional development schools serve as universities' partners during teacher training (Callahan & Martin, 2007; Frampton et al., 2003; Greany & Brown, 2015). Another notable example is offered by Finland, which ranks as one of the most successful countries in terms of education; its approach to initial teacher education and the use of TSs are cited as reasons for its success (Tryggvason, 2009). Given the different types of school-university partnerships found among, and also within, countries, partnerships can be divided into any one of five models (Maandag et al., 2007). As explained by Loock & Gravett (2014), these include the following models:

1. work placement (school as workplace);

2. coordinator (school with a central supervisor);

3. partner (trainer in the school as a trainer of professional teachers);

4. network (trainer in the school as leader of a training team in the school);

5. training school (training by the school).

School-university partnerships bring into play a number of complex issues. A core issue relates to the quality and nature of the learning experiences that can be derived from partnerships (Mukeredzi, 2014). I concur that schools provide authentic learning experiences – whether good or bad. Given the stark realities of inefficiencies in school-based education in

South Africa, one should remain mindful of the effect constraints have on programme delivery. This is largely due to the inefficiencies and lack of best practice we note at many former black schools. As noted above, given policy requirements affecting initial teacher education, we have little choice other than to engage with schools. This challenges higher education institutions (HEIs), including the university where I currently work, to consider the best possible approaches to experiential learning.

The *Integrated Strategic Planning Framework for Teacher Education and Development in South Africa: 2011–2025* details the South African government's revised vision for initial teacher education. It envisages that TSs will strengthen *"the teaching practice/school experience component of teacher education"* in South Africa (RSA, DBE & DHET, 2011). Following from experiences with the TS concept at UJ, Loock *et al.* (2014) explain that this vision requires a robust school-university partnership – one that must be governed by a memorandum of agreement (MOA). The MOA binds the university and the relevant provincial department of education under whose jurisdiction the schools fall to a set of responsibilities and obligations. These are all aimed at ensuring that best practice would be the norm at the TS and not the exception.

Loock *et al.* (2014) explain that depending on how TSs will be integrated into the curriculum design of teacher education programmes in South Africa, the TS collaboration model will fall within the category of a partner or network model, or a hybrid of the two. Based on the description in Maandag *et al.* (2007), the Finnish model of university training schools, also referred to as university practice schools or teacher training schools, falls within the broad classification of a partner or network model.

I maintain that the basic requirement for a school that wishes to serve as a TS remains "best practice". It is at this juncture that the university as principal partner may – and indeed does – lay down sets of requirements. The TS must perform at a consistently high level, since it has to serve as an example of the ideal. It follows that a TS would institute a cycle of perpetual improvement. After all, its close ties with a university, where theory is emphasised together with research, make it part of the knowledge creation process. I explore this factor in greater detail later, where the notion of organisational learning is discussed.

Approaches to Experiential Learning: Exposure to Best Practice

The notion of "best practice" and ways to achieve excellence at classroom level characterise school-university partnerships. Differences between theory and practice, however, mean that partners need to manage relational tensions. Indeed, finding a common view of "best practice" in terms of classroom-based teaching is difficult at the best of times. It is thus pertinent to have a deep understanding of the dynamics among partners in a school-university partnership. Reddy *et al.* (2008) cite Cochrane-Smith (1991), who reports three main categories of activities: consonance, critical dissonance, and collaborative resonance, and I concur that these might serve to "reinvent" the practicum process. These three categories can be explained as follows:

1. consonance: This entails that partners maintain a common understanding of what is expected in terms of "good teaching". It entails other questions, for example: "What does it mean to be a teacher?" and brings into play issues related to identity and professionalism (Nygaard *et al.*, 2008);

2. critical dissonance: This requires a critical stance towards schooling and teaching, especially in cases where it is necessary to interrupt the influence of the school during WIL in an effort to follow a more transformative stance towards cultivating best practice among student teachers;

3. collaborative resonance: This approach resonates with the type of school-university partnership that is envisaged with TSs. It is based on the assumption that joint efforts involving the school and the university would create opportunities that are richer than the opportunities that neither of the two could provide alone (Reddy *et al.*, 2008).

Partnering schools offer opportunities for powerful learning. This is not unlike the notion of situated knowledge that has been traditionally used in other areas of study, for example medicine, health, the legal profession, and business studies. In following Piihl's (in this volume) metaphor of curriculum as a perforated tube, situated knowledge raises a number of issues related to quality, authenticity, and value, since it involves partnerships with entities that reside outside the full control of the university. Following up on the research findings of Gibson *et al.* (2002), I consistently question issues related to quality assurance. This is particularly relevant to the assessment of our students' micro-teaching lessons, whether at our local TS or at outside partnering schools. As I explain in this chapter, quality is an issue at outside partnering schools, but unlike a TS, our direct involvement is minimal.

Apart from learning, I emphasise the issue of assessment and experiential learning. The questions that we rightfully ask are: "What gets assessed?" and "What weight do the assessors' opinions carry?" (Sedumedi & Mundalamo, 2012; Smith, 2010). After all, we are trying to improve education through more rigorous training, which includes assessment *for* learning, and assessment *of* learning. Both training and assessment require experienced teachers who are called upon to mentor student teachers in the "art of teaching". This is done using reflective practices, as explained in more detail in the next sub-section.

Relationships between In-Service Teachers and Student Teachers: Minding the Gap

When student teachers attend schools for their experiential learning, in-service teachers are required to serve as mentors (Kwan & Lopez-Real, 2005; Ming See, 2014; Tomlinson, Hobson & Malderez, 2010). The purpose is to help foster deep learning through active engagement – the type mentioned by Nygaard and Serrano (2009). Invariably, a triad is formed between academic staff members, students, and in-service teachers. Like coaching and instruction, mentorship requires a complex skill set, which is instrumental for deep learning (Ambrosetti, 2010; Kwan & Lopez-Real, 2005; Liu, 2014). Successful mentoring involves reflection, which is used as a mechanism to elicit the type of insights that one associates with deep learning.

As alluded to elsewhere in this chapter, the delivery of a credible experiential learning component relies upon amicable working relationships with high-functioning schools that would result in collaborative resonance. That is why we favour the notion of a TS where the level of proficiency is considerably higher than in outside partnership schools.

However, in neither instance is it easy to maintain amicable working relationships; two very different types of organisations are partners in a school-university partnership.

Each organisation is governed by its own sets of legislative frameworks, policies, and cultures (Allen & Wright, 2014; Darling-Hammond, 2006; Loock & Gravett, 2014). On the one hand, one deals with a university, which is steeped in its own traditions and emphasises theory. On the other hand, one deals with a partnered school which focuses on teaching and learning *in practice*. During initial teacher education – in following the metaphor of curriculum as a perforated tube – both entities contribute knowledge and experience of teaching and learning, albeit from different perspectives. It is thus easy to understand why pre-service students might experience a gap between theory and actual classroom practices during their education (Perrow, 2013).

Tensions can thus be expected among the various stakeholders in school-university partnerships. I maintain, however, that like all partnerships, learning at an organisational level remains the *raison d'être* for a collaborative partnership (Fenwick, 2007; Tsui et al., 2008). Collaborative resonance, I believe, can be achieved by instituting mechanisms aimed at organisational learning. Consequently, learning is not aimed solely at students but at all members involved in a school-university partnership, including academic staff and in-service teachers. Organisational learning (OL) is, however, often elusive. Efforts to help achieve it can easily end in frustration, as attested by partnerships between institutions in other economic sectors. The same applies to school-university partnerships, which exist for the sole aim of training student teachers in the art of "becoming" teachers (Bierly et al., 2000; Callahan & Martin, 2007; Choy & Delahaye, 2011).

Section 2: Experiential Learning and the Main Components of our BEd Foundation Phase Programme

Our BEd FP programme, it has been noted, draws upon two types of experiential learning: 1) learning *from* practice through observation, and 2) learning *in* practice through active teaching, namely micro-teaching. Careful scheduling ensures that students are afforded opportunities to spend time in "real-world" classrooms where both these types of learning are used. Furthermore, I explained in the introduction that two types of partnering schools are used for purposes of our experiential learning component. Both are stated as requirements at the Council for Higher Education, our national accreditation body. Apart from an intense practicum programme involving a TS (Mareleng Primary School), each student also selects a public school in the vicinity of their homes where they complete their work-integrated learning sessions. Given the rural nature of the Mpumalanga province, where the Siyabuswa Campus is situated, this approach is followed in order to circumvent problems with accommodation and transport.

The two types of partnerships with schools differ in a number of ways. This factor has an impact on the nature of students' experiential learning and how it manifests in terms of programme delivery. As evident from Figure 2, students spend more time at the TS, where we exercise a greater influence through direct involvement with it. We aspire to maintain control over processes aimed at ensuring that the school becomes – and remains – a high-performing school. As explained later, we employ mechanisms to ensure organisational learning as a way to cultivate and diffuse best practice at Mareleng Primary School. Efforts have been underway since 2014 to ensure it becomes a fully functional school. In time, it should become an exemplary TS along similar lines as UJ's Funda Ujabule School.

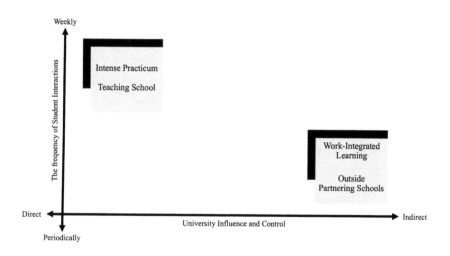

Figure 2: University influence and frequency of interactions. Type of Partnering Schools.

It is noteworthy that students spend a limited amount of time at outside partnering schools. Moreover, currently the University of Mpumalanga's (UMP) influence at outside partnering schools in the province remains minimal. No programmes are in place to develop those in-service teachers who engage with our pre-service students during their WIL sessions; we acknowledge that this should be our long-term goal. We realise that it will require substantial investments through long-term partnerships with the business sector, among others. Closer collaboration with other universities that also engage with public schools along similar lines is on the cards.

	Teaching school	Outside partnering schools
Proximity to campus	Close: walking distance	Varied: spread across the province
Nature of university's influence	Direct: governed by MOA (to be negotiated and finalised at time of writing)	Indirect: loose arrangement with the school
Frequency of student visits	Weekly programme	1st year: no WIL 2nd–3rd years: at start of school year before university opens; twice during the year when university is on recess 4th year: three WIL sessions of 21 days each
Learning *from* practice	All year groups: observation programme	Observation programme; alternate with micro-teaching
Learning *in* practice	Micro-teaching programme for second-, third-, and fourth-year students	Micro-teaching programme for second-, third-, and fourth-year students
Assessors	Lecturers and teachers	Teachers at local schools 4th year: one lesson assessed by provincial official
Mentoring	Teachers and lecturers	Teachers
Best practice	Under development	No formal programme
Quality control	Direct oversight through university involvement (COPs)	Dependent upon provincial department of education
Controlling authority	Mpumalanga Department of Education with the university as principal partner	Mpumalanga Department of Education

Table 1: Comparison between a teaching school and outside partnering schools.

For students at our Siyabuswa Campus, the following organisational arrangements are made. This division is also maintained during WIL at outside partnering schools, although it does happen from time to time that students are placed in other grades in the foundation phase depending on the situation at the outside partnering school. Our practicum programme at the TS has four cycles. A new cycle starts when Group 1 is scheduled again after Group 20 has completed its session. Careful coordination helps ensure alignment between the university calendar and the school terms.

Year group	Classroom level at teaching school
First-year level	Grade R, 5- to 6-year-old learners
Second-year level	Grade 1, 6- to 7-year-old learners
Third-year level	Grade 2, 7- to 8-year-old learners
Fourth-year level	Grade 3, 8- to 9-year-old learners
100 students per year group, divided into 20 groups	Four classes per grade

Table 2: Year-level grouping and school grade association.

With reference to Figure 2, we achieve our goals with learning from practice, while the focus remains the observation of learners, not only in class but also on the playground. Therefore, the observation time slot at the TS coincides with a short break. However, once back in class, students invariably also observe teachers in action. This is incidental and not a planned focus, unlike practices elsewhere that require student teachers to observe in-service teachers and not necessarily the learners (Jenkins, 2014).

By linking observation with assignments for some of the theoretical modules (see Addendum A), particularly Education Studies (EDS) and Methodology and Teaching Practicum (MPR), we constantly try to link students' learning from practice at the TS with their theoretical knowledge. Other modules also draw upon students' interaction with learners and teachers. In terms of the TS, the Teaching Studies module (TSD) that is offered during the first semester of the first year includes a service learning (SL) project. Service learning also features in other modules, such as English (EFP). Another aspect that we consider to be essential when "becoming a teacher" relates to classroom management and discipline – something students often find difficult during work-integrated learning sessions.

Observation and the Role of Reflection

Reflection forms an integral part of observation and is done using a set structure. Leading questions help instil the principles of enquiry. We start this process at first-year level (Mule, 2006). Structured observation, we believe, helps students think critically about what it is they observe in terms of the developing child, since students do not focus on in-service teachers' practices. By instilling critical enquiry, we aim to equip students for lifelong learning, research, and continuous scholarship. This is in accordance with one of the seven roles and competencies originally listed in the *Norms and Standards for Educators* (Government Gazette, 2000).

For first-, second-, and third-year students, a timetabled slot requires groups to write down their reflection narratives upon completion of the observation sessions. A Google form is used to collect answers for questions aimed at soliciting deep thinking about their observations. Since feedback is electronic, such narratives can then be collated and shared with academic staff as well as with teachers at the TS. The platform used for such discussions is the weekly community of practice (COP) session. Details about COPs are presented elsewhere in this chapter.

By writing their reflections students are also prepared for an action research project in their fourth year. This project draws upon classroom practice in a Grade 3 classroom at the outside partnering schools. Students use the first WIL session to identify a problem, provide a clear problem statement, and define their research questions. Between the first and second WIL sessions, students engage with literature surveys and continue to prepare for the next phase in their research. This includes designing survey instruments to test the effect of their recommended solutions. During the second WIL session, students apply their solutions and test the effectiveness of their suggested teaching practices. They report upon this in true action-research fashion once they return from their second WIL session.

Micro-Teaching Experiences: Learning in Practice

In this section, I focus on our involvement at the TS, although learning in practice also takes place at outside partnering schools, especially for the fourth-year students (explained below). Learning *in* practice runs parallel to our observation schedules. Following the same four cycles and student groupings, so-called micro-teaching at the TS draws from different modules that represent the theoretical component of the programme: Culture and Natural Environment (CNE) which corresponds with Life Skills, English (EFP), African Home Languages, and Mathematics (MFP). Depending on the practicum cycle, micro-teaching can be done as either individual work or in groups. Micro-teaching entails a four-step process that starts with planning. This is followed by lesson preparation, lesson presentation, and, finally, reflection and feedback. These steps occur over a two-week period, giving students ample time to prepare lesson plans and resources.

Year level	Observation	Micro-teaching schedule Takes place on Thursday mornings Four cycles during the year
First year	Grade R Monday–Thursday	n/a
Second Year	Grade 1 Monday–Wednesday	Cycle 1: individual Cycle 2: at Mareleng Cycle 3: peer teaching Cycle 4: peer teaching
Third year	Grade 2 Monday–Wednesday	Cycle 1: individual Cycle 2: at Mareleng Cycle 3: peer teaching Cycle 4: peer teaching
Fourth year	Grade 3 Monday–Wednesday	Cycle 1: individual Cycle 2: at Mareleng Cycle 3: peer teaching Cycle 4: peer teaching

Table 3: Observation and micro-teaching schedule.

During Cycle 1, the second- and third-year students attend individual sessions with lecturers (when teachers at Mareleng Primary School are sufficiently developed, they will fulfil this role). Discussions are held on campus in venues that resemble typical school classrooms. The focus is deep thought about lesson planning. Students are required to explain their approaches to a specific lesson topic and reflect upon their decisions in terms of approaches to teaching strategies and assessment. We aim to identify the development of their respective knowledge domains and use the technological pedagogical content knowledge (TPACK) framework. Students are given 30 minutes during individual reflective sessions. A rubric is included with their lesson plan templates. While individual sessions take place, the rest of the group remains occupied in the same venue, where they engage in handwriting exercises as well as practise their board-writing skills. Senior student tutors assist the lecturers in this regard.

During Cycle 2, the second- and third-year students teach at Mareleng Primary School. Micro-lessons last approximately 45 minutes. Although these are currently overseen by lecturers, the aim is that Mareleng teachers would eventually be adequately skilled to serve as assessors and mentor teachers. This would be in accordance with the TS model (Gravett, 2014; Mathews & Berwick, 2013; Niemi & Jakku-Sihvonen, 2011).

We also use peer teaching (students teaching each other in groups), although this is not ideal in an FP setting. One reason for this is the language mismatch between the university and the TS. The language mismatch results from the fact that Mareleng Primary School offers only Sesotho sa Leboa and isiNdebele. At the campus, however, siSwati and isiNdebele are offered, although we introduced Sesotho sa Leboa in 2017. Peer teaching is therefore used when students need to present micro-lessons in siSwati. Given the demographics of South Africa, the closest school that offers siSwati is approximately 200 km away from the Siyabuswa Campus. When students go to outside partnering schools, however, they must select schools where their home language is offered. This provides them with additional opportunities for micro-teaching lessons in their home language. It remains a point of concern that micro-teaching in real classroom environments cannot be done in the presence of lecturers for siSwati home language students. Another reason to use peer teaching relates to time and scheduling. During the 2017 academic year, the school term and university calendar do not allow for adequate shared time at the TS; five weeks are necessary for a complete cycle, but in 2017 there are only three weeks of shared time with the school towards the end of the year. Consequently, during the fourth cycle, we resort to peer teaching, since it excludes the school. Such arrangements vary from year to year. Apart from subject-related content that links with school-based subjects, the BEd FP programme also includes aspects such as classroom management and discipline. This is taught in both the Teaching Studies (TSD) modules as well as the Teaching Methodology and Practicum (MPR) modules. These too, draw upon experiences gained during students' interactions with learners and teachers in real classroom environments.

Unique Learning Opportunities at the Teaching School: A Longitudinal Study

A school-university partnership that involves a TS offers a number of unique learning opportunities unlike those involving outside partnering schools. A TS serves as an open laboratory that makes ongoing research possible. Moreover, constant, high intensity engagement provides opportunities for longitudinal studies. In our case, we try and capitalise on opportunities to observe and engage with the "developing child". Student-learner associations are made during the first year, when a grade R learner at the TS is assigned to a first-year student. Through sets of activities, students are guided to discover and make sense of various aspects related to the developing child from grade R to grade 3. Associated largely with the Education Studies module (EDS), students are required to complete assignments that span their four-year curriculum.

However, a number of realities make longitudinal research difficult at Mareleng Primary School. First, not all learners pass their grade each year. This means that some students cannot continue to observe their associated learners during observation times when they are promoted to the next year. Moreover, at each new academic year, the school reorganises their learners into different classes. This is necessary because some learners leave the school to attend other schools; new learners are also enrolled in grades other than the first grade, which is grade R. In comparison, enrolment at UJ's Funda

Ujabule School is largely stable, allowing students to focus on new enrolments at grade R level only.

Apart from a few organisational challenges concerning student-learner association, we value the longitudinal research component because it sets the student teacher on the path of becoming a researcher. It also includes the development of the notion of teacher-as-theorist – something that is explored in their teaching studies module (first-year level, first semester). This addresses one of the seven roles of teachers mentioned at the outset of this chapter. The skills and insights attained during the longitudinal research component also form an integral part of an action research project in the fourth year. This is explained elsewhere in this chapter.

Section 3: Lessons Learned

Initial teacher education is complicated, given the necessity to include schools as partners. Ascribing to the metaphor used by Piihl et al. (in this volume) that curriculum is a perforated tube means that the university does not have sole control over all aspects of curriculum delivery. School-university partnerships vary in terms of function and form; hence, we can expect a range of possible challenges.

The Quest for Best Practice and Concerns about Quality

Arrangements with outside partnering schools differ considerably in comparison with that of a TS. This has an impact upon students' learning, since issues of quality and a display of best practice along the TPACK framework vary from school to school. In general, the reasons for this are related to the realities of school-based education in South Africa. As explained in this chapter, the levels of underdevelopment in many formerly black schools, and in particular rural schools, remain a point of grave concern for teacher education programmes (Reddy et al., 2008).

The level of control and degree of direct influence over partnering schools affect the delivery of our experiential learning component (see Figure 2). Among others, it determines the cultivation of best practice in accordance with the requirements of the university. The main concern for curriculum design at this juncture is the fact that student teachers mostly come from the same outside partnering schools or from schools with similar dire circumstances, where teaching and learning are largely of questionable standards. To unlearn that which students have experienced for twelve years during their own schooling can hardly be done within the span of a four-year undergraduate degree programme. Our efforts to ensure exposure to best practice ought to be clear then, given UJ's successes with the Funda Ujabule School. It offers irrefutable evidence in favour of TSs in the South African context (Gravett et al., 2014).

The concerns we have about the quality of teaching at outside partnering schools relate closely to the complexities involved in training students to become effective teachers. In the first place, we focus on the development of the seven roles of educators as envisaged by the Department of Higher Education and Training (DHET) (Government Gazette, 2000). Furthermore, we emphasise the development of best practice within the TPACK framework, as alluded to elsewhere in this chapter. Based upon a constructivist approach, learning through experience allows students to construct meaning from authentic real-life environments. However, we remain cautious about the quality and credibility of student assessment. Partnerships of this nature subscribe to the view of curriculum as a perforated tube – one that allows for direct influences from outside. We also endeavour to reach collaborative consonance with our partners, although we recognise the existence of tensions due to the theory-practice divide.

TPACK and the Lack of Technological Integration

Ever since I joined the Siyabuswa Campus in 2013, efforts to establish best practices along the TPACK framework have proven particularly difficult. This concurs with studies in other parts of the world. In fact, given the challenges resulting from the so-called digital divide, integrating technology into the TPACK framework seems well-nigh impossible. This is especially true for outside partnering schools in remote areas. Evident from surveys that were conducted among students, these schools offer very little in terms of real opportunities for students to practise their pedagogical content knowledge, let alone technological integration. The lack of, and need for, substantial investment to ensure that South African teachers embrace technology is explored in the literature but not discussed further in this chapter (Chigona et al, 2010; Jin & Bagaka, 2005; Ndlovu & Lawrence, 2012; Sherman & Howard, 2012.) South African learners, particularly in schools with limited resources, have continuously underachieved in the gateway subjects like Mathematics and Science. The government has turned to modern technology to strengthen teaching and learning and to redress past inequalities in its schools. This intervention has made little or no progress despite the availability of information and communication technologies (ICTs).

It is evident, however, that what I teach students in the teaching studies module during the second semester of their first year (Computers for Foundation Phase) hardly ever manifests itself in their micro-lessons (Du Plessis, 2017). The reasons for this relate to a number of factors at play in schools: low levels of self-efficacy in terms of the use of technology for pedagogical purposes, few examples to draw from and thus limited modelling, infrastructure shortcomings, and a lack of access to mobile devices such as laptops and smartphones. Bandwidth and reception also remain obstacles that effectively prohibit students from accessing the Internet and its myriad resources. Although not the case at the TS, at some schools even the electricity supply is not assured.

In fact, students are at pains to report their experiences to me when they are away for work-integrated learning at outside partnering schools. We use WhatsApp group discussions and often engage in interesting live sessions while they experience "real-life" problems in actual classroom situations. Short video clips and pictures shared on the WhatsApp group help to instil a feeling of "I am not alone". This brings a new dimension to engaging with students in an effort to support them during experiential learning in a (near) real-time fashion.

Classroom Management and Approaches to Discipline

An example of "support-on-the-go" which translates to "learning-on-the-spot" relates to classroom management. In South Africa, corporal punishment was abolished in 1994 by the new democratically elected government. However, when they are away on work-integrated learning at outside partnering schools, students are at pains to share their views with me about ways to discipline "unruly" children. It is evident that corporal punishment is still meted out at some schools, especially in deep rural areas. Such realities offer opportunities for powerful learning, given that this differs from what is being taught by the university.

At the time of writing this chapter, a WhatsApp group chat allowed me to converse with fourth-year students who were away for their WIL at outside partnering schools. Some students remarked how difficult it was to control their learners. Upon suggesting approaches to classroom management and discipline that we had covered during lectures, some students remarked that Western approaches to classroom discipline are ineffective in deep rural South African environments. In rural schools, most students maintain, children can only be controlled through corporal punishment, since this is also the way that their parents mete out discipline. These views were again explored in face-to-face focus group discussions that I recently had with the current final-year students. Such views allow for lively topical discussions, especially since the issue of decolonising South Africa's curricula is currently under discussion.

Recognition of Diversity among Partnering Schools

Given the university's reliance on partnering schools for the WIL component, considerable efforts are being made to help ensure that school-university partnerships remain fully functional. Curriculum designers, academic staff, in-service teachers, together with administrative and support staff members all play a role to help ensure that we do not forfeit opportunities for authentic, quality learning. In fact, we endeavour to embrace experiential learning from the "real world". We do recognise that these are often far removed from the ideal. Concurring with the views of Nygaard and Serrano (2008), as head of school, I often remind the academic team of context and the importance of recognising diversity in the process of identity formation. While students' WhatsApp conversations, for example, afford us opportunities for "live" engagement, we particularly value their reflective narratives. These narratives are used as key artefacts for deep analysis, given that they use reflection as a way to achieve deep learning.

Through discussions based upon their narratives, we guide student teachers with their identity formation. In the process of becoming a teacher, experiential learning, together with theoretical knowledge, offers opportunities for becoming a professional teacher. Students are encouraged to actively construct new meanings in terms of "Who am I?" Hence, we aid them to find answers to questions such as: "What does it mean to be a teacher?" It is with this in mind that the process view of curriculum design has proven to be the most appropriate avenue to take for experiential learning in our BEd FP teacher training programme. One of the modules (i.e., Teaching Studies) taps into this by expecting students to craft a personal teaching philosophy at first-year level. By blogging about this and commenting on each other's teaching philosophies, students and lecturers alike are afforded opportunities for much-needed discussions. I believe these discussions are key to deep thinking akin to a constructivist approach. By their fourth year, students are required to revisit their teaching philosophies, since these public statements require constant revisions.

Organisational Learning and School-University Partnerships

The notion of learning in a school-university partnership has been investigated by Matoba *et al.* (2007), who explored the ways in which teachers learn from each other. Despite this, few studies focus on learning among the partners as a core focus of their partnership. However, after exploring the literature and following up on personal experiences, I argue that organisational learning (OL) lies at the heart of interactions among members of a school-university partnership (Crossan *et al.*, 1999; Easterby-Smith & Lyles, 2011). This is surely the case at a TS, since the university's sphere of influence and intensity of its involvement with outside partnering schools are far less. Where a partnership involves a TS, organisational learning can help to ensure that best practice is identified, developed, and diffused. In this regard, the power of connections is deemed important (see Hartge & Branch, in this volume).

While research on organisational learning involving school-university partnerships is limited, the same cannot be said of studies about organisational learning in private-sector partnerships or public-private partnerships. From the literature review, it is evident that numerous studies have been conducted that investigate different aspects of OL (Crossan *et al.*, 1999; Dodgson, 1993; Huber, 1991). Despite voids in research about OL and school-university partnerships *per se*, a central theme remains: learning at both an individual and group level (Callahan & Martin, 2007). It is in this regard that the so-called 4-I knowledge framework takes centre stage in my approach to manage the school-university partnership with the Mareleng Primary School. Given that the school is at an early stage of development in terms of functioning as a TS, the use of mechanisms such as communities of practice (COPs) are key to our success. In time, I hope to expand the deployment of the 4-I knowledge framework to outside partnering schools by increasing COPs that would also involve the development of teachers at far-flung schools. COPs draw upon the strength and quality of ties – an idea that is echoed by Hartge & Branch (in this volume).

Sharing Knowledge through COPs

Following difficulties from 2013 with working closely with in-service teachers at the Mareleng Primary School, by mid–2015 I had instituted a COP – or professional learning network – for each of the year levels and their associated school levels. A lecturer from the academic corps serves as the chairperson for a particular COP (e.g., "COP year level 1:R". A common time is scheduled for COP sessions on the timetables of each institution and attendance is compulsory. Initial successes have been limited for numerous reasons. Among others, an open agenda proved to be too unstructured.

From 2017, all COP meetings have followed a set structure. These include discussions about operational matters related to the observation programme: students' absenteeism, general behaviour, and other matters that affect teachers during their interactions with students. Discussions ought to turn to teaching and learning: teachers reflecting upon their work during the past week, and during these discussions we envisage that learners' workbooks would be showcased. Academics can thus gain first-hand insight into the teaching activities of each teacher. Learning from each other is being emphasised here: academics gaining insights into how teachers teach at a rural school destined to become a TS.

Pace of Curriculum Delivery

The pace of delivery of the school-based curriculum should also be noted at this point (in South Africa, the so-called CAPS curriculum is to be followed closely with set pacesetters provided by each provincial depart-ment). Synchronisation with the university's schedules is of paramount importance. However, lost teaching days are a reality for many South African schools, including Mareleng Primary School. Falling out of sync with the pacesetter is further exacerbated by teachers who do not observe the scheduled topics; reasons for this vary, such as teaching days lost due to unforeseen events. Deviating from the provincial schedule has implications for the university programme, since the students' micro-lessons must be synchronised with the topics of the teacher.

Knowledge Cultivation and Dissemination

Through their active involvement with in-service teachers and as leaders of their respective COPs, academics at the Siyabuswa Campus become active co-constructors of (new) knowledge. It is envisaged that the COPs and the learning which emanates from focused conversations will go further by utilising the notion of knowledge cafés. Teachers from surrounding schools and other role players are to meet for discussions that would focus on any number of relevant areas. The objective is to cultivate best practice through the dissemination of knowledge and insights, but above all to nurture wisdom. As proposed by the 4-I knowledge framework, the cultivation of best practice starts at an individual level and only becomes institutionalised once it has been diffused through groups and integrated among its members (Table 4). It is through such efforts that the university gives meaning to its mandate to contribute to knowledge creation and dissemination. It also suggests that the notion of curriculum as process, together with Piihl's (in this volume) metaphor of curriculum as a perforated tube, presuppose active interaction between university and schools – one that values learning among all its stakeholders.

What ought to be clear is that as far as school-university partnerships are concerned, learning becomes a mantra for all stakeholders. Learning ought to be fostered at an organisational level to help ensure that value is added through the "third space", which comes into existence as a result of partnerships. Given that academics and in-service teachers engage in deep learning for the sake of knowledge creation, the wisdom that they finally gain must also find its way to student teachers and the broader education fraternity. After all, *good teaching requires wisdom*" (Alias & Alias, 2010:152).

Learning/Renewal in organisations: Three levels and four processes		
Level	Process	Inputs/Outcomes
		Experiences
	Intuiting	Images
		Metaphors
Individual		
		Language
	Interpret	Cognitive map
		Conversation/dialogue
		Shared understandings
Group	Integrating	Mutual adjustments
		Interactive systems
		Routines
Organisation	Institutionalising	Diagnostic systems
		Rules and procedures

Table 4: 4-I knowledge framework.

Conclusion

The transformation that has characterised education globally since the turn of the 20th century influenced decisions in South Africa, which must be seen against the background of the need to bring about a just and equitable society. Efforts to increase the quality of education in South Africa include changed approaches to initial teacher education, entailing a revised vision for the role of schools during initial teacher education. In-service teachers offer experience and knowledge about what it means "to be a teacher". Careful consideration is given during curriculum design to ensure that students derive maximum value from their experiential learning at schools. For this reason, various sets of activities bind modules with practical work.

Following the successes of UJ with the TS concept, their revised BEd Foundation Phase programme was used to help launch the University of Mpumalanga's campus at Siyabuswa in 2013. This resulted in the establishment of the second TS in South Africa, namely Mareleng Primary School. Unlike UJ's Funda Ujabule School, Mareleng Primary School is an existing public school that has to be transformed through a developmental programme into a high-performing school. At the time of writing this chapter, the lessons learned from our experiences while working with the staff at Mareleng Primary School mirror problems with school-university partnerships generally. In our case, we depart from a low base, which means that developing best practice along the TPACK framework will require a considerable amount of time and resources.

We do recognise that, in our case, the TS concept is still in its infancy. Once fully developed, the TS will be unlike outside partnering schools where experiential learning often takes place in less than ideal circumstances. If the problems we experience with the TS are anything to go by, students' experiences during their WIL sessions at outside partnering schools confirm the need for large-scale, intense interventions that would result in well-trained and fully equipped mentor teachers. This is unlikely to happen any time soon due to service delivery problems and budgetary constraints. The university has limited capacity to engage with far-flung schools. This necessitates collaboration with other universities that are already active at some schools along similar lines to those that we envisage. Despite numerous problems, our efforts are aimed at putting into practice the revised vision for teacher education in South Africa. In this, the learning-centred approach remains central to our curriculum design.

Addendum A

In this addendum, a detailed overview is given of the different modules and their foci.

Year level	Semester courses offered as modules	Year course
First year Second year Third year	Culture and Natural Environment (CNE) Education Studies (EDS) English 1st additional language for FP (EFP) Mathematics for FP (MFP) Methodology and Practicum for FP (MPR) IsiNdebele Home Language for FP (NFP) SiSwati Home Language for FP (SFP) Sesotho sa Leboa Home Language for FP (SEP) Teaching Studies for FP (TSD)	n/a
Fourth year	n/a	Selection from semester courses; Action research project

Table 5: Modules in the Foundation Phase programme.

Class attendance throughout the four years is compulsory because the University of Mpumalanga (UMP) is a comprehensive residential university offering contact tuition. In terms of progression, a module at one year level is not a requirement for entry to the next year level. However, by the end of the third year, a student should have successfully completed all modules before proceeding to the fourth and final year. It is thus impossible for students to carry any modules from their first three years, since the fourth-year modules are year courses; time is also mostly spent away from the campus to complete three sets of work-integrated learning (WIL) sessions at outside partnering schools. This is over and above time that is spent at the TS as part of the intense practicum component. The WIL component involving outside partnering schools forms an integral part of the curriculum at each year level and is spread across the four years. This is explained in the following subsection. In all respects, assessment as well as theoretical knowledge are augmented with knowledge and insights gained from interactions at Mareleng Primary School.

Culture and Natural Environment

Culture and Natural Environment (CNE) relates to a subject called Life Skills in the Foundation Phase at school level.

Year level	Semester one	Semester two
First year		Physical education Supervision of sports activities for FP
Second year	Arts and craft, music, drama	Social science Personal well-being
Third year	Natural science, space science, earth and environmental science	n/a
Fourth year	Production of a play with schools in vicinity of campus	

Table 6: Culture and Natural Environment.

Education Studies

Education Studies (EDS) has no equivalent subject at school level. Throughout the programme, the EDS modules form an integral part of the WIL component. Assignments for the various EDS modules spread across semesters; all draw upon data obtained from observation at the TS and/or outside partnering schools.

Year level	Semester one	Semester two
First year	Theoretical framework of child development	Physical and sensory development of young children
Second year	Childhood cognitive development from birth to 12 years	Social and emotional development from birth to middle childhood
Third year	Language and literacy development from birth to middle childhood	Barriers to learning and development
Fourth year	Inclusive education and barriers to learning	

Table 7: Education Studies (EDS).

English for Foundation Phase

English for the Foundation Phase (EFP) is offered as first additional language (FAL). English is particularly important since it becomes a medium of instruction from grade 4 onwards; it is offered during every semester at each year level. During the first semester of the first year, the focus falls upon students developing their own English language competence and the requisite subject knowledge in English; it is to enable them to support English language learning in the Foundation Phase classroom.

Year level	Semester one	Semester two
First year	Grammar, spelling, diagnostic testing, youth and children's literature, language through games and play, social networks and Internet for language learning	Academic literacy, structure of academic texts, visual literacy, social networks and internet for language learning
Second year	Grammar; diagnostic testing, discourse and genre, children's literature, blogs and social networks for language learning	Academic literacy: cohesion and coherence, visual literacy, literary theory, book club, reading and writing
Third year	Grammar, diagnostic testing, youth and children's literature, blogs and social networks for language learning	Submission of academic essay, visual literacy, book club, literary theory
Fourth year	FP English teaching methodology: handwriting, chalkboard writing, review of grade R	

Table 8: English for Foundation Phase.

Mathematics for Foundation Phase

Like English, mathematics is also offered during each semester at every year level. Historically, mathematics poses particular problems, given that English becomes a language of instruction from grade 4. Like English, mathematics is a particular focus area during micro-teaching.

Year level	Semester one	Semester two
First year	Understanding of numbers and numerical systems	Algebra and fractions
Second year	Space and shapes	Measurement: mass and weight
Third year	Measurement of shapes, scales and units of measurement	Handing of data
Fourth year	Methodology of teaching mathematics at FP level	

Table 9: Mathematics for Foundation Phase.

Methodology and Teaching Practice

Methodology and Teaching Practice (MPR) is offered throughout the four years, since it is a core module. MPR is closely related to the WIL component at the TS. Assessment tasks usually refer students to the TS at Mareleng Primary School and/or require them to draw from their experiences at the outside partnering schools.

Year level	Semester one	Semester two
First year	Grade R methodology	Linguistic components in teaching children to read
Second year	Linguistic components in reading from perspective of African home languages modules	n/a
Third year	Develop understanding of methodology for teaching numeracy, literacy and language in grades 2 and 3; provide opportunities to practise	Develop understanding of methodology for teaching numeracy, practise and develop teaching skills in mathematics learning. Develop understanding of pedagogy for teaching literacy and language in grades 2 and 3
Fourth year	Classroom as a learning community, assessment tasks based on experiences at Mareleng TS and outside partnering schools	

Table 10: Methodology and Teaching Practice (MPR).

African Languages on Home Language Level: isiNdebele, siSwati or Sesotho sa Leboa

Of the eleven constitutionally recognised official languages, nine are African languages. Students may choose any one of three African language courses currently on offer at home language level. During the first year, the purpose of this module is to guide students in developing language competence, knowledge, and application in isiNdebele, siSwati, or Sesotho sa Leboa. This is to enable basic communication and requisite subject knowledge to support language learning in the Foundation Phase classroom.

Year level	Semester one	Semester two
First year	Historical overview of development of the language in its formal forms, written forms after colonisation	Parts of speech (noun classes with C. M. Doke and Meinhof classifications), noun position in sentence, noun as subject, concord, pronouns, adjectives, relatives, enumeratives
Second year	Noun class system and noun prefixes (classes 1–3), noun class system and noun prefixes (classes 4–17), subject morphemes of noun classes, object morphemes of 3rd person, youth literature	Novel (structure, themes, characterisation, and setting), semiotics (signs), essays, differences between a short story and other literary texts, literary theory, analysis and structure of a short story
Third year	Aspects related to orality, drama, and poetry; emphasis on teaching methodology and practice	

Table 11: African languages offered on home language level.

Teaching Studies

A subject with modules at each year level is Teaching Studies (TSD). As is the case with Education Studies (EDS), this module does not have an equivalent at school level. During the first semester at first-year level, the purpose of the module is to guide students in developing a conceptually coherent viewpoint of the interplay of the various roles that underpin a teacher's professional practice. An emphasis is placed on the teacher's community and citizen roles. For their assignments, students are referred to their experiences at the TS as well as their experiences when at outside partnering schools.

Year level	Semester one	Semester two
First year	Personal teaching philosophy, teaching as practice of citizenship, teaching for CARE (community, agency, responsibility, education), service learning	ICT for Foundation Phase: MS Word, MS Excel, PowerPoint
Second year	n/a	Development of educational leadership, management and administrative skills for the classroom and between school and home
Third year	n/a	
	Teaching for motivation and engagement; developing an orderly, purposeful learning environment; repairing and restoring behaviour	
Fourth year	Refreshment of ICT skills in three lectures	

Table 12: Teaching Studies.

During the second semester, the TSD module at first-year level covers ICT for the foundation phase. Students are introduced to word processing, spreadsheets, and presentations as well as some multimedia formats. Google applications for education (GAFE) are used, since these Google services are also used in other modules for which I am responsible (Du Plessis, 2017).

About the Author

Andries Du Plessis is a senior lecturer in the School of Early Childhood Development at the University of Mpumalanga, South Africa. He can be contacted at this e-mail: andries.duplessis@ump.ac.za

Bibliography

Abeysekera, I. (2006). Issues relating to designing a work-integrated learning (WIL) program in an undergraduate accounting degree program and its implications for the curriculum. *Asia-Pacific Journal of Cooperative Education*, Vol. 7, No. 1, pp. 7–15.

Alias, N. A. & N. A. Alias (2010). Technology to Enhance the Affective Learning Outcomes of Teacher Trainees. In J. Yamamoto (Ed.), *Technology Implementation and Teacher Education: Reflective Models*. Hersey PA: Publisher: Information Science Reference, pp. 146–163.

Allen, J. M. & S. E. Wright (2014). Integrating theory and practice in the pre-service teacher education practicum. *Teachers and Teaching*, Vol. 20, No. 2, pp. 136–151.

Ambrosetti, A. (2010). Mentoring and learning to teach: What do pre-service teachers expect to learn from their mentor teachers? *International Journal of Learning*, Vol. 17, No. 9, pp. 117–132.

Atkinson, G. (2016). *Work-based learning and work-integrated learning: Fostering engagement with employers*. Adelaide: NVCER.

Bierly, P. E.; E. H. Kessler & E. W. Christensen (2000). Organizational learning, knowledge and wisdom. *Journal of Organizational Change Management*, Vol. 13, No. 6, pp. 595–618.

Blunden, R. (2000). Rethinking the place of the practicum in teacher education. *Australian Journal of Teacher Education*, Vol. 25, No. 1, pp. 1–16.

Burton, S. L. & G. R. Greher (2007). School-university partnerships: What do we know and why do they matter? *Arts Education Policy Review*, Vol. 109, No. 1, pp. 13–24.

Callahan, J. L. & D. Martin (2007). The spectrum of school-university partnerships: A typology of organizational learning systems. *Teaching and Teacher Education*, Vol. 23, No. 2, pp. 136–145.

Carney, S. (2003). Learning from school-based teacher training: Possibilities and constraints for experienced teachers. *Scandinavian Journal of Educational Research*, Vol. 47, No. 4, pp. 413–429.

Chigona, A.; W. Chigona; P. Kayongo & M. Kuasa (2010). An empirical survey on domestication of ICT in schools in disadvantaged communities in South Africa. *International Journal of Education and Development Using Information and Communication Technology*, Vol. 6, No. 2, pp. 21–32.

Chisholm, L.; J. Daniel, R.; Southall & J. Lutchman (2004). *The state of South Africa's schools*. Cape Town: HSRC Press.

Chitpin, S. (2011). Can mentoring and reflection cause change in teaching practice? A professional development journey of a Canadian teacher educator. *Professional Development in Education*, Vol. 37, No. 2, pp. 225–240.

Choy, S. & B. Delahaye (2011). Partnerships between universities and workplaces: Some challenges for work-integrated learning. *Studies in Continuing Education*, Vol. 33, No. 2, pp. 157–172.

Cochran-Smith, M. (1991). Reinventing Student Teaching. *Journal of Teacher Education*, Vol. 42, No 2, pp. 104–118.

Cohen, E.; R. Hoz & H. Kaplan (2013). The practicum in pre-service teacher education: A review of empirical studies. *Teaching Education*, Vol. 24, No. 4, pp. 345–380.

Crossan, M. M.; H. W. Lane & R. E. White (1999). An organizational learning framework: From intuition to institution. *Academy of Management Review*, Vol. 24, No. 3, pp. 522–537.

Darling-Hammond, L. (1994). *Professional development schools: Schools for developing a profession*. New York: Teachers College Press.

Darling-Hammond, L. (2006). Constructing 21st-century teacher education. *Journal of Teacher Education*, Vol. 57, No. 3, pp. 300–314.

Dodgson, M. (1993). Organizational learning: A review of some literature. *Organization Studies*, Vol. 14, No. 3, pp. 375–394.

Du Plessis, A. S. (2017). Modelling the use of Google Applications for Education and Social Media as building blocks for student teachers' TPACK. In J. Branch; S. Hayes; A. Hørsted & C. Nygaard (Eds.), *Innovative Teaching and Learning in Higher Education*, Oxforshire: Libri Publishing, pp. 399–412.

Easterby-Smith, M. & M. A. Lyles (2011). *Handbook of organizational learning and knowledge management*. West Sussex: John Wiley & Sons.

Edwards, A. & T. Mutton (2007). Looking forward: Rethinking professional learning through partnership arrangements in initial teacher education. *Oxford Review of Education*, Vol. 33, No. 4, pp. 503–519.

Fataar, A. (2003). Higher education policy discourse in South Africa: A struggle for alignment with macro development policy and perspectives on higher education. *South African Journal of Higher Education*, Vol. 17, No. 2, pp. 31–39.

Fenwick, T. (2007). Organisational learning in the "knots": Discursive capacities emerging in school-university collaboration. *Journal of Educational Administration*, Vol. 45, No. 2, Vol. 138–153.

Frampton, P. ; V. L. Vaughn & M. Didelot (2003). The professional development school partnership: Is practice improving? Teachers and principals respond. *Journal of Educational Administration*, Vol. 41, No. 3, pp. 292–309.

Gibson, E.; S. Brodie; S. Sharpe; D. K. Wong & E. Deane (2002). *Towards the development of a work integrated learning unit. Celebrating teaching at Macquarie*. Sydney: Macquarie University.

Gravett, S. (2012). Crossing the "theory-practice divide": Learning to be (come) a teacher. South *African Journal of Childhood Education*. Vol 2, No 2, pp. 1–14.

Gravett, S.; N. Petersen & G. Petker (2014). Integrating foundation phase teacher education with a "teaching school" at the University of Johannesburg. *Education as Change*, Vol. 18, No 1, pp. S107–S119.

Greany, T. & C. Brown. (2015). *Partnerships between Teaching Schools and Universities: Research Report*. London: Centre for Leadership in Learning, UCL IOE.

Grudnoff, L. (2011). Rethinking the practicum: Limitations and possibilities. *Asia-Pacific Journal of Teacher Education*, Vol. 39, No. 3, pp. 223–234.

Huber, G. P. (1991). Organizational learning: The contributing processes and the literatures. *Organization Science*, Vol. 2, No 1, pp. 88–115.

Jenkins, J. M. (2014). Pre-service teachers' observations of experienced teachers. *Physical Educator*, Vol. 71, No. 2, pp. 303–319.

Jin, S. & J. Bagaka (2005). The role of teacher practices and classroom characteristics on the "digital divide" in students' usage of technology tools: A multilevel analysis. *Contemporary Issues in Technology and Teacher Education*, Vol. 5, No. 3, pp. 318–329.

Kwan, T. & F. Lopez-Real (2005). Mentors' perceptions of their roles in mentoring student teachers. *Asia-Pacific Journal of Teacher Education*, Vol. 33, No. 3, pp. 275–287.

Liu, S. (2014). Excellent mentor teachers' skills in mentoring for pre-service teachers. *International Journal of Education*, Vol. 6, No. 3, pp. 29–42.

Loock, C. & S. Gravett (2014). Towards a governance and management model for teaching schools in South Africa. *South African Journal of Childhood Education*, Vol. 4, No. 3, pp. 174–191.

Maandag, D. W.; J.F. Deinum; A. W. Hofman & J. Buitink (2007). Teacher education in schools: An international comparison. *European Journal of Teacher Education*, Vol. 30, No. 2, pp. 151–173.

Mathews, P. & G. Berwick (2013). *Teaching schools: First among equals.* Nottingham, England: National College for Teaching and Leadership.

Matoba, M.; Y. Shibata & M. R. Sarkar Arani (2007). School-university partnerships: A new recipe for creating professional knowledge in school. *Educational Research for Policy and Practice,* Vol. 6, No. 1, pp. 55–65.

Ming See, N. L. M. (2014). Mentoring and developing pedagogical content knowledge in beginning teachers. *Procedia – Social and Behavioral Sciences,* Vol. 123, pp. 53–62.

Mukeredzi, T. G. (2014). Re-envisioning teaching practice: Student teacher learning in a cohort model of practicum in a rural South African context. *International Journal of Educational Development,* Vol. 39, pp. 100–109.

Mule, L. (2006). Pre-service teachers' inquiry in a professional development school context: Implications for the practicum. *Teaching and Teacher Education,* Vol. 22, No. 2, pp. 205–218.

Ndlovu, N. S. & D. Lawrence (2012). The quality of ICT use in South African classrooms: Strategies to overcome poverty and inequality. Presented at the *Towards Carnegie III,* Cape Town.

Niemi, H. & R. Jakku-Sihvonen (2011). Teacher education in Finland. In Zuljan, M.; Z. Vogrinc & J. Vogrinc (Eds.), *European Dimensions of Teacher Education: Similarities and Differences,* Faculty of Education, University of Ljubljana, Slovenia and The National School of Leadership in Education, Kranj, Slovenia, pp. 33–51.

Nygaard, C.; T. Højlt & M. Hermansen (2008). Learning-based curriculum development. *Higher Education,* Vol. 55, No. 1, pp. 33–50.

Nygaard, C. & M. B. Serrano (2009). Students' identity construction and learning. Reasons for developing a learning-centred curriculum in higher education. In L. Kattington (Ed.), *Handbook of Curriculum Development.* New York: Nova Science Publishers.

Osman, R. & R. Casella (2007). Learning through fieldwork: Undergraduate research and teacher education in South Africa. *Education as Change,* Vol. 11, No. 2, pp. 33–43.

Perrow, M. (2013). "Welcome to the real world": Navigating the gap between best teaching practices and current reality. *Studying Teacher Education,* Vol. 9, No. 3, pp. 284–297.

Reddy, C.; H. Menkveld & E. Bitzer (2008). The practicum in pre-service teacher education: A survey of institutional practices. *Southern African Review of Education with Education with Production: A Review of Comparative Education and History of Education from SACHES,* Vol. 14, Nos. 1 & 2, pp. 143–163.

Rorrison, D. (2010). Assessment of the practicum in teacher education: Advocating for the student teacher and questioning the gatekeepers. *Educational Studies*, Vol. 36, No. 5, pp. 505–519.

RSA (Republic of South Africa) (2000). *Norms and Standards for Teacher Educators*. Government Gazette, No. 20844. Pretoria: Government Printer.

RSA (Republic of South Africa) (2011). *National Qualifications Framework Act 67 of 2008 Policy on the Minimum Requirements for Teacher Education Qualifications*. Government Gazette, No. 34467. Pretoria: Government Printer.

Rusznyak, L. (2015). Knowledge selection in initial teacher education programmes and its implications for curricular coherence. *Journal of Education*, No. 60, pp. 7–30.

Sedumedi, T. D. T. & F. J. Mundalamo (2012). Understanding field assessment of pre-service teachers on school practicum. *Africa Education Review*, Vol. 9, No. 1, pp. S73–S90.

Sherman, K. & S. K. Howard (2012). Teachers beliefs about first- and second-order barriers to ICT integration: Preliminary findings from a South African study. In P. Resta (Ed.), *Proceedings of Society for Information Technology & Teacher Education International Conference*, 5–9 March 2012, Austin, Texas, pp. 2098–2105.

Smith, K. (2010). Assessing the practicum in teacher education: Do we want candidates and mentors to agree? *Studies in Educational Evaluation*, Vol. 36, No. 1, pp. 36–41.

Stenhouse, L. (1975). *An introduction to curriculum research and development*. London: Heinemann.

Tabak, E. (1962). *Curriculum development: Theory and practice*. New York: Harcourt, Brace & World.

Tomlinson, P. D.; A. J. Hobson & A. Malderez (2010). Mentoring in teacher education. In P. P. B. McGaw (Ed.), *International Encyclopaedia of Education* (Third Edition), Oxford: Elsevier, pp. 749–756.

Tryggvason, M. T. (2009). Why is Finnish teacher education successful? Some goals Finnish teacher educators have for their teaching. *European Journal of Teacher Education*, Vol. 32, No. 4, pp. 369–382.

Tsui, A. B.; G. Edwards; F. Lopez-Real; T. Kwan & D. Law (2008). *Learning in school-university partnership: Sociocultural perspectives*. Routledge. Retrieved from https://books.google.co.za

Welch, T. (2002). Teacher education in South Africa before, during and after apartheid, an overview. In J. Adler & Y. Reed (Eds.), *Challenges of Teacher Development: An Investigation of Take-up in South Africa*, Pretoria: Van Schaik, pp. 17–35.

Chapter 8

Using the ECTS for Learning-Centred Curriculum Design

John Branch & Timothy Hartge

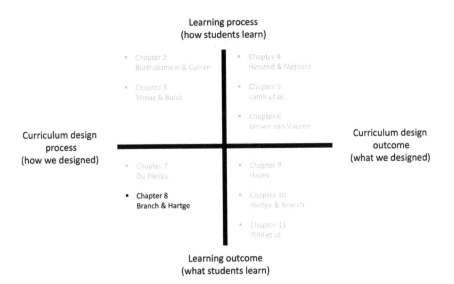

Introduction

We contribute to this book *Learning-Centred Curriculum Design in Higher Education* by illustrating that the ECTS is itself learning-centred, and that the ECTS can be used to aid learning-centred curriculum design. In relation to the central model of the book, we position our chapter in section three – Curriculum Design Process/Learning Outcome – because we focus on how we design curriculum using ECTS, and how that will enable us to focus on what students learn.

Charles Eames, who along with his wife Ray Eames became famous in the mid–20th century for their modern architecture and furniture, believed that design depends on constraints. Rather than viewing them in the negative, Eames suggested that constraints are not only normal but also necessary...perhaps even hinting at a fundamental difference between art and design – that artists enjoy unbounded creativity, whereas designers must operate within prescribed or self-imposed limits. When asked to elaborate, Eames responded: *"Here is one of the few effective keys to the Design problem: the ability of the Designer to recognize as many of the constraints as possible; his willingness and enthusiasm for working within these constraints. Constraints of price, of size, of strength, of balance, of surface, of time, and so forth. Each problem has its own peculiar list."* (Interview of C. Eames by L. Amic at the Musée des Arts Décoratifs, Palais de Louvre). And so it is with curriculum design. Indeed, any curriculum design exercise almost always begins with constraints (see Bartholomew & Curran; Lamb *et al.*, in this volume, for examples). The university year, for example, has (somewhat arbitrarily) been divided into trimesters or semesters or other circumscribed periods of time. A committee somewhere, sometime might have decided that, irrespective of their focus and content, all courses in a degree programme will be standardised to 3 credits. Or maybe the department chairperson has restricted enrolment in a course to students who have met certain prerequisites, has already written the course's learning outcomes, and has even mandated a specific course textbook.

In 1999, the European Union undertook a bold initiative that erected a new set of constraints for institutions of higher education across Europe. Named the Bologna Process after the Italian city in which the founding declaration was signed into effect, the initiative aimed to create a single transparent and competitive higher education 'market' out of the diverse national higher education systems (Bennett *et al.*, 2010). Its main features are 1) a standardised three-cycle bachelor-master-doctoral progression, and 2) a common unit of measurement for educational attainment that has subsequently been dubbed the European Credit Transfer and Accumulation System (ECTS). The result of the Bologna Process has been the emergence of the European Area of Higher Education (EAHE), the educational equivalent of Europe's currency-based Eurozone. We contend that the ECTS specifically – as a constraint – serves as a very useful tool for learning-centred curriculum design in higher education by providing both intrinsic and extrinsic guidance for designing lessons, courses, and even entire degree programmes. After reading this chapter, you will be able to:

1. situate curriculum design within the broader educational enterprise;

2. describe the principles of the ECTS;

3. use the ECTS for learning-centred curriculum design.

We have structured our chapter in three sections. In section one, we introduce a model of pedagogy that helps situate curriculum design. In section two, we then review the tenets of the Bologna Process, and details the ECTS. In section three, we demonstrate the use of the ECTS for learning-centred curriculum design with two examples: 1) an undergraduate marketing management course, and 2) a new MBA programme.

Section I: Pedagogy

Defined as the art, science, or profession of teaching, pedagogy (or its Latin equivalent education) focuses broadly on the context of teaching and learning, and more narrowly on the specific operations therein. As such, pedagogy can be thought of as involving the three primary activities: curriculum, instruction, and assessment (see Figure 1, below). Like writing, do-it-yourself, or other practices, pedagogy features, among other things, design and executional elements. In brief, curriculum refers to the specific subjects or topics of a lesson, course, or programme of study. A lesson on weather, for example, might warrant discussion of atmospheric conditions, forecasting, and the seven influences on weather: latitude, altitude, nearness to large bodies of water, ocean currents, prevailing winds, and air masses. It follows, therefore, that curriculum design, taking a learning-centred perspective of pedagogy, is the specification of the particular subjects or topics of the lesson, course, or programme of study. It addresses *what* the student ought to learn. Indeed, curriculum design can be considered as the intentional activity of answering the question "What ought students to know at the end of this learning event?"

Instruction is a fancy word for teaching (of the curriculum). From a learning-centred perspective of pedagogy, however, it might be defined better in terms of the methods for learning. In other words, instruction focuses on *how* students will learn. Instructional design, therefore, concerns the choice of learning tools; it is about selecting specific instructional methods (lectures, videos, textbook readings, cases, simulations, etc.) from the instructor's 'bag of tricks' (see Lamb et al., in this volume, for a similar idea). Like curriculum design, it is an intentional activity,

223

but aimed at answering the question "How can students' learning be facilitated?"

Assessment is about measuring the learning which has transpired. It addresses *if* students have learned. Assessment design, perhaps obviously, is the specification of methods for identifying whether the learning objectives have indeed been met. And like both curriculum design and assessment design, it is also intentional and attempts to answer the question "Have students achieved the learning objectives which were set?" Although, to be fair, assessment has in recent years been expanded to include the learning process and not only the learning outcomes (summative versus formative assessment).

As highlighted in Figure 1, these three primary activities of curriculum, instruction, and assessment are interrelated – self-reinforcing and self-informing. Consequently, the model intimates that there ought to be an improvement in the pedagogy with each iteration of the curriculum, instruction, and assessment cycle. Poor student results following an assessment, for example, ought to lead to reflections on the suitability and success of the assessment methods. However, they also raise concerns about the design and execution of both the curriculum and the instruction.

Similarly, the model intimates that no one activity stands alone. Indeed, each of the three activities is dependent on the other activities. Curriculum design, for example, must consider both instructional design and assessment design. That is to say, the subjects or topics of a lesson, course, or programme of study must consider how they can be both learned and assessed. Our colleague Julian Lamb (in the volume) went further, suggesting that curriculum, instruction, and assessment might be analogous to the 'holy trinity' or quantum physics, in which the elements exist independently but are simultaneously inseparable.

Now, in our experience, the other two activities in Figure 1 are seemingly less prominent in higher education – although no less valuable. Indeed, they are worthy of attention first, because the terms *assessment* and *evaluation* are often, but erroneously, used interchangeably. They are also important considerations from a learning-centred perspective, because any learning event exists within a broader context. The first activity, *needs*, points to the motivation for learning – needs address *why* the student must learn. Needs analysis, therefore, is a diagnosis of sorts, whose aim is to identify the purpose of the learning event. Evaluation gauges the impact of the learning event. It addresses the *so what*. In effect, it is testing whether or not the needs have been met by the learning event. As before, there is also an interrelationship between needs analysis; the 'holy trinity' of curriculum, instruction, and assessment; and evaluation, likewise suggesting the iterative and interdependent nature of the pedagogy overall.

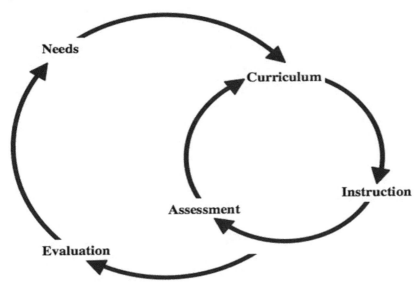

Figure 1: A model of pedagogy.

An example here might be useful. Consider a company whose employee turnover rate has been increasing. A needs analysis identifies that employees are not satisfied with their jobs, especially because they do not receive feedback from their managers. These managers, therefore, *need* training on delivering feedback to their employees. Thus, this leads to the design of a training programme for managers, which includes a curriculum (*what* the managers ought to learn about feedback), instructional methods (*how* they will learn that curriculum), and assessment methods (*if* they have learned that curriculum). After the training programme, the company ought to evaluate its effectiveness (the *so what*), by examining if the training programme has indeed led to reduced employee turnover.

Similarly, but in a more salient higher education context, corporate recruiters have recently complained that the graduates of the MBA programme at the Stephen M. Ross School of Business are unprepared for the indistinct and often nebulous nature of business problems. Consequently, the core curriculum committee, which advises on the required courses of the first year of the MBA programme, has been meeting to identify the specific knowledge, skills, and abilities (KSAs) which are required of MBA graduates in order to be prepared for the vagaries of the business world upon graduation. The curriculum committee has likewise been tasked with the development of 1) cross-disciplinary instructional methods for 'teaching' these KSAs, and 2) assessment methods for ensuring that the KSAs are indeed mastered. No discussion has occurred about the "So what?", however, but presumably the associate dean of the MBA programme will circle back to the corporate recruiters, as a check on the effectiveness of the curriculum committee's recommended course of action.

As a final thought, a syllabus can be considered as the tangible documentation of the five activities of pedagogy (well, sort of). A good syllabus often highlights the needs to some degree, usually in the form of a "Why this course?" rationale in the course overview...although, this rationale is rarely based on a formal needs analysis. Much attention has been paid in the past decade to the construction of learning objectives, and consequently most syllabi do an admirable job with curriculum through the use of elaborate statements of overall course and specific learning objectives. Most syllabi, however, pay much less attention to instruction and assessment, and almost always skirt evaluation altogether, abdicating responsibility to administrators further up the food chain.

Section 2: The Bologna Process

The Bologna Process is a voluntary framework whose primary purpose is to increase the compatibility and quality of higher education in Europe. It has now been adopted by some 50 countries and has resulted in a single higher education market across Europe and Eurasia – the so-called European Higher Education Area (EHEA). The Bologna Process began in earnest in 1999 with the signing of the Bologna Declaration by 29 European countries. It was foreshadowed, however, in 1998 when education ministers from France, Germany, Italy, and the United Kingdom committed, in the Sorbonne Declaration, to the harmonisation of European higher education. The Bologna Process has evolved over time with additional ministerial meetings and declarations and now encompasses ten broad policy aims, or 'action lines' (see Table 1).

Established in the Bologna Declaration of 1999	Adoption of a system of easily readable and comparable degrees
	Adoption of a system essentially based on two cycles
	Establishment of a system of credits
	Promotion of mobility
	Promotion of European co-operation in quality assurance
	Promotion of the European dimension in higher education
Added after the Prague Ministerial Conference of 2001	Focus on lifelong learning
	Greater inclusion of higher education institutions and students in the Bologna Process
	Promotion of the attractiveness of the European Higher Education Area
Added after the Berlin Ministerial Conference of 2003	Doctoral studies and the synergy between the European Higher Education Area and the European Research Area

Table 1: Action Lines of the Bologna Process (UK Parliament, 2012).

The first and foundational action line of the Bologna Process requires that signatory countries adopt the Anglo-Saxon sequence of bachelor-master-doctor. The traditional French system of higher education, for example, began with a two-year post-secondary DEUG diploma, followed by a one-year license, followed by a one-year maîtrise, and so on and so on. Under the Bologna Process, these multiple diplomas have been replaced with only three degrees: bachelor, master, and doctor. Within this first and foundational action line, it is also stipulated that a master degree will typically be awarded upon completion of five years of post-secondary education. Interestingly, the action line allows institutions the flexibility to specify if the five years will be 3+2 or 4+1. That is to say, institutions can opt to have bachelor degrees either three or four years in length, followed accordingly by two-year or one-year master degrees.

The more impactful action line – at least from a curriculum design perspective – concerns the European Credit Transfer and Accumulation System (ECTS). It serves as a kind of common currency of higher education within the European Union – the educational equivalent of the EURO. It pre-dates the Bologna Process; its roots can be traced to 1988, when the European Union devised the ERASMUS programme (European Community Action Scheme for the Mobility of University Students) in support of student exchanges with the European Union (Enders, 1998).

ECTS begins with the stipulation that one academic year of full-time study is equivalent to 1,800 hours (the ECTS, in fact, allows for a range of 1,500 to 1,800 hours, but for simplicity we shall use 1,800 hours). Using a full-time 'work week' of 40 hours, 1,800 hours represent an academic year of 45 weeks. Note that hours in the ECTS do not mean face-to-face classroom hours. On the contrary, the ECTS has switched the focus of higher education away from the instructor to the student, away from teaching to learning. Hours, therefore, refer to *learning* hours – that is to say hours that the average student spends learning, irrespective of the learning activity. Learning activities include reading, project work, discussions, assignments, examination preparation, lectures, and any other instructional method. The ECTS also equates one academic year of full-time study to 60 ECTS credits. One ECTS credit, therefore, equals 30 learning hours. To reiterate, these hours are not face-to-face, classroom hours but instead learning hours.

Probably the most important takeaway from the ECTS is that it allows for dramatically different instructional designs. One instructor, for example, could teach a two ECTS credit course in marketing by having its 60 learning hours spread over only two learning activities: 59 hours of face-to-face classroom lectures, and a 1-hour examination. Another instructor, however, might have 20 hours of readings, 10 hours of cases, 20 hours of a team consulting project, and 10 hours of online discussions. In the eyes of the ECTS, the two courses are equivalent.

The intention of the ECTS, as you might conclude, is largely to facilitate student mobility by creating course transparency for institutions. Indeed, students can receive credit more easily for courses that are taken while on exchange, because course credits can be compared directly. A more important consequence, however, is that the ECTS gives instructors (and thereby institutions) extreme flexibility in how courses are designed. Even more, it pushes instructors to think more about learning and less about teaching. Indeed, the ECTS demands that instructors think of themselves not as teachers, but as 'architects' of learning – that a course is a collection of learning activities that instructors 'curate', and whose efforts sum to the ECTS learning hours total. Finally, it ought to be mentioned that the learning hours are inclusive – that is to say, all learning events, including classroom face-to-face lectures, readings, examinations and other assessments, self-study (everything) make up the learning hours. The learning hours must not exceed 40 hours per week, and they must not begin before, or extend beyond, the designated learning period.

Section 3: Examples of Learning-Centred Curriculum Design Using the ECTS

As mentioned previously, we contend that the ECTS serves as a very useful tool for learning-centred curriculum design in higher education by providing both intrinsic and extrinsic guidance for designing lessons, courses, and even entire degree programmes. This section supports this contention by demonstrating the use of the ECTS for learning-centred curriculum design with examples from our own experiences. It begins with an example of the design of a single course, followed by an example of an entire degree programme.

BBA Marketing Management

In 2013, the Stephen M. Ross School of Business bachelor of business programme (BBA) was completely overhauled. As part of the new curriculum design, all students would be required to complete a 'capstone' course, which, the logic went, would provide a subject-specific integrative experience in the final year of study. Each of the different subject groups (e.g., strategy, operations, management) committed to developing and offering a capstone course.

In the 2016/2017 academic year, I (John) was tasked with teaching the capstone course for the marketing group, dubbed MKT401 Marketing Management II. No guidance was provided in terms of specific subject requirements or even broad learning objectives – not an uncommon practice in North American universities in which instructors are given a wide berth as part of so-called academic freedom (see introduction of this volume). Start and end dates, national holidays, final exam period, and the grade deadline were set. The '4' in MKT401 designated it as an upper-level course, and the course was valued at 3 credits. But otherwise, I was on my own to design the course as I saw fit.

So, I began the course design by first attempting to identify if the School had any ECTS learning hours equivalent. American institutions of higher education are still concerned primarily with face-to-face contact hours, and often allocate credits accordingly. An inquiry at the dean's office gave no solid answer. Colleagues looked at me like an alien. But after some searching, I discovered an official document from the registrar that provided guidelines for independent study courses: 1 credit = 48 hours of independent work. A 3-credit course, therefore, requires 144 learning hours. Note that this is substantially higher than the 90 learning hours of the typical 3-credit European course. Our speculation is that the hours coincide with the 40-hour workweek which is the norm in Europe...but it is speculation.

I then pulled out the calendar to calculate the number of weeks in the semester. Recall that ECTS mandates that learning hours must not begin before, or extend beyond, the designated learning period. The answer was 14 weeks, which created my first challenge: 144 is not divided neatly by 14. A little number play led me to a decision: 12 weeks of 11 hours and 2 weeks of 6 hours, for a total of 144 hours. But how to allocate these hours across various learning activities?

First, as a general rule at the School, a 3-credit course consists of 36 face-to-face contact hours. The scheduling of these hours is usually dictated by the registrar: 14:00 to 15:40 on both Mondays and Wednesdays, for example (the School has a 10-minute settling-in period at the beginning of each session, which results in the ubiquitous University euphemism for being late as 'Michigan time'). That was easy – the challenge was filling the remaining hours.

Recalling that ECTS specifies that learning hours are inclusive of all learning activities (including assessments), it was at this point in the design of the course that the interrelationship between the three primary activities of curriculum, instruction, and assessment was illustrated. Indeed, as I enumerated the learning objectives for the course (*what* the students ought to learn), I also considered different instructional tools (*how* they would learn). I experimented with different ideas, allocating learning hours that were commensurate with the different learning objectives. Likewise, I began to think about appropriate assessment methods (*if* the students had learned), aligning them with the learning objectives, and ensuring that the learning hours that would be spent on any specific assessment would be proportional to its contribution to the final grade.

Figure 2 shows the result of this exercise. Note the 36 hours of face-to-face sessions. The four assessments contribute another 80 hours. The remaining hours were allocated to reading and other independent activities, all in service of the course learning objectives. And as mentioned above, the learning hours for the four assessments that I decided to use were made proportional to the contributions of the four assessments to the final grade:

1. RISK Exercise: 10%

2. Examination: 10%

3. Consulting Project: 40%

4. Simulation: 40%

I continued the course design concurrently by allocating learning hours across each of the 14 weeks of the semester, ensuring that the total learning hours of any specific week corresponded to six hours or eleven hours, as described above. Figure 3 shows the course schedule and learning activities of the syllabus. Note that there are no learning activities that occur prior to the first face-to-face session because, as per ECTS, learning hours must not begin before, or extend beyond, the designated learning period. The course design must account for holidays; for example, Martin Luther King Day occurred in week 2, thereby limiting the week to only one face-to-face session. However, the total learning hours must remain at 11, and the learning hours in the course schedule refer to all learning hours, irrespective of the learning activity, face-to-face session, reading, assessment, etc.

Course Effort

You ought to spend 144 hours on this course—6 hours in the first week of the semester, 6 hours in the last week of the semester, and 11 hours per week in the remaining 12 weeks of the semester. This breakdown will help you allocate these hours.

Learning Activity	Hours
24 Face-to-Face Sessions	36
RISK Exercise	8
Examination	8
Consulting Project	32
Simulation	32
Reading and Other Independent Activities	28
Total	144

Figure 2: Course effort for the BBA Marketing Management course.

Luxembourg School of Business MBA

In 2014, at a pizzeria in Zagreb, Croatia, a friend and colleague, Marin Njavro, and I (John) discussed the possibility of establishing a business school in Luxembourg. Over the past two decades, the country had transformed itself from a sleepy agricultural and industrial economy into the world's services Mecca. Today, its capital city harbours many multinational corporate headquarters, it is a haven for young professionals, and it hosts almost 300,000 daily migrant workers from neighbouring Belgium, France, and Germany.

Less than six months later, the Luxembourg School of Business (LSB) was founded, with a small, rented office, a shiny website, and some branded business cards and other promotional collateral. Marin took the reins as the School's managing director, and I was 'appointed' as its inaugural dean. First up was a series of one- and two-day open enrolment executive education seminars, which, despite the limited brand recognition of LSB, attracted participants from several large companies in Luxembourg. I then began the task of designing the School's MBA programme, starting from a blank slate.

Week	Learning Activities (Learning Hours)
Week 1. Monday 9 January to Sunday 15 January (6 hours)	1. Attend Face-to-Face Session 1. Introduction to Marketing Strategy (1.5 hours) 2. Attend Face-to-Face Session 2. Competition (1.5 hours) 3. Read and understand thoroughly the RISK® instructions (1 hour) 4. Read this guide to military strategy, and then plan your RISK® strategy (2 hours): • Strategy and Tactics: A Primer (Canvas)
Week 2. Monday 16 January to Sunday 22 January (11 hours)	1. Attend Face-to-Face Session 3. RISK® (1.5 hours) 2. Complete RISK® Exercise (8 hours) 3. Watch the following YouTube talks, and then consider the link between purpose/vision and marketing (1.5 hours): • Start With Why: How Great Leaders Inspire Action (Canvas) • Profit With Purpose: Corporate Social Responsibility (Canvas)
Week 3. Monday 23 January to Sunday 29 January (11 hours)	1. Study this tutorial on the resource based view of the firm, and articulate the role of marketing (1 hour): • Resource Based View (Canvas) 2. Attend Face-to-Face Session 4. Company (1.5 hours) 3. Read these articles on the importance of marketing, and then contemplate the challenge which marketing has in companies (2 hours): • Marketing Concepts and Orientations (Canvas) • Marketing in the Driver's Seat (Canvas) • The Decline and Dispersion of Marketing Competence (Canvas)

Figure 3: Course scheduling and learning activities of the BBA Marketing Management II course.

A survey of business schools revealed that most MBA programmes in Europe vary from 45 to 75 credits, despite the ECTS requirement that postgraduate degrees must have a minimum of 60 credits. I decided that the LSB MBA would be 60 credits, in part because it was the average credit total but also because 60 credits is a more easily divisible number – not an inconsequential issue in curriculum design. Simple arithmetic, therefore, means that, with 30 learning hours per credit, the MBA would require 1,800 learning hours. I also decided that the LSB MBA would be structured into 15-week modules. Again, simple arithmetic resulted in 20 credits per module (40 learning hours per week) if studied full-time, or 10 credits per module (20 learning hours per week) if studied part-time.

As for curriculum, I also surveyed other MBA programmes, noting the variety of subjects and topics that they included. And I called on my 20+ years of experience teaching and training around the world.

As a starting point, I drew up a wish list for the curriculum:

1. a broad foundational curriculum to enable students to master the fundamentals of business;

2. a grounding in general management, but international in perspective and entrepreneurial in spirit;

3. leadership woven throughout the programme;

4. flexible enough to allow full- or part-time study; and

5. experiential-learning opportunities.

Finally, I wanted the curriculum to have a narrative. That is to say, I wanted the courses to cluster in themes that were not only logical but also furnished an outsider with a sense that the curriculum follows a 'story'. See Figure 4 for the LSB MBA programme.

Now, I was keenly aware that as a new higher education institution, LSB was constrained in terms of human resources. Consequently, I knew that any curriculum design had to plan for instructors flying in to Luxembourg for the face-to-face sessions, and probably no more than twice per module, considering both time and cost. After some back-and-forth debate with Marin, I decided that face-to-face classroom sessions ought to be scheduled on alternating weekends – in my experience, every weekend was too 'busy' for students, and once a month, although normal for executive MBA programmes, was too infrequent to create a strong student culture. Additionally, with alternating weekends, students could conceivably attend the LSB MBA full-time by completing modules 1 and 4 simultaneously, modules 2 and 5 simultaneously, and modules 3 and 6 simultaneously. I also decided that face-to-face classroom sessions ought to be scheduled Friday evenings and Saturdays, thereby avoiding any conflicts that might arise between students and their employers. With this scheduling, the classroom space also remained free during the week-days, allowing LSB to continue operating its series of one- and two-day open enrolment executive education seminars.

The ECTS was particularly useful when mapping out the modules. As an example, consider module 1: Foundations. A 3-credit course has 90 learning hours, a 1-credit course 30 learning hours. In total, this module (like all six modules) represents 300 learning hours. These 300 learning hours are evenly spread over the 15-week module, with 20 learning hours per week. The leadership course is 'front-loaded', with 10 learning hours allocated to face-to-face activities on the first weekend of the module. The three other courses each have two weekends of face-to-face activities situated elsewhere in the module. These courses, therefore, require instructors to develop self-study learning activities for the weeks leading up to their first face-to-face contact. But these learning activities must be designed so that together they do not add up to more than 20 learning hours in total for any single week.

LSB / **Luxembourg School of Business**

The LSB MBA Curriculum

Module 1. Foundations (10 credits)
The Global Economy (3 credits)
Competitive Markets (3 credits)
People and Organisations (3 credits)
Leadership (1 credit)

Module 2. Functions (10 credits)
Marketing (3 credits)
Operations (3 credits)
Finance (3 credits)
Leadership (1 credit)

Module 3: Tools (10 credits)
Financial Reporting (3 credits)
Business Law and Ethics (3 credits)
Managerial Economics (3 credits)
Leadership (1 credit)

Module 4. Directions (10 credits)
Strategy (3 credits)
Power and Persuasion (3 credits)
Data Analysis and Decision-Making (3 credits)
Leadership (1 credit)

Module 5: Extensions (10 credits)
International Business (3 credits)
Technology and Innovation (3 credits)
Entrepreneurship (3 credits)
Leadership (1 credit)

Module 6: Applications (10 credits)
Simulation (3 credits)
Practicum (5 credits)
Leadership (2 credits)

Figure 4: The LSB MBA programme.

Conclusion

Theodor Geisel, more commonly known as Dr Seuss, wrote his now famous *Cat in the Hat* children's book with only 50 words. Yes, 50 words! Although counterintuitive, it seems that constraints, rather than constraining human activity, might provide some degree of freedom. Indeed, consider your productivity on the day before your vacation begins, or the economy of your words when the number of pages which you are allowed is limited. In this chapter, we reviewed the European Credit Transfer and Accumulation System (ECTS), contending that the ECTS specifically – as a constraint – serves as a very useful tool for learning-centred curriculum design in higher education by providing both intrinsic and extrinsic guidance for designing lessons, courses, and even entire degree programmes. Examples of curriculum design for an undergraduate marketing management course and a new MBA programme demonstrate this usefulness. The examples also confirm the idea of freedom through constraints. Indeed, the ECTS, as a constraint, provides freedom to the curriculum designer to escape the traditions of face-to-face contact hours, and, more importantly, to design lessons, courses, and entire degree programmes with any activities that situate learning at the centre.

About the Authors

John Branch is academic director of the part-time MBA programmes and assistant clinical professor of business administration at the Stephen M. Ross School of Business and faculty associate at the Center for Russian, East European, and Eurasian Studies, both of the University of Michigan in Ann Arbor, USA. He can be contacted at this e-mail: jdbranch@umich.edu

Timothy Hartge is a lecturer of business communication at the College of Business at the University of Michigan in Dearborn, USA, and an intermittent lecturer at the English Language Institute at the Stephen M. Ross School of Business, University of Michigan, in Ann Arbor, USA. He can be contacted at this e-mail: thartge@umich.edu

Bibliography

Bennett, P.; S. Bergan; D. Cassar; M. Hamilton; M. Soinila; A. Sursock; S. Uvalic-Trumbic & P. Williams (Eds.) (2010). *Quality assurance in transnational higher education*. Helsinki, Finland: European Association for Quality Assurance in Higher Education.

EHEA (1998). *The European Higher Education Area Joint Declaration of the European Ministers of Education*. Online Resource: http://www.ehea.info/ Uploads/about/BOLOGNA_DECLARATION1.pdf [Accessed on 29 May 2017].

Enders, J. (1998). Academic staff mobility in the European community: The ERASMUS experience. *Comparative Education Review*, Vol. 42, pp. 46–60.

UK Parliament (2012). *The Modernisation of Higher Education in Europe— European Union Committee*. Online Resource: https://www.publications. parliament.uk/pa/ld201012/ldselect/ldeucom/275/27505.htm [Accessed on 29 May 2017].

Section 4: Learning Outcome/Curriculum Design Outcome

Chapter 9
Introducing the Concept of "A Corresponding Curriculum" to Transform Academic Identity and Practice

Sarah Hayes

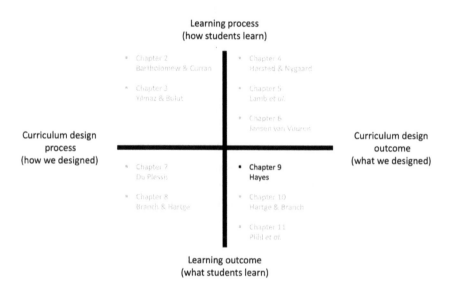

Learning process
(how students learn)

* Chapter 2
  Bartholomew & Curran

* Chapter 3
  Yilmaz & Bulut

* Chapter 4
  Horsted & Nygaard

* Chapter 5
  Lamb et al.

* Chapter 6
  Jansen van Vuuren

Curriculum design
process
(how we designed)

Curriculum design
outcome
(what we designed)

* Chapter 7
  Du Plessis

* **Chapter 9
  Hayes**

* Chapter 8
  Branch & Hartge

* Chapter 10
  Hartge & Branch

* Chapter 11
  Plihl et al.

Learning outcome
(what students learn)

Introduction

I contribute to this book *Learning-Centred Curriculum Design in Higher Education* by introducing the concept of a *corresponding curriculum,* dynamically developed by the participants themselves on a master in education (MEd) programme at Aston University in England. In relation to the central model of the book, I position my chapter in section four –Learning Outcome/Curriculum Design Outcome – because I describe both students' learning outcomes and the outcome of our curriculum design process following from working with the corresponding curriculum. Readers may be familiar with the notion of a "hidden curriculum", which is frequently discussed in a negative way. To respond to this imbalance, I describe forms of learning (both group and individual) that take place in parallel to the declared curriculum as a corresponding curriculum. This makes the lived experiences of learners transparent, placing emphasis on self-knowledge and deeper engagement with personal and professional identity. Thus, I define a *learning-centred curriculum*, firstly, as a dynamic and "contextualised practice", where design and delivery encompass knowledge, principles, values, teaching, learning, assessment, and evaluation (Pokorny & Warren, 2016:12). At the same time, "curriculum" is considered as a "contested space" of possibility for participant transformation and resistance, via *praxis*, which I interpret as "living" research (Hayes, 2015). Through praxis, curriculum becomes a more flexible vehicle for promoting human emancipation, respect for others via critical pedagogy (Freire, 1973), and acknowledgement of personal learning journeys.

If we are developing a learning-centred curriculum, then room should be negotiated for shared critical consciousness to be constructed collaboratively. I therefore draw inspiration from *arts-based research* and apply techniques such as mindfulness and contemplation to the teaching and indeed design of the curriculum. This challenges participant assumptions and develops a sense of community, even love (see Lamb *et al.*, in this volume), where curriculum content becomes co-constructed as part of daily life. A negotiated assessment for the 60-credit MEd module helps to encourage a model of praxis. Whilst a distinct and rigorous design was applied in the construction of the Aston University MEd during 2014, with participant consultation and quality approval for the intended taught content – flexibility is key. The MEd design framework offers scope as a shared space, where as a group of colleagues, we converse with the curriculum, making room for the intimate, painful, and pleasurable aspects of life that inform the ways in which we learn and teach. This helps to resist the more alienating and de-humanising elements of consumer-focused education and fosters a re-conceptualisation of the curriculum and the body. I ask readers to re-imagine the role of the human body (emotions, aches and pains, panic, sweat, joy, dancing, even love) and not simply the mind in learning and teaching and to link their practice with their different identities.

I have learned from participants that "they can only start from where they are." By adopting the term *corresponding curriculum*, I imply that the visible, planned, "intended" curriculum (that is often set in stone – and in this case is designed to support an individual structured research inquiry) is, in practice, something we all communicate with on a regular basis. However, in parallel, we collectively and curiously pursue an "actual", emotionally engaging, and "lived" transformative curriculum that we, as a group, mindfully co-construct. In reading this chapter, you will gain insights into:

1. what constitutes a curriculum and how to develop a curriculum that is learning-centred, with space for participant contribution. Also, why "curriculum theorising" on what counts as knowledge is worthwhile is explored through curriculum ideologies (Schiro, 2013), arts-based research, and my own reflexive development, as personal praxis;

2. principles applied in the design and enactment of the MEd Negotiated Project, taught by colleagues in the Centre for Learning, Innovation and Professional Practice (CLIPP), Aston University, and participant feedback. An inclusive and contemplative approach adopted towards the taught content, allows "social intelligence" to emerge (Sfeir, 2014), based on personal narratives and popular culture (Jubas *et al.*, 2016);

3. opportunities to consider how you might develop a *corresponding curriculum* for yourself, or your students, as you read short extracts from a set of abstracts that the 2016 MEd group have produced for a special issue. These draw out key points that emerged through our corresponding curriculum.

The chapter has three main sections. In the first section, *Curriculum*, I explore this as a socially constructed and sequenced set of decisions about what to include or omit. However, this reveals what is "delivered" as curriculum, but it says little on what is "received" by students, let alone collectively developed, particularly as we begin to adopt a teaching excellence framework (TEF) in the UK. Instead of treating curriculum as a broad body of knowledge that exists independently of students and staff, this makes space for what Fraser and Bosanquet (2006:276) call an *"interaction of knowledges"* that fosters *"belonging"*. In section two, *The MEd Participant-Negotiated Project*, I share the negotiated nature of the learning outcomes and assessment portfolio. This offers "scaffolding" for staff participants to follow a critically self-reflexive journey, aware of their "intended", and eventually "actual", learning outcomes. In defining "curriculum", we should not restrict this to *considerations only of that which is planned"* (Kelly, 2009:6) but acknowledge and make room for "living" aspects shaped by the groups we teach (Hayes, 2015:125). Community has a critical role to play in developing academic careers, identity, and agency (Sutherland & Taylor, 2011). In academic staff development programmes, the curriculum does not sit only within the classroom, it extends into cross-collaborations, resource sharing, mentoring, and recognition. In section three, *A Corresponding Curriculum*, I draw distinctions between a "hidden curriculum" that may reinforce instrumental values within a capitalist context and a more empowering approach where participants might *correspond* with the curriculum to collectively develop it. In the sections that follow, I explore these ideas through my own lived experience as programme director for the Master in Education (MEd) at Aston University, Birmingham, UK.

Section I: Curriculum

Curriculum is an expansive term. It is a social construction that results from a set of decisions about what will be learned by students within a particular time frame (see Branch & Hartge, in this volume). Therefore, curriculum is always subject to pressures and complications in relation to the diverse communities and social contexts in which participants gain self-understanding (Samuel *et al.*, 2016). Essentially, in curriculum theory and design there is an interplay among the major components of education: subject matter, learning, teaching, larger social, political, and economic contexts, and the immediate instructional situation (Samuel *et al.*, 2016). Yet in discussing development of a curriculum, emphasis may lean only towards a simple ordering of materials and content for learning, or it may assume a focus on curriculum design principles and theory about how learning is planned, guided, and assessed. Important though these elements are, such explanations *alone* may imply a static and chronological approach, where intended learning is specified in advance and packaged up weekly for students to undertake. This tells us about what is "delivered" as curriculum, but little about what is "received" by students. Furthermore, in higher education (HE), teacher values and beliefs can strongly influence what is considered relevant to include as topics (Weller, 2016:61). There are few opportunities for students to question who put the schedule together and what wider purposes influenced the choice of what to include or exclude. Thus a "hidden curriculum" (see Yilmaz & Bulut, in this volume) shapes what students receive.

If little space is left for students to actively contribute to curriculum, it is not hard to see why attendance in classes may drop. This feeds an instrumental model where students are only required to take from their education what they believe they need for future employment, rather than to invest themselves in what HE can offer more holistically for the whole of life (Hayes, 2015:126). Therefore, curriculum design as a concept needs to acknowledge the personal narratives and social intelligence that correspond with any given design, rather than simply construct and present a completed package to students. Grundy (1987) and Cornbleth (1989) suggest that such a model classifies curriculum as if it were a *"product"* to be delivered to students. This model raises questions about *who* decides on the boundaries that are to be placed around this "product" and what is valued as "knowledge" in relation to a certain course or programme of study. Given that in recent decades HE has needed to respond to the demands of a global economy and a new emphasis on "students as consumers", it is perhaps not surprising that a curriculum model of discrete and deliverable products (modules) is often widely adopted (Molesworth, Nixon, & Scullion, 2009). Yet "curriculum" is derived from the Latin verb *currere*, which means to run, referring to a race or race course (Goodson, 1997). This implies motion and acknowledges the context of time and space surrounding individuals and groups on a learning journey.

Working with the metaphor of "journey", people travelling may do so together or alone, they may drive, walk, run, or be transported by others as they move at different paces. They may browse websites, watch films, listen to music, read, or meditate and exchange ideas en route. I therefore suggest we pay more attention to how students progress, in correspondence with the curriculum, via their dynamic and ongoing experiences, emotions, and links with popular culture. If we only consider student engagement with the curriculum to be about observable and measurable practices, then we omit the *"private, silent, unobserved and solitary practices"* of engagement (Gourlay, 2015:410). If what we expect students to achieve is only that which is declared ahead of teaching and we simply advise them on meeting these goals, dynamic opportunities may be overlooked, both in terms of recognising transformative learning for students and staff and for the ongoing shaping of any future curriculum.

Curriculum Theorising

Rarely do I personally find that creative thought or contemplation takes place for me in my office or within the physical space of the University. Instead, learning in these ways is usually realised in the "spaces" that occur on my way to work, whilst out walking, exercising, driving, gardening, or even during sleep. I will awake with a start and commit to paper a clarification of thought to take forward exciting ideas that have only taken shape when my mind and body have been permitted relaxation. Deeply personal and contemplative practices have their place in the lives of the individuals we teach, but they hold a different form of power when there is space left in the curriculum for collective, spontaneous experimentation. Schiro (2013) points to four visions of curriculum that embody distinct beliefs about the type of knowledge that should be taught: the *scholar academic* ideology, the *social efficiency* ideology, the *learning centered* ideology, and the *social reconstruction* ideology. These ideologies are said to influence people's ways of thinking about curriculum and what counts as knowledge in the same powerful ways that their political beliefs might influence their stances on political issues (Schiro, 2013:2). Based on these ideas, it is worth imagining how we might design curriculum to intermingle with the daily lives of students and staff, placing all aspects of their learning at the centre and not just what we believe they need to know. Here, we can apply arts-based research techniques to challenge and question our assumptions about curriculum (see Lamb *et al.*, in this volume). This can aid us in moving beyond simple disciplinary and epistemological differences. Shaun McNiff defines art-based research as: *"The systematic use of the artistic process, the actual making of artistic expressions in all of the different forms of the arts, as a primary way of understanding and examining experience by both researchers and the people that they involve in their studies."* (McNiff, 1998:29).

Facilitating approaches to activate these elements may at first involve discussion, but may later involve artistic, poetic, contemplative activities, or those that are sensory or involve movement. Savin-Baden & Wimpenny (2014) discuss a branch of arts-based inquiry that they refer to as *arts-engaging inquiry*: *"A use of art that engages communities, marginalised groups and diverse and different audiences. The focus of this typology is in community engagement and provoking change."* (Savin-Baden & Wimpenny, 2014:10).

MEd colleagues are required to undertake a structured inquiry, but in order to approach this authentically and reflexively, *"autobiographical reflexivity is a vital part of the production of qualitative research."* (Dean, 2017:114). Introducing arts-engaging inquiry into sessions provides disruptions. It enables us to re-establish the role of our human bodies and a sense of being, as well as our minds, in the processes of knowing within the curriculum. Most authors tend to focus on these techniques as part of the research process (Kara, 2015). Less seems to have been written about applying art-based research into teaching, let alone to specifically seek to do this at the point of curriculum design. I would argue that if programme teams seeking to develop a learning-centred curriculum reflect on the role of contemplation and mindfulness, it would be valuable at the point of developing the programme philosophy, as well as in the design phase, to think more holistically. Rather than simply ask how students will experience curriculum, we can ask: how will students correspond with the curriculum, to input into it, have a stake in it, and indeed collectively develop it?

Phelan (2015:6) suggests that if teacher education, as a field of study, is to contribute to revitalising education, then "curriculum theorising" is necessary. This engages concerns about subjectivity, human agency, and action to inform new debates about policy and practice. I emphasise a need not to lose sight of the relationship between "intended" and "actual" learning outcomes – the actual reflecting the lived "reality" of what really takes place for learners: *"Curriculum Studies must ultimately be concerned with the relationship between these two views of the curriculum between intention and reality, and, indeed, with closing the gap between them, if it is to succeed in linking the theory and the practice of the curriculum."* (Stenhouse, 1975:56).

I suggest that in defining curriculum, we should not restrict this to *"considerations only of that which is planned"* (Kelly, 2009:6). By linking the theory and practice of curriculum, we avoid losing the *"living"* aspects of what is both experienced and indeed shaped by the groups we teach (Hayes, 2015).

Curriculum as Product or Process

Grundy (1987) argues that both teacher and learner negotiate the content of the curriculum to confront the real problems of their existence and relationships (Bates, 2016). However, individuals can have very different perspectives about what constitutes a curriculum, which according to Weller (2015:57) might be:

+ a *broad body of knowledge*, such as texts, concepts, and protocols;

+ a *means to an end*, expressed through pre-determined learning outcomes;

+ a *learning-centred approach*, via critical student-teacher engagement;

+ a *co-construction of knowledge*, as an iterative, dynamic engagement where teacher and student experience mutual transformation of identity/perspective.

There are colleagues who would argue that these perspectives are really all part of a continuum that runs from the "product-focused", means-to-an-end approach that stresses consistency of outcomes, to a more "process-focused" conception of a learning-centred curriculum, involving co-construction of knowledge (Fraser & Bosanquet, 2006).

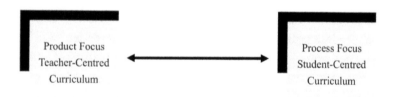

Figure 1: A product- or process- focused curriculum (Fraser & Bosanquet, 2006).

In considering the perspectives above, if curriculum is a *broad body of knowledge*, then the suggestion is that knowledge exists independently of students and staff. This approach would sit at the "product-focused" end of the spectrum above, because a student would be expected to assimilate the content of the curriculum. If curriculum is a *means to an end*, this moves a little more towards the "process-focused" end, because knowledge is discerned in response to precise statements of what a successful learner should be able to do. The student's performance is assessed against these. A *learning-centred approach* treats knowledge as personally constructed, based on prior experiences and learning, and so is further again towards "process-focused". Assessments require students to apply discipline knowledge to contextually focused questions. Finally, where curriculum is treated as *co-construction of knowledge*, the content is "negotiated", mutually evaluated, and critiqued, and so this is student-centred and "process-focused". Assessment tasks encourage transformative potential.

Teaching Excellence and a Learning-Centred Curriculum

These ideas have further significance, given recent rapid changes in the UK to introduce a *teaching excellence framework* (TEF) (BIS, 2016). The framework focuses on particular metrics: 1) *teaching quality*, 2) *learning environment*, and 3) *student outcomes and learning gain*. Whilst these are student-focused considerations, it would be easy to assume what we believe students will experience, and then design a curriculum that is so "declared" and packed with content that there is little room for any meaningful dialogue with our students. This has implications too in terms of how and what we assess and indeed how "ready" students may be to move from a university context into a dynamic and pressured place of work. Sitting passively in a lecture theatre does not enable students to practice the less tangible skills that employers seek. Therefore, enabling students to correspond with the curriculum is a powerful way to build forms of negotiation for later life. A recent focus on *learning gain* by the Higher Education Funding Council for England (HEFCE) presents complex challenges (Scott, 2016), and so I would argue that returning to fundamental principles around learning-centred curriculum design is now a necessity if students are to be empowered as critical-thinking and autonomously acting employees. As long ago as 2002, in a book about learning-centred teaching, Weimer (2002) pointed out five recommended changes to practice:

1. The role of the teacher: to facilitate student learning, not simply "go over" the syllabus;

2. The balance of power: faculty should share decision-making about learning with students (e.g., assignment choices and policy setting);

3. The function of content: to build a knowledge base and develop learning skills and learner self-awareness so that teachers cover less and students learn more;

4. Responsibility for learning: faculty create learning environments that motivate students to accept responsibility for learning;

5. Processes and purposes of evaluation: promote learning via participation to develop self- and peer-assessment skills.

Weimer's suggested changes remain highly relevant today, and alongside this more active partnership approach, others would suggest we should also cultivate a sense of "belonging" (Thomas, 2012; May, 2013). Belonging involves much more than academic engagement; it includes social activities, respect for personal autonomy, and acknowledgement of the heterogeneity of any student body (Thomas, 2012). However, I would take this further to emphasise "bodily" experience as an integral part of belonging for students and staff.

The "Body" of a Curriculum

In both HE policy and in teaching, we use a lot of words, but we leave little space in which to acknowledge the role of our human bodies. We readily refer to the "body" of the curriculum or the student body as if these were fixed, unchanging entities, yet demographics and educational politics remind us that this cannot be so. Furthermore, our minds do not exist separately from our bodies, and knowledge has to be personally "embodied". May (2013) cites the example of driving a car, where at first we think hard about the accelerator, clutch, and mirrors, but as these activities become embodied, we perform them without thinking consciously and they become part of our bodily memory and skills.

Academic work within a neoliberal context is strongly constructed, and indeed constricted, around *"managing time in a demonstrably efficient manner."* (Walker, 2009:486). This has direct effects on our bodies, whether we acknowledge this or not. We may break into a sweat when we realise we are late for deadlines, ache from sitting too long over a laptop, avoid comfort breaks in order to complete a task, feel emotions at time spent away from family, and dance with joy in writing something that is published. In seeking to "outsmart" time to achieve many things, we may also marginalise the role of our human bodies and emotions in the practices of teaching and learning, treating the body *"as relevant only as a vessel that houses the brain."* (Ng, 2008:4).

Carillo Rowe (2012) argues that this mind/body split goes far beyond a simple intellectual exercise, as she seeks to reclaim the *"process of loving and learning as erotic."* (Carillo Rowe, 2012:1032). Controversially, she labels the affective ties between teachers and learners as potentially tantalising and exciting. She suggests we might re-appropriate the term "erotic" from neoliberal connotations linked to pornography and remind ourselves that pedagogy that is erotic is also transformative. I therefore question where we make space for emotions in a designed curriculum, given the lesser role that the body and its related vulnerabilities is now "assigned" within neoliberal HE. These examples link to a central ethos on the MEd that we can only begin from *"where people are in the world"* (Smith, 1987:87,89).

A Model of Praxis

When attending either physical or virtual classes to learn, participants bring with them anxieties and emotions, as well as traces of the multi-modal streams from popular culture and life that surround their learning journeys as physical beings. Given such considerations, rather than a *"product"*, curriculum might be better understood as a *"process"* for meaning-making, in dialogue with wider experiences and spaces to experiment (Grundy, 1987; Cornbleth, 1989; Pokorny & Warren, 2016). However, this can be taken further into a model where, through the exercise of "critical pedagogy" (Freire, 1973) and a shared focus on *process*, the curriculum also supports *praxis*. Through praxis, the design approach undertaken engenders both critical reflection on the political context in which education takes place and also action that seeks to change undemocratic social practices. Critical pedagogy involves an ongoing personal commitment towards inclusivity and co-creation of emancipatory learning environments (Grundy, 1987). If this becomes our starting point as designers of the curriculum, then we can apply praxis from the moment we begin as a team to create a programme and a related philosophy. Going forward, whilst clear design principles should be adopted in creating a programme, a shared philosophy can be infused throughout, and classes can be reminded at regular intervals of the reflexive nature of the curriculum in relation to this philosophy.

In developing the Aston University MEd for teaching staff, a form of curriculum design to enable co-construction of knowledge was particularly important. Firstly, it contributes to colleagues recognising what influences their own development and it supports them to critically question different forms of knowledge to effect change. Particularly important is a recognition of academic and researcher identities. Secondly, it aids staff to recognise the importance of understanding the social construction of their own students' consciousness and values, motivations and emotions. From here, they can begin to develop what Fraser and Bosanquet (2006:276) call an *"interaction of knowledges."* We share a commitment to "critical pedagogy" (Freire, 1973) in CLIPP, and so we wish to encourage praxis amongst our participants. This includes critical reflection on the political context of HE and an ongoing commitment towards inclusivity and co-creation of emancipatory learning environments (Grundy, 1987). This approach is risky, as it calls into question any knowledge that is brought into sessions, but it is exciting too, as it opens shared space for a collaborative construction of meaning.

Constructive Alignment as a Key Design Principle

At Aston, like many institutions, our curriculum design principles are based on the theory of constructive alignment (CA). This approach is taught to teaching staff who complete our PG Certificate in Higher Education (PGCert), before they progress through to PGDip and MEd. CA is defined as: *"an approach to teaching in which learning outcomes students are intended to achieve are defined before teaching takes place."* (Biggs, 2014:5). The teaching and assessment methods are then designed: *"to best achieve those outcomes and to assess the standard at which they have been achieved."* (Biggs, 2014:5). CA supports a consistent approach to provide clarity by emphasising the following:

+ *Constructive*: students socially construct their own knowledge. Whatever the topic, students arrive at their understanding of it by drawing on a combination of their prior knowledge, experiences, and reflection;

+ *Alignment*: as shown in Figure 2, below, the learning outcomes, learning activities, and assessment should all be aligned. One way to build clarity is to write learning outcomes in such a way that these can be easily measured by an assessment.

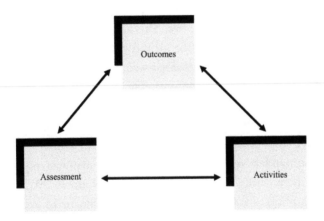

Figure 2: Constructive alignment (Biggs, 2014).

For CA to work well, it requires programme teams to all agree that they will design their modules in this way, with measurable learning outcomes (see Bartholomew & Curran, in this volume). Whilst this could result in a "product-focused" and more teacher-centred design, it is actually linked by Biggs to the idea of *learning-centred* curriculum design in HE, because it raises the question of *what a student needs to do* in order to meet the learning outcomes.

However, this may be interpreted by students as: *what is the minimum I need to do (in order to pass)?*, moving back along the continuum then towards a product, rather than a process focus. Valuable learning opportunities may not be noticed. Critics have also argued that the large scale on which CA has been unquestioningly adopted in a modular and standardised educational system (see Branch & Hartge, in this volume) is flawed and built on *"managerial logics from the business world"* (Pettersen, 2015:23). Formal quality assurance initiatives (Harvey & Williams, 2010) are said to have led to a shift in focus from process to "outcome evaluation" (Pettersen, 2015).

Certainly, if the learning experiences of students become too broken down, in terms of discrete modules and chronologically presented tasks, opportunities for students to "live" what they are learning in a way that is "transformative" become diminished (Hayes, 2015). I have written previously about designing a curriculum that is not simply chronological but that instead encourages students to see their studies more holistically *across time* as a choice of how to *live*. This approach incorporates the body as well as the mind. It speaks to an individual student's past, bringing identity and ontology into the research-writing process, rather than simply confining learning experiences into weekly folders that are rarely revisited (Hayes, 2015). It resists the adoption in HE policy of "buzz phrases", where *"student subjective diversity is contained in a singular universal representation: the student experience"* (Hayes, 2016:32) and words appear to enact our human labour for us (Hayes, 2016). It also has implications for "professionalism" and "professionality" (Bartholomew, 2015) as learner participants prepare for work or change direction in routes of life-long learning. What is potentially received by those we teach is an important aspect of a curriculum planner's responsibility. Whilst critically acknowledging these arguments, there is no intention in this chapter to suggest that CA should be discredited as a very useful design principle. Instead, I will explain how CA was applied in the design of the MEd, enabling us to retain a curriculum allowing co-construction of knowledge as praxis.

Section 2: The MEd Participant-Negotiated Project

To explain the design of the MEd Participant-Negotiated Independent Project, below in Figure 3, I share our wider structure of taught programmes tailored for PhD students and staff at Aston, in which this 60-credit module sits. When designing these programmes, we took both a "holistic" and "distributed" approach. Holistically, we gathered initial resources and wrote a programme philosophy and aims. Our overall philosophy is related to the values we share across the colleagues who teach on our programmes and those who participate:

"This work-based learning programme is designed from the perspective that learning is a social activity, best undertaken within a multi-disciplinary community. We see learning as a product of discussion and debate. Using conceptual modules and theoretical perspectives of learning and teaching to underpin debate we intend to be provocative and so enhance critical reflection upon tacit assumptions about professionalism and 'power' within higher education. We uphold diversity of identities and approaches to teaching within an anti-oppressive and anti-discriminatory context. We support the development of creative academic practice and innovation." (Our Programme Philosophy Statement).

In a more distributed approach, we designed modules and created our programme specification. Each module has its own philosophy statement that articulates with our overall philosophy and is constructed in line with university-level agreed curriculum design principles:

+ four learning outcomes;

+ two assessments;

+ assessment criteria in the form of an assessment brief and a rubric.

ILTP

Introduction to Learning and Teaching Practice (20 credits)

PGCert

Evolving your Teaching Practice (20 credits)

Becoming a Designer of Academic Programmes (20 credits)

Becoming a Research-led Innovator in Higher Education (20 credits)

PGDip

Promoting Quality Processes in Academic Programmes (20 credits)

Enhancing Academic Provision through University-wide Collaboration (20 credits)

Embedding Technology into Campus-based and Distance Learning Programmes (20 credits)

MEd

Participant-negotiated Independent Study (60 credits)

Figure 3: The CLIPP taught programmes structure at Aston University.

The MEd, however, is a little different. MEd has:

+ one declared learning outcome.

On successful completion of the module, a participant will be able to transform their academic practice through structured enquiry. Participants are then expected to work towards defining:

+ two negotiable learning outcomes.

One should relate to the production of their final research artefact and one should relate to the evaluation of this and their personal transformation. With such a design, the process of constructive alignment is shifted into the hands of participants. Colleagues on the MEd are required to draft and continually shape their two negotiable learning outcomes as they refine their ideas for their structured research inquiry. In the Biggs model, learning outcomes are fixed from the start, but MEd participants declare their *intended* learning outcomes in their presentations to the group (see the assessments below). Later, as the transformative projects progress towards completion, they produce their own assessment rubric and *actual* learning outcomes to be assessed against. Participants are each allocated a discussant from CLIPP who acts as a critical friend in helping them to shape their project.

1	Self-audit of research experience (i.e., to report on what is new to the participant).	1,500 words.	15% weight.
2	Proposal for research/structured enquiry (to include two negotiated LOs aligned to design of research product).	3,000 words.	25% weight.
3	Risk assessment (i.e., Ethics proposal).	1,000 words.	0% weight (proceed/don't proceed decision).
4	Peer review (e.g., Grand round or review without right ro respond).	10-minute oral presentation.	10% weight.
5	The research/study artefact.	6,000 words or equivalent.	50% weight.

Figure 4: The MEd assessments.

Assessment items 1–4 form a portfolio intended to support participants in developing what they will "produce" for 5: their research artefact. From the outset, our participants are challenged to consider producing something other than a written artefact. Whilst writing forms a part of MEd, to enact or create something (e.g., a play, documentary, garment, policy, toolkit, or event) is considered part of the change process. When they review what they have produced, their final learning outcome includes evaluation of their personal transformation through the whole process. One participant later commented:

"My understanding was that we needed to demonstrate how we have been transformed in terms of how we teach. But now I can see that the transformation is about our academic practice so it is much broader than I first thought and encompasses teaching, learning and pretty much everything we do as academics."

Now that the design structure of the MEd has been explained, I will discuss the way in which the taught content in sessions is co-constructed by participants.

Popular Culture, Social Intelligence, and Personal Narratives

The MEd ran for the first time at the start of 2016. There are nine taught half-days that run from January to September, and each morning ends in a shared lunch in order to continue debates and build the community. Arriving at the first session, I took a very incomplete session plan along for the group (just 12 participants during 2016) to develop. It seemed incongruous to arrive with a detailed plan for a negotiated module; however, there are some topics that are fundamental to any research inquiry, such as the position a researcher takes towards knowledge, epistemology, ontology, and critical reflexivity (Dean, 2017).

By Day 2, we explored these and other terms in some depth of argument, despite the varied, multidisciplinary backgrounds of the group. For all taught sessions at any level, our participants observe the "Chatham House Rule". This means that participants may use information they receive during the class, but the identity of the speaker(s) may not be revealed. This creates a safe space so that honest and authentic forms of disclosure might be exchanged. I asked the group the question: *how do you know where you are starting from?* A variation of this has since become the title for a special issue that the 2016 MEd group are contributing to: *"We can only begin from where we are."*

Hart (2004:28) suggests: *"how we know is as important as what we know."* This suggests a *process* of "knowing", rather than something static and simply "known". The element of "movement" in *knowing as a process* permits ontology and epistemology to be brought into dialogue together, through fluid cultural and art-based interventions. Therefore, during the first year of the MEd, we explored some of our discussions through critical pedagogy and popular culture. *"Critical pedagogy of popular culture offers a tremendous amount of educational benefits such as expanding thinking about others, finding alternative narratives about one's own life, enhancing cultural synchronisation, building culturally responsive awareness, building consumer awareness, and scaffolding social intelligence."* (Sfeir, 2014:24). By simply discussing a film or piece of music that holds interest for a member of the group, this can intertwine with a variety of relevant themes linked to personal transformation. One of the 2016 MEd group played *Twelve Angry Men* in class, drawing analogies with the ways in which knowledge is developed across a group. The social media system Yammer (see Figure 5) provides a way to share such resources between sessions and to build collaborative understandings about what people's experiences might mean. Following Week 4, of individual presentations, with no right to reply, a number of comments were posted to Yammer:

"I want to thank everybody for sharing their work today; it went beyond just interesting, the sheer breadth of topics and the dedication to teaching was gob-smacking. I think we all deserve a huge pat on the back, if for no other reason than we managed to keep our mouths shut for 5 minutes afterwards!! Hiya, thank you for today. I have to say my head is spinning. Here is the book I mentioned about academics being actively reflexive. I hope it helps."

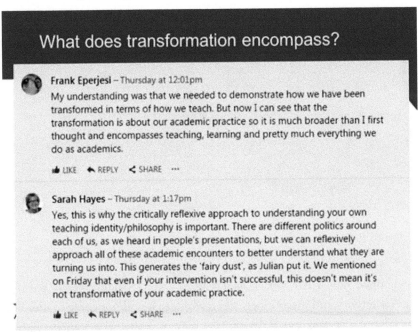

Figure 5: Making sense of transformation on our Yammer social media space.

Free Writing

By Week 5, the 2016 group had really developed as a community. They seemed ready to trial some contemplative techniques as a group, particularly as the topic of "procrastination" (Ellis, 2012) in beginning to write for the first of the assessments, had arisen in class and on Yammer: *"My experience is that difficult work leads me to procrastinate. Everything seems more appealing (vacuuming, washing the car, weeding the lawn, claiming expenses, marking, posting on Yammer) than making a start".*

In introducing the Day 5 session, I included some of their Yammer comments as a way to reconnect with discussions in the previous session. Then I shared a (carefully taken) photograph of me at home writing whilst taking a bath.

Figure 6: Personal self-disclosure (discreetly, of course!).

I explained how I use a bath as a way to counterbalance really painful mental activity and discomfort, when words just will not come to me. We considered just how much discomfort may be a part of a transformative process. Then I set the *free-writing* task detailed below for the group to do. We all sat around one table, and participants insisted I also join in. We set a timer for 10 minutes, and the group were asked the following:

1. Write for 10 minutes about your proposed artefact and your identity in reply to the question: *What is transformative about your project/process?*;

2. Don't stop. Keep writing, even if you write: "I don't know what to write";

3. Write in any order, write anything, use the questions below if they help;

4. Use single words, phrases, sketches, diagrams, pictures;

5. Don't worry about spelling/grammar;

6. Don't cross anything out;

7. Even writing down what you don't know can be a great starting point.

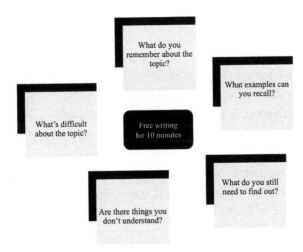

Figure 7: Some prompts you might use when setting a free-writing task.

We wrote and wrote without stopping, until our arms ached and our minds became tired too. As a group, we noticed that our bodies, as well as our minds, were a part of this collaborative yet individual process. No one was disengaged, everyone wrote, and then we gathered what we had written together in a pile. The sheets were passed anonymously around for a peer to comment. Everyone received freely written peer feedback. Then we discussed what had just taken place. Most astonishingly, it was a member of the group who until now had said little whose words spilled over with energy to talk about what we had just done. Later on Yammer, others added their views:

"I too liked the free writing session and thank you to the colleague who commented on my writing."

"I have found free writing useful in the past when faced with a difficult piece that I need to write. Usually I can just about get myself to start 'a mind dump' to just get something down on paper. There is often poor or no grammar most words are spelt incorrectly and a nine year old would do better but at least my thoughts are captured and I can't forget them. Later I can edit, add, fix, polish and weave in high brow words. But at least I have made a start. The difficulty is then keeping the momentum."

"Thinking again about procrastination. May be that's part of my process. Thinking about the piece, locking down gems and discarding duds until I'm ready to write."

"Yesterday I felt ready to write more on the bus but the journey was bumpy and I couldn't write properly so I had a free writing session in the bus stop when I got off. I got some strange looks. Will add yesterday's thoughts to my work after I've posted this. Honest."

By Week 6 though, it was also interesting to observe some reverting back to more instrumental approaches amongst the staff. This was commented on by a participant:

"I couldn't help but notice that the looming assessments have driven some or perhaps all of us into 'student assessment mode'. By this I mean the bigger picture of learning to get better at what we do so we can help students and colleagues (that's my bigger picture) takes a back seat and is replaced for a short while by a mechanistic narrow view that revolves around deadlines, word counts and getting over the pass mark."

When planning for the new MEd intake, it seemed worth bearing this in mind and designing in shared experiences to mitigate against a mechanistic approach.

Contemplative Techniques

At the time of writing, the new 2017 MEd group have recently given their Day 4 and Day 5 presentations. In the lead up to these, we have shared fascinating insights from classical music and Twitter, as well as resources from literature through Yammer. Integrating texts from popular culture into our debates has caused participants to negotiate *"their own perspectives on the connections between learning, personal experiences and social values"* (Sfeir, 2014:24). Yet we have gone further in adding a number of other contemplative techniques to our activities. Ahead of Day 1, I wrote the following to the new 2017 MEd participants:

> "I started this email several times this week....always things have intervened. Now I am completing it whilst travelling to Scotland for the weekend. This sums me up right now....every project and task is begun – then it stalls as other demands cut in. If this sounds familiar....then practicing techniques of contemplation under such circumstances may seem mad, or a luxury.
>
> On MEd we are exploring, through your first learning outcome, personal transformation in relation to practice. Some authors draw close links with changes in identity (Illeris, 2014), whilst others suggest transformation is provoked as you question, via a range of contemplative techniques, 'how do I really know...what I believe I know?' (Hart, 2004).
>
> So in preparation for our first session, which I have called 'Accommodating Transformation', think about what forms of contemplation enable you to pause and refocus your mind and body, before you begin to imagine what your MEd project experience (and you) might become (Dall'Alba, 2009). Perhaps some of you already practice techniques we might explore, and it will be great to share these. In the meantime, have a go at the following:
>
> 1. Dip into anything that interests you in the attached articles: 'To get students to focus, some professors are asking them to close their eyes', 'Opening the Contemplative Mind' and 'Transformative Learning re-defined: as changes in identity'. No need to read a lot, just pick up on anything you might enjoy discussing or arguing about, when we meet. ☺

2. *Give one of the techniques you read about a trial.*

   • *For example, try to breathe meditatively (inhale, hold, exhale) and focus on feelings and causes of stress or hurt, let go of negativity.*

   • *Or, if you prefer, try giving your full attention to something for a period of time where you do nothing else at all. Ziegler suggests 'beholding' an artefact of some sort leads to care and the capacity to focus on what's valuable in art, nature, and human life*

   • *Or simply bring to mind things you enjoy in life generally – if you have a hobby, favourite film, a book, article, image or pastime that feels a part of you, consider sharing it with the group when we meet.*

   • *Think about the research inquiry you hope to undertake. Challenge yourself about what this might 'become' in terms of a creative artefact you identify with and produce. Jot a few notes and we can discuss further.*

Whilst I have developed a schedule for our MEd sessions, where we explore creative research approaches and techniques for contemplation, it is entirely flexible. We will negotiate the content as we go and I will respond to any requests. But much of it you will provide yourselves, through your interaction together as a group. "

Turning up on Day 1, I imagined it might be a few weeks before we would actually trial any forms of contemplation as a group in class. I opened a discussion where we considered what it means to be "fearless at work". Shortly after, I asked if anyone would like to share contemplative techniques they had tried. It was only half an hour into the first session when a participant suggested that we as a group get out of our seats and walk around with our eyes shut and our fingers in our ears. In response, participants followed her lead to move around the room in this way and to comment on how it made them notice different things. Another participant then talked us through some breathing and gentle movements from her yoga techniques. To breathe in this way is interesting because it can challenge the instrumentality of neoliberal institutional environments and renew our interest in connections between our bodily functions and our minds (Shahjahan, 2015). Thus, it provides a simple but effective way for individuals who may not feel they hold much power in the university to effect change, to establish control over how they breathe, and to ask what this means. Controlling our breathing means we contemplate our inner worlds rather than simply accept that the structure we find ourselves in is the only norm. Drawing on these techniques from yoga prompted other ideas, resulting in one participant agreeing to take us through the early meditative stages of hypnosis when we next met.

On Day 2, we first heard from each person about their ideas for their projects so far. It was a rich exchange and I was struck by the early creativity of thought across the entire group, including one participant who brought along two ceramic vases to materially illustrate a point about his project. The interventions people were considering undertaking were diverse and fascinating and brought forth support, comments, and suggestions of further resources from the group. Then, before lunch, people were given the option to stay or leave during the hypnosis part. Most of the group remained. We were talked through the process by the participant who conducts hypnosis professionally. Half an hour passed in what felt like only moments, as we each imagined a place we would wish to visit in order to relax and then gradually returned to recall that there were others in the room.

Having once more explored some free-writing techniques during Day 3 and then heard individual presentations during Days 4 and 5, on Day 6 we had the privilege to be present at the "submission" of a completed artefact created by a participant from last year's MEd. She had negotiated with us the creation of a garment inscribed with elements of her academic and personal life that she wore to a session she delivered to this year's MEd group. Below, she is pictured presenting the session, which she called "Narration Beyond Voice", and the listening participants are colouring.

Figure 8: A participant "submits herself", wearing the artefact she created.

Section 3: A Corresponding Curriculum

The notion of a "hidden curriculum" can often carry negative connotations. It is a concept associated with maintaining the political and institutional status quo through education by reinforcing hierarchies within capitalist society. Yet not all forms of hidden learning are restrictive or negative. Some may be autonomous, collective, and liberating in that they challenge existing norms and institutions (Cornbleth, 1990:50). When curriculum is treated as a contextualised social process, a hidden curriculum gives way to personal or collective meaning-making. Curriculum becomes something we might *correspond* with, rather than simply adhere to. Such a correspondence can embrace the principles of critical pedagogy and popular culture and go well beyond platitudes in HE policy, such as the overused buzz phrase "the student experience", to uncover assumptions and recognise the experiences of both learner and teacher as problematic (Grundy 1987:105). By exposing problems and encouraging open and respectful dialogue, critical consciousness can be developed collaboratively to build emancipatory learning environments that acknowledge the process of "coming to know" (Barnett, 2009).

To illustrate this, the following short excerpts are from a set of abstracts that the 2016 MEd group have produced for a special issue. These draw out key points that emerged through our corresponding curriculum:

Self-disclosure:

"'self-disclosure' is the tool by which a teacher can maintain balance; however, whilst enacting self-disclosure and being one's self can create powerful connections with students, it also puts the teacher in a vulnerable position."

Critical reflexivity:

"The official line is it's about journeying into not-knowing with an openness to fresh possibilities. A recognition that all assumptions and preconceptions about reality could be limiting or flawed. For me it's about being middle-aged and playing football (trying) against 20 year olds."

Ontology and Epistemology:

"Ontology is the nature of reality and refers to the study of existence or being. The epistemological question is driven by your ontological view and examines how we come to know what we know. How the public comes to believe what is true when we are told lies and to feel like they have knowledge in this post truth world has fascinated me."

The MEd process is the transformative part:

"It is the process itself and ever evolving nature of our collaborative group conversations that is the transformative part. The unexpected discussions and revelations, the challenges and questioning are by far more important to me that the actual MEd itself. The research project which was once central feels a side line, where once completion of the project and answering the research question was the goal, the aim now is to discover the questions and how to maintain our collaborative learning environment."

As participants on the MEd learned to correspond with these riskier elements of the curriculum, they described transformative experiences:

> *"This was a fantastic experience; through meeting staff from outside my School I feel I have learned a significant amount about how other people from different disciplines approach learning and teaching in HE. The nature of the sessions made me reflect deeply on who I am and what I do as a teacher in HE. It has had a profound impact on both my current teaching practice and my ambitions for the future. The whole team responsible for delivering this module should receive a hearty round of applause."*

When asked what they liked about the MEd module, they commented:

> *"Flexibility, nothing is prescribed."*

> *"The group work and the non-risk averseness of the group members."*

> *"The atmosphere, how we were treated, with consideration, great respect the great listening skills of our tutors who then steered the module in our direction."*

> *"The fact that I could tailor the assessment to support my personal development needs and ambitions. Not only was this more interesting but it was also immensely valuable to my needs and the needs of my school/ university."*

At the point of writing, I am about to facilitate a creative and contemplative workshop for participants at the British International Studies Association (BISA) conference, taking place in Brighton, UK, between 14–16 June 2017. My body is reacting, as I feel butterflies in my stomach at the prospect of trialling this form of work with strangers outside of Aston University. Yet in the process of marking five MEd projects this weekend that will go through our exam board in the coming week, I have found myself drawing inspiration for what I might do. The panic I feel at not being ready and organised with a well-constructed plan for Brighton is replaced by a fluid excitement, as the journeys of the MEd group lay before me. They are not easy to grade. Indeed the 2016 participants argued that their transformation is evident and does not require formal assessment. However, by documenting what they have achieved through our formal quality processes and verified by our new external examiner, this programme becomes even more powerful as a vehicle for institutional change (see Bartholomew & Curran, in this volume). The participants have changed, and they will take their inspiration from their MEd into their leadership roles at Aston. The 2017 group have just submitted their first assessments, and I am moved once more by the honesty and deeply personal accounts of these new participants. Their topics range from new approaches towards student attendance, to support for students from non-traditional backgrounds, to a greater sense of belonging for distance learners, research into "third space" professional/academic roles, teacher loss of memory, and developing a yoga module for colleagues. The topic of "academic identity" is a common theme explored across the projects in diverse and original ways. Comments from peers on each other's presentations have been fascinating, and I have a strong sense that as individuals, and as a community, we are deeply engaged in corresponding with the MEd curriculum.

Conclusion

As programme director for the MEd, I have learned from participants that "they can only start from where they are". Human learning experiences that cause the flesh to tingle, the body to dance, or that lead to submissions that draw tears from a lecturer marking them (yes, this happens often) are not forms of engagement that can be packaged and delivered to students and staff. They cannot be marketed or embedded, because they need to be "lived" (Hayes, 2015:147). Furthermore, these should not be overlooked in terms of their value. This excerpt from my abstract for the special issue describes my own reflections on my lived experience of this course:

"From day one of MEd, I knew they would own it. I just didn't know where they would take it...as they 'went rogue' to blur all the boundaries. As a Sociologist, I formerly encouraged my undergraduates to creatively 'live' their research, as personally intertwined with daily experience and political environment. Since working in academic staff development, 'reflection' seemed too detached from human context. So for me, critical reflexivity, related to ontology and epistemology, felt important for any MEd group to debate. 'That's just jargon' they told me, yet they didn't let go of these terms, they re-negotiated their meaning, in respect of their MEd 'artefacts' and their personal, intimate and often painful experiences. Moving from discussion into the collective act of 'free writing' developed their individual 'voices', but also sealed their 'becoming' as an ongoing community."

As a designer of curriculum who is also required to lead others in this craft, I suggest we consider, firstly, the context around our learners (see Hørsted & Nygaard, in this volume) and how to scaffold "social intelligence" (Sfeir, 2014:15). If this is mindfully imbued in the philosophy for the programmes we create, then we make "room" in the curriculum for an inclusive body of human experience. We leave space for personal narrative and culturally responsive awareness of broader popular culture to shape the journeys our learners take. Secondly, we can encourage an "interaction of knowledges" (Fraser & Bosanquet, 2006:276) if we share a commitment to "critical pedagogy" (Freire, 1973) and praxis with our participants. This includes critical reflection on the political context of HE and an ongoing commitment towards the co-creation of emancipatory learning environments (Grundy, 1987). Lastly, we can draw some elements of the intimate, personal, pleasurable, and affective into learning contexts (Maudlin, 2006). This helps resist the more alienating and de-humanising elements of consumer-focused education and fosters a re-conceptualisation of the curriculum and the body (Maudlin, 2006). This chapter has revealed how the MEd group nurtured these values into a collective process, *a corresponding curriculum*, which led to transformation, in parallel to the enactment of their assessed research projects.

About the Author

Dr Sarah Hayes is a senior lecturer in the Centre for Learning, Innovation and Professional Practice at Aston University, Birmingham, UK. She can be contacted at this e-mail: s.hayes@aston.ac.uk

Bibliography

Barnett, R. (2009). Knowing and becoming in the higher education curriculum. *Studies in higher education*, Vol. 34, No. 4, pp. 429–440.

Bartholomew, P. (2015). Learning through Auto-Ethnographic Case Study Research. In C. Guerin; P. Bartholomew & C. Nygaard (Eds.), *Learning to Research – Researching to Learn*. Oxford: Libri Publishing Ltd., pp. 241–267.

Bates, B. (2015). *Learning Theories Simplified:... and how to apply them to teaching.* London: Sage.

Benson, P. & A. Chik (Eds.) (2014). *Popular culture, pedagogy and teacher education: International perspectives.* Routledge.

Branch, J.; S. Hayes; A. Hørsted & C. Nygaard (Eds.) (2017). *Innovative Teaching and Learning in Higher Education.* London: Libri Publishing Ltd.

Business Innovation & Skills (BIS) (2016) Teaching Excellence Framework Technical Consultation, Online Ressource: https://www.gov.uk/government/uploads/system/uploads/attachment_data/file/523340/bis–16–262-teaching-excellence-framework-techcon.pdf [Accessed 16 December 2016]

Carrillo Rowe, A. (2012). Erotic pedagogies. *Journal of homosexuality*, Vol. 59, No. 7, pp. 1031–1056.

Cornbleth, C. (1990). *Curriculum in Context*, Basingstoke: Falmer Press.

Dean, J. (2017). *Doing reflexivity: An introduction.* Policy Press.

Ellis, C. (2012). The Procrastinating Autoethnographer Reflections of Self on the Blank Screen. *The International Review of Qualitative Research*, Vol. 5, No. 3, pp. 331–337.

Fraser, S. P. & A. M Bosanquet (2006). The curriculum? That's just a unit outline, isn't it?. *Studies in Higher Education*, Vol. 31, No. 3, pp. 269–284.

Freire, P. (1973). Pedagogy for critical consciousness. New York: Seabury Press.

Goodson, I. F. (1997). The changing curriculum. *Studies in social construction.* New York: Peter Lang.

Gourlay, L. (2015). Student engagement and the tyranny of participation. *Teaching in Higher Education*, Vol. 20, No. 4, pp. 402–411.

Grundy, S. (1987). *Curriculum: Product or praxis*, Lewes: Falmer.

Hayes, S. (2015). Encouraging the intellectual craft of living research: tattoos, theory and time. In C. Guerin; P. Bartholomew & C. Nygaard (Eds.), *Learning to Research – Researching to Learn.* Oxford: Libri, pp. 125–150.

Hayes, S. (2016). Learning from a Deceptively Spacious Policy Discourse. In T. Ryberg; C. Sinclair; S. Bayne & M. de Laat. (Eds.), *Research, Boundaries, and Policy in Networked Learning.* Springer, pp. 23–40.

Jubas, K.; N. Taber & T. Brown (Eds.) (2016). *Popular Culture as Pedagogy: Research in the Field of Adult Education* (Vol. 95). Springer. Online Resource: https://www.sensepublishers.com/media/2486-popular-culture-as-pedagogy.pdf [Accessed on 26 March 2017].

Kara, H. (2015). *Creative research methods in the social sciences: A practical guide.* Policy Press.

Kelly, A. V. (2009). *The curriculum: Theory and practice.* Sage.

McNiff, S. (1998). *Art-based research.* London: Jessica Kingsley Publishers.

May, V. (2013). *Connecting self to society: Belonging in a changing world.* Palgrave Macmillan.

Maudlin, J. G. (2006). *Teaching bodies: Curriculum and corporeality.* Online Resource: http://digitalcommons.georgiasouthern.edu/cgi/viewcontent.cgi?article=1469&context=etd [Accessed on 19 December 2016].

Molesworth, M.; E. Nixon & R. Scullion (2009). Having, being and higher education: The marketisation of the university and the transformation of the student into consumer. *Teaching in higher Education,* Vol. 14, No. 3, pp. 277–287.

Ng, R. (2008). *Toward an integrative embodied critical pedagogy through Qi Gong,* Paper read at The Scope of Interdisciplinarity Symposium, Edmonton, AB: Athabasca University.

Phelan, A. M. (2015). *Curriculum theorizing and teacher education: Complicating conjunctions.* Routledge.

Samuel, M. A.; R. Dhunpath & N. Amin (2016). *Disrupting Higher Education Curriculum: Undoing Cognitive Damage.* Rotterdam: Sense Publishers.

Savin-Baden, M. & K. Wimpenny (2014). *A practical guide to art-based research.* Rotterdam, The Netherlands: Sense Publishers.

Scott, J. (2016). Measuring learning gain in higher education is a complex challenge. *Times Higher Education.* Online Resource: https://www.timeshighereducation.com/blog/measuring-learning-gain-higher-education-complex-challenge [Accessed on 28 June 2017].

Schiro, M. S. (2013). *Curriculum theory: Conflicting visions and enduring concerns.* Sage Publications.

Sfeir, G. (2014). Critical Pedagogy Through Popular Culture. *Education Matters: The Journal of Teaching and Learning,* Vol. 2, No. 2.

Shahjahan, R. A. (2015). Being 'lazy' and slowing down: Toward decolonising time, our body, and pedagogy. *Educational Philosophy and Theory,* Vol. 47, No. 5, pp. 488–501.

Slattery, P. (2000). Popular culture and higher education: Using aesthetics and seminars to reconceptualise curriculum. *Popular culture and critical pedagogy: reading, constructing, connecting,* pp. 210–217.

Smith, D. E. (1987). *The everyday world as problematic: A feminist sociology.* University of Toronto Press.

Stenhouse, L. (1975). *An Introduction to Curriculum Research and Development,* London: Heinemann.

Sutherland, K., & L. Taylor (2011). The development of identity, agency and community in the early stages of the academic career. *International Journal for Academic Development.* Vol. 16, No. 3, pp. 183–186.

Thomas, L. (2012). *Building student engagement and belonging in Higher Education at a time of change.* Online Resource: https://www.heacademy.ac.uk/system/files/what_works_summary_report_1.pdf [Accessed on 28 June 2017].

Walker, J. (2009). Time as the fourth dimension in the globalisation of higher education. *The Journal of Higher Education,* Vol. 80, No. 5, pp. 483–509.

Weimer, M. (2002). *Learner-centered teaching: Five key changes to practice.* John Wiley & Sons.

Weller, S. (2015). *Academic practice: Developing as a professional in higher education.* Sage Publications.

Academic Rigour: Harnessing High-Quality Connections and Classroom Conversations

Timothy Hartge & John Branch

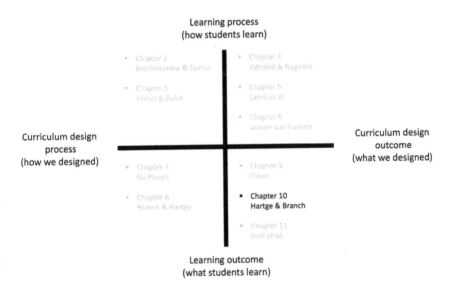

Learning process
(how students learn)

Chapter 2
Bartholomew & Curran

Chapter 4
Hørsted & Nygaard

Chapter 3
Yilmaz & Bulut

Chapter 5
Lamb et al.

Chapter 6
Jansen van Vuuren

Curriculum design
process
(how we designed)

Curriculum design
outcome
(what we designed)

Chapter 7
Du Plessis

Chapter 9
Hayes

Chapter 8
Branch & Hartge

Chapter 10
Hartge & Branch

Chapter 11
Piihl et al.

Learning outcome
(what students learn)

Introduction

We contribute to this book Learning-Centred Curriculum Design in Higher Education by exploring the impact which high-quality connections can have on the learner, and subsequently on classroom conversations. In relation to the central model of the book, we position our chapter in section four – Learning Outcome/ Curriculum Design Outcome – as we focus on how students learn academic rigour, and how we have designed the curriculum to achieve this.

The TV-series *The Office* – in both its British and American forms – might be considered a modern masterpiece for its sardonic take on modern management. But for more than ten years before the first television episode aired in the United Kingdom, the cartoon *Dilbert* was capturing the Kafkaesque nature of business bureaucracy. Indeed, its creator Scott Adams had the seemingly incomparable ability to chronicle the corporate culture of the time, with all its fads and fashions, catchphrases and crazes. Consider one cartoon strip in which Dilbert's pointy-haired boss comments on the inefficacy of the new management style which he had adopted "*My new management style is exhausting me. I heard some people talking about 'MBWA' or 'Management by Walking Around'. I walked all the way to the park and back. But I can't say that I see much improvement around here.*"

Higher education could doubtless be criticised for the same folly (although the crimes often go unrecorded). Take experiential learning, for example, which in the 1990s was doubtless the 'soupe du jour'. Not long ago, blended learning epitomised the educational zeitgeist of the day, and the flipped classroom has become all the rage in recent years. Another contemporary buzzword in higher education is rigour, as in academic rigour. Indeed, we both have countless examples from formal faculty meetings, curriculum committee assignments, and even casual hallway conversations that were laden with such indisputable conclusions as "That course needs to be more rigorous" or "We must add rigour to these degree requirements" or "This book is not rigorous enough for an MBA-level course".

Like many concepts in higher education, however, the term rigour has not been defined well. It is often associated with the traditional dictionary notion of unyielding rigidity, suggesting that academic rigour is about 'sticking to the syllabus'. The term rigour has sometimes been used to describe teaching and learning environments that are harsh, controlled, or prescriptive – the 'rigorous classroom'. And colleagues in our business schools, especially those with economics or other mathematics-oriented disciplinary backgrounds equate rigour, very simply, with difficulty, the result of which, we have heard it said, has been the 'push-down and pile-on syndrome' in higher education (and in education more broadly).

The purpose of this chapter, therefore, is to explore academic rigour. It adopts a broad stance that views academic rigour as that fine line between challenging and frustrating. Academic rigour is about pushing students to think in different ways. It means stimulating them, engaging them, and supporting them. And consequently, academic rigour ought to be learning-centred and a defining feature of curriculum design. Indeed, academic rigour, as outlined here, requires instructors to provide rich, deep, and relevant experiences for students that are 'suitably challenging', or, to paraphrase Goldilocks, which are not too difficult, not too easy, but just right.

With this chapter, we make an important contribution to this anthology on *learning-centred curriculum design in higher education*, because we provide a kind of touchstone for learning-centred curriculum design. That is say, we suggest that academic rigour and its associated mechanisms furnish both the guidelines for designing, and the criteria for judging, learning-centred curricula. After reading this chapter, you will be able to:

1. define academic rigour;

2. describe its associated mechanisms;

3. apply the concept of academic rigour to your learning-centred curriculum design activities.

We have structured our chapter in three sections. In section one, we define academic rigour, in particular with respect to the theories of academic optimism and academic press. In section two, we introduce the concept of high-quality connections, suggesting that academic rigour in the classroom is based to some extent on the relationships that are developed between instructors and their students. In section three, we review classroom conversations as one possible method for developing and improving these relationships.

Section 1: Academic Rigour

Academic rigour is more than a buzzword in higher education. Indeed, academic rigour has garnered attention from both practitioners and theoreticians alike. From a practical perspective, academic rigour is about setting high performance standards for students. It is similar to the effect of a production supervisor who demands more effectiveness and efficiency from a production process. From a theoretical perspective, academic rigour is modelled as the synthesis of two theories: academic optimism and academic press. It is thought to be at the core of student achievement in modern-day higher education.

Academic optimism can be viewed in terms of the relationships between instructors and students. It is comprised of three working concepts: 1) instructor efficacy, 2) instructor trust, and 3) instructor expectations. Hoy *et al.* (2006) describe collective efficacy as the power that instructors have to affect student outcomes. They maintain that instructor trust is a contributor to academic rigour. Instructor trust includes reciprocal relationships in which each stakeholder believes that the other stakeholder will continually act in each other's best interest. The theory of academic optimism emphasises a cognitive and behavioural construct consisting of high academic goals for students and an orderly learning environment. The construct also includes motivated students, respect for all stakeholders, and academic achievement. Both instructors and students require a high quotient of self-efficacy to achieve academic optimism.

Self-efficacy is the belief that one can be successful at the task or in the field; more than just a positive disposition about the task, it also involves an accurate assessment of both the task requirements and one's abilities. Both instructors and students must possess a belief in their abilities to complete tasks and achieve goals. These beliefs and abilities are critical as both move forward to explore learning. Bandura's (1994) unifying theory of self-efficacy and behaviour presents evidence from a theoretical perspective about how behaviour is acquired and regulated through cognitive processes, and how self-efficacy is achieved.

Using academic optimism as the theoretical lens, it is expected that:

1. the instructor sets high expectations;

2. instructors do not ignore students but exert effort toward them, and students towards instructors;

3. both students and instructors persist in the face of learning difficulties;

4. instructors provide frequent, quality feedback;

5. instructors ensure that students are engaged with and focused on their work; 6. instructors often use collaborative and authentic tasks that place students at the centre of the learning process;

7. instructors arrange student seating so that they are clustered, varied, and functional with multi-instructional areas;

8. instructors are actively engaged with different groups, and students are anxious to approach their various tasks or assignments;

9. both students and instructors have a joyful feeling of purposeful movement and industrious thinking within a vital, vibrant atmosphere, and environment.

Another theory thought to play a role in establishing academic rigour is academic press. Academic press theory emerged as early as the 1980s. The academic press compact is between the academic organisation, the teaching culture, and a curriculum driven by academically oriented beliefs, values, and norms. Some academic cultures might be oriented more toward other kinds of outcomes, such as student self-esteem, a sense of belonging, or the establishment of supportive and caring social relationships. Shouse (1995) described academic press as a climate consisting of high-status courses and the assignment of meaningful homework. Although not proven, Shouse also posited that academic press might exist as a 'statistically significant' predictor of academic achievement, and concluded that relevance and earned grades, in combination with disciplinary climate, are part of the theory of academic press. Other components of academic press might be high rates of attendance, positive behaviour, and instructors' instructional practices, including the setting of high standards and the provision of meaningful student feedback. In the classroom, academic press might be expressed as output-driven daily activities, practices, experiences, and understandings, complementing and reinforcing the importance of academic achievement. However, to realise this high standard of learning, instructors and students must form a bond of mutual trust and confidence.

Positive Organisational Scholarship

Allied to academic rigour is the theory of positive organisational scholarship, which originated with the positive psychology movement and which today is making large waves in business and organisational studies. Positive organisational scholarship links two veins of positive psychology. First, positive organisational scholarship looks at how organisations in a macro-context shape positive states and outcomes for organisations, groups, and individuals. Second, positive organisational scholarship concentrates on the cultivation of collective and individual strengths. Narrowly stated, the theory looks at how developing a positive psychological state enhances the group and the individual (see Lamb *et al.*, in this volume.).

Positive organisational scholarship illustrates the critical contexts and positive dynamics that individuals perform in organisations (e.g., colleges, companies, and community organisations), emphasising that positive collective strength is vital to understanding how organisations work. An organisation flourishes through the interplay of positive cognitive, emotional, and relational mechanisms. Building these mechanisms serves to create new collective and individual resources such as energy, respect, optimism, and insight. These resources, in turn, all contribute to the collective and individual growth of an organisation.

Positive meanings and emotions have an optimistic effect on relationships, which can ripple through an entire organisation and produce large effects on a collective scale. Positivism spirals, as these effects have been described, moving upwards and outwards, serving to infuse, connect, and energise whole networks of organisations and individuals. The transference of positive organisational scholarship occurs through methods devised by leadership, most notably those methods set forth by the theory of appreciative inquiry.

Appreciative Inquiry

According to Whitney & Trosten-Bloom (2002), appreciative inquiry (AI) is the exploration of that which gives life to human systems that are functioning at their best. Appreciative inquiry theory postulates that human organising and change is ultimately a relational process of inquiry and appreciation, grounded in affirmation. Whitney & Trosten-Bloom state further that appreciative inquiry theory is about the dynamic of the 'positive' in human systems change.

The positive strengths perspective of appreciate inquiry theory argues that human systems do not flourish under conditions of manufactured urgency, trauma, or fear. Under these conditions human systems do not embrace change; in fact, the opposite might be true, because anger and fear tend to constrict cognition. Positivity, on the other hand, tends to open up thought-action repertoires whereby individuals see the best in the world. Human systems might well become more resilient and capable of realising their potential if they engage less with negative emotions and more with positive emotions. For example, resiliency may stem from intrinsic hope, inspiration, and joy. Positive emotions tend to broaden, build, and open minds.

Appreciative inquiry works on the principle of positivism and treats people as people rather than machines. Humans are social beings creating their identities and knowledge in relationship to one another. Humans are curious and like to tell and listen to stories. Commitment comes from human values and beliefs that are communicated through the wisdom in the stories. Humans like to learn and practice that which they have learned. They delight in doing well in the eyes of others whom they respect and for whom they care. Appreciative inquiry enables leaders to create humanitarian organisations that are naturally rich in knowledge, based on strength and adaptability, and that, consequently, become learning organisations.

The theory of appreciative inquiry posits six working mechanisms:

1. building relationships, enabling people to be known in the relationship;

2. creating opportunities for people to be heard, recognised, and mutually respected;

3. promoting opportunities for people to dream and to share their dreams;

4. creating environments in which people may choose their methods of contribution;

5. providing people the discretion and support to act;

6. encouraging and enabling people to be positive.

At its core, therefore, appreciate inquiry seeks to be transformational. Whether the agenda is change or personal development, appreciative inquiry activates the human cognition to be creative and to excel. Words create worlds, and the words applied by appreciative inquiry are no exception. Appreciate inquiry can be a powerful tool for instructors in higher education, forming a lens for recalibration and establishing a standard for learning. Appreciate inquiry creates opportunities for future change that is built upon past and present strengths, engaging the actors in a "dance" of enacting change.

Although appreciate inquiry theory was initially applied to commercial organisations, the theory may also be adapted readily to the higher education classroom. Appreciative inquiry is a wrap-around for one dimension of academic optimism – a belief in the assumption that students are clever and capable of being active participants in their learning, rather than simply passive recipients of knowledge. That notion is a positive, self-fulfilling prophecy, because it is a phenomenon in which one's beliefs about the situation are not only reflected but created. The reality might be that active participation in the learning process is possible and rewarded. High expectations increase the likelihood that instructors will encourage active participation rather than passive learning. Appreciate inquiry can help shape experiences and focus student attention and reflection, both on the dynamic complexity of their world and on the means that are available to create change. Essentially, appreciate inquiry functions to reframe inquiry toward matters of importance. These efforts are accomplished through words and actions, leading to the instructor enabling learning.

Task-Enabling

Another concept that is useful for unpacking academic rigour is task-enabling. According to Dutton (2003), task-enabling is a mutual investment process in which both people in a relationship benefit from the relationship. It is being attentive to the other person's needs and alert to opportunities to help the person improve and grow. It is the act of giving something of oneself in service of another's success.

Task-enabling behaviours are related to empowerment and self-efficacy. Task-enabling, empowerment, and self-efficacy are all linked to a psychological sense of personal control, influence, and power. In higher education, the concept of task-enabling is also linked to scaffolding learning for students, enabling and motivating students to appreciate learning. The pedagogy and curriculum of the instructor, therefore, ought to be organised around concepts that students find important and valuable, thereby encouraging them to derive motivational benefits in addition to knowledge and skills. Instructors who seek to task-enable students are those who give honest feedback and who encourage growth through interactions. Students learn to benefit from instructor and peer feedback, and to value professional counsel. A powerful mechanism for task-enabling, therefore, is a high-quality connection between the instructor and the student.

Section 2: High-Quality Connections

Human connections are vital to organisational systems, and the quality of these connections, in turn, affects how organisations function. Dutton & Heaphy (2002) characterise the quality of connections using a human tissue metaphor: high-quality connections are those that allow the transfer of vital nutrients and are flexible, strong, and resilient; by contrast, in low-quality connections, ties exist but the connection is damaged, and thus there is a little death in every interaction.

High-quality connections are discrete positive social interactions between at least two people in which participants in the relationship are aware of the interaction (Dutton, 2003). The mutual experience of an interaction implies that individuals have affected one another in some way. Connections might occur as the result of a momentary encounter, but they might also have cumulative effects over a longer period of time. The power of a high-quality connection forms the foundations of longer-term relationships – it has lasting implications for the individuals, and often for the organisation.

There are two types of connections that define high-quality connections: those that build the relationship, and those that strengthen the relationship. Both types revolve around the interaction between two people and require both individuals to realise that they are experiencing the interaction. Behind both types of connections are three foundational mechanisms: cognitive, emotional, and behavioural (see Bartholomew & Curran, in this volume). Cognitive mechanisms denote both conscious and unconscious thoughts that predispose people to build high-quality connections. Emotional mechanisms represent the extent to which one's feelings are involved in shared connections with other people. Behavioural mechanisms highlight the role of actions that help define the quality of the connection being formed.

High-quality connections share three subjective qualities: a sense of vitality, perceived positive regard, and a degree of felt mutuality. Students involved in a high-quality connection are likely to feel positively aroused to a sense of heightened positive energy or vitality (Quinn & Dutton, 2005). The second quality present in the interaction is a 'felt sense' of positive regard, a sense of feeling known, loved, respected and cared for in the connection. The third connection quality is marked by the degree of felt mutuality, capturing the subjective feeling of potential movement in the connection. The potential movement represents building and strengthening the initiation of a high-quality connection and the movement toward a connection with greater quality (Stephens et al., 2011). People experience the moment with both mutual vulnerability and responsiveness as they engage in the connection. These subjective indicators help to explain why high-quality connections are attractive, pleasant, and at the same time life-giving. One has a sense of being more alive in a human-to-human high-quality connection.

The quality and structural aspects of high-quality connections are experienced in three primary ways: 1) through connections versus relationships (e.g., involved interaction and mutual awareness), 2) through subjective experiences (e.g., a sense of aliveness, positive regard, and felt mutuality), and 3) greater emotional carrying capacity (e.g., the ability to carry more emotions, both positive and negative emotions, or the ability to yield, adjust, bend, withstand the strain of difficult learning). Finally, high-quality connections are represented by a connectedness, an openness to new ideas. Connections are produced by changes in people's behaviour, feelings, or thinking, or within the ecosystem. Social processes and connections are also key elements of how work is performed and accomplished in organisations. The quality of the connection can vary with inputs and feedback. Differences in connection quality may reflect variations in the health and well-functioning of the living tissue or dyadic relationship. These variations may be filtered by internal or external noise or by life experience.

The structural aspect of a high-quality connection is measured by the degree to which the connection strengthens the relationship or bond. This aspect is also characterised by subjective cognitive, emotional, and behavioural experiences. The cognitive impact is evidenced by the tensile strength of the connection; that is, the capacity to bend and withstand the strain of learning in a variety of circumstances. This feature builds resiliency and the capacity to bounce back from setbacks. The emotional impact implies that there is a greater emotional carrying capacity attached to the relationship. Finally, the behavioural component is experienced as connectivity, in this case, defined as the level of openness to new ideas and influences.

The theoretical lens of high-quality connections is useful for viewing academic rigour. Indeed, high-quality connections provide the energy (emotions) and the behavioural characteristics that give life to the connections. Instructors and students in the classroom form vital relationships that are critical to self-efficacy. It is this connective tissue that is situated at the core of creating self-efficacy.

Communication, interactions, and connections between instructors and students in the classroom are dynamic. To expand upon the tissue metaphor, high-quality connections are living tissue, muscle and tendon that require mutual awareness and interconnection to be sustained. The muscle provides the vigour to make the body move and function; the tendons or sinew connect to the structure. Often relationships refer to two people in association with one another. Further, people and connections are dynamic, and feelings might change during any given interaction.

Instructors can build high-quality connections (and thereby student self-efficacy) through a variety of pedagogical techniques, some of which might involve content pedagogy and some of which do not. For example, instructors can increase the quality of connections in the classroom by executing micro-communications that might be content-oriented or non-content pedagogical words, actions, or activities that students recognise cognitively, emotionally, or behaviourally. Such micro-interactions might include learning students' names, approaching students respectfully, providing time and space for students to respond to classroom questions or ideas fully, or avoiding the embarrassment of students in any way.

Deepening or strengthening the connection might be achieved when instructors encourage – or students choose of their own volition – to go deeper into the learning, or step outside their comfort zones. Examples of such interactions might include instructors requiring academic service learning work outside of the classroom or when students feel comfortable presenting their ideas publicly in the classroom, such as writing on a whiteboard. In doing so, students become task-enabled, trust the instructor, and become willing to step outside their comfort zones.

High-quality connection theory effectively describes how the student-instructor communication connection develops the quality and strength of the bond that subsequently leads to shared meaning. As a story in the classrooms unfolds, the instructors' actions serve as small-scale, short-duration micro-interactions that connect the instructor and student. In a short period, these micro-interactions build student trust in the instructor, leading to higher self-efficacy and thereby task-enabling the student to move on to more difficult learning.

However, both the instructor and student must be resilient and self-reliant, and must have a positive belief system in order to withstand the rigours of learning. Beard *et al.* (2010) concluded that the instructor's academic optimism becomes a single latent construct, reflective of the students' psychological state. Through the formation of dyadic relationships, instructors and students form lasting bonds of trust. These relationships are closely linked to student learning, academic tasks, and instructor academic optimism. Social cognitive theorists Usher & Pajares (2008:785) state further that *"optimistic people are equipped with self-enhancing biases needed to sustain resilience. They also have a strong belief in their efficacy, sustaining them in the times of trouble".*

It might also be posited that classroom instructors set the stage for positive learning experiences. Indeed, the vehicle for modelling and transference of optimism is wrapped up in the instructor's dominant characteristics or methods. Classroom instruction is not simply inanimate speech. The instructor's actions and professional traits have the power to cause students to desire to learn or create a strong predisposition toward learning. Motivation, in the form of the instructor's academic optimism, might provide the basis for student self-efficacy and learning.

Section 3: Classroom Conversations

Words create our worlds; words are transformational. More formally, the constructivist philosophy postulates that reality is linguistic in nature, organised and structured in meaning that is comprised of words. Therefore, reality is 'made through conversation'. And in the classroom, meaning is produced through conversations. Knowledge is imparted, to some degree, through the instructor's language and other communicative actions.

Content pedagogy is unique to the instructor and forms the basis for the manner in which the instructor relates his/her knowledge. Essentially, content pedagogy is what he or she knows about teaching, and about applying that knowledge in order to 'transfer' that knowledge (subject knowledge) to students. Shulman (1986) argued that being an instructor requires more than memorising facts and figures. An instructor must also understand organising principles and structures in the classroom, and comprehend the rules for establishing student learning.

Dewey (1916/1964) believed that good instructors could recognise and create 'genuine intellectual activity' in students. He argued that methods of such activity were intimately tied to instructors. Subjects, he believed, were the embodiments of the mind, the product of human curiosity, inquiry, and the search for truth. Therefore, instructors must be able to communicate their study subject matter by delving back to its 'psychical roots'.

Instructors must contemplate which tasks and subjects, in combination with the use of classroom devices, constitute intellectually stimulating content and whether that pedagogy will drive student learning. This contemplation might take the form of which content, device, or method, the instructor must ask, will be worthwhile in terms of what students might learn. At the very least, the instructor must know, for instance, if a specific video reinforces the learning objective of that class. Or is the use of a classroom prop important cognitively? Does it foster student cognitive activity and/or problem solving? This sort of analysis and preparation is essential for any instructor and ought to be adapted for each unique classroom context.

Teaching methods are different for different subjects and for different instructors. Both Schulman (1986; 1987) and Dewey (1916/1964) argue that, depending on the characteristics of the subject matter, instructors will often use different methods to develop knowledge in learners. Expert instructors have the ability to recognise environmental, personal, and instructional patterns both quickly and accurately. This helps instructors recognise the needs of the learning and the students.

Recognising that relationship connectedness is critical for a positive learning environment, instructors also use a variety of instructional/

motivational/non-content strategies. Among those delivery strategies are lectures, real-world examples, metaphors and analogies, feedback, discussion questions, modelling behaviour, and role-playing. Instructors often attempt to establish a link between students' prior knowledge and the information they are being presented in order to move learning forward. Ball *et al.* (2008:673) concurred, stating that teaching is *"everything that instructors must do to support the learning of their students"*. It follows, therefore, that the interactive work of classroom teaching requires instructors to plan carefully when designing curricula.

Today's classroom, however, is a complex environment, which, in turn, requires complex interactions between content, instructor, and students. Alonzo (2012) also argued that there is a relationship between pedagogical content knowledge and student motivation. Therefore, helping students contextualise content, in the light of their own experiences and of their knowledge of the instructors' teaching goals, adds to the learning experience and forms one of the hallmarks of effective teaching.

Conclusion

Successful classroom conversations play a significant role in academic rigour. Indeed, instructors have positive effects on student task-enabling, suggesting a connection between self-efficacy and an instructor's liberal application of high-quality connections in the classroom. Students of instructors who use high-quality connections self-report that they experience a greater sense of self-confidence, relatability of the content, enjoyment, and a strengthened sense that the knowledge they gain is applicable in their future lives. It suggests, therefore, that instructors ought to learn to develop high-quality connections in the classroom. Additionally, teaching evaluations that are administered to higher education students ought to include questions that are aimed at assessing the quality of the personal relationships that instructors develop with students. For creating such measures, the work of Beard *et al.* (2010), who developed constructs to assess academic optimism, might be a useful starting point.

In our experience, most curriculum design is focused on content and measurable learning outcomes – with the instructor's gauge of success being student test scores. This chapter, on the contrary, argues that more difficult-to-measure soft skills, such as relationship- and trust-building, are equally important. Creating classrooms that promote relationships and high-quality connections, both within and outside the curriculum, would be valuable. A high-quality connection framework might help to describe the actions in the classroom that instructors might use to increase student success. Many of these actions might be the product of instructor personality traits such as humour, charm, or charisma – traits that are not teachable. But other actions that help students feel respected and cared for (e.g., learning students' names, talking to them before a classroom session, or being approachable) are teachable characteristics that might improve learning outcomes.

About the Authors

Timothy Hartge is lecturer of business communication at the College of Business at the University of Michigan in Dearborn, USA, and intermittent lecturer at the English Language Institute at the Stephen M. Ross School of Business of the University of Michigan in Ann Arbor, USA. He can be contacted at this e-mail: thartge@umich.edu

John Branch is academic director of the part-time MBA programmes and assistant clinical instructor of business administration at the Stephen M. Ross School of Business, and faculty associate at the Center for Russian, East European, & Eurasian Studies, both of the University of Michigan in Ann Arbor, USA. He can be contacted at this e-mail: jdbranch@umich.edu

Bibliography

Alonzo, A.; K. Mareike & T. Seidel (2012). Pedagogical content knowledge as reflected in instructor-student interactions: analysis of two video cases. *Journal of Research in Science Teaching*, Vol. 49, No.10, pp. 1211–1239.

Ball, D. (1995). Transforming pedagogy: Classrooms as mathematical communities. A response to Timothy Lensmire and John Pryor. *Harvard Educational Review*, Vol. 65, No. 4, pp. 670–677.

Bandura, A. (1994). Self-efficacy. In V. S. Ramachaudran (Ed.), *Encyclopedia of human behavior*, Vol. 4, pp. 71–81. New York: Academic Press.

Burke, K. (1945). *A grammar of motives*. New York: Prentice-Hall.

Dewey, J. (1964). *John Dewey on education.* Chicago: University of Chicago Press. (Original work published 1916).

Dutton, J. (2014). Creating high quality connections as a pathway for cultivating purpose. *People & Strategy,* Vol. 37, No. 2, p. 9.

Dutton, J. & E. Heaphy (2003). The power of high-quality connections. In K. Cameron; J. Dutton & R. Quinn (Eds.), *Positive organizational scholarship.* San Francisco: Berrett-Koehler, pp. 263–278.

Hoy, W.; C. Tarter & A. Woolfolk-Hoy (2006). Academic optimism of schools: a force for student achievement. *American Educational Research Journal,* Vol. 43, No. 3, pp. 425–446.

Schulman, L. (1987). Knowledge in teaching: Foundations of the new reform. *Harvard Educational Review,* Vol. 57, No. 1, pp. 1–22.

Shouse, R. (1995). Academic press and sense of community: conflict, congruence, and implications for student achievement. *Social Psychology of Education,* Vol. 1, No. 1, pp. 47–68.

Stephens, J.; E. Heaphy & J. Dutton (2011). High-quality connections. In G. Spreitzer & K. Cameron (Eds.), *The Oxford handbook of positive organizational scholarship.* New York: Oxford.

Whitney, D. & A. Trosten-Bloom (2002). *The Power of Appreciative Inquiry.* San Francisco: Berrett-Koehler.

Chapter 11

Curriculum Design for Enhancing Employability through Learning Experiences with External Stakeholders

Jesper Piihl, Anna Marie Dyhr Ulrich & Kristian Philipsen

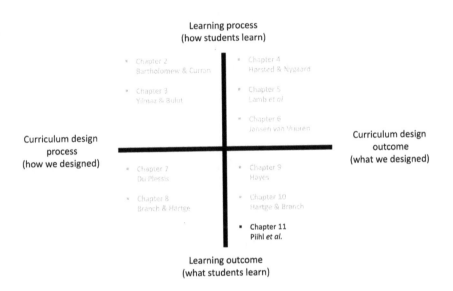

Learning process
(how students learn)

Chapter 2
Bartholomew & Curran

Chapter 4
Horsted & Nygaard

Chapter 3
Yilmaz & Bulut

Chapter 5
Lamb et al

Chapter 6
Jansen van Vuuren

Curriculum design
process
(how we designed)

Curriculum design
outcome
(what we designed)

Chapter 7
Du Plessis

Chapter 9
Hayes

Chapter 8
Branch & Hartge

Chapter 10
Hartge & Branch

Chapter 11
Piihl *et al.*

Learning outcome
(what students learn)

Introduction

We contribute to the book *Learning-Centred Curriculum Design in Higher Education* by offering three metaphors for understanding the role of and relationship with external stakeholders, who play an important role in designing and delivering the curriculum. Further, we discuss how learning activities within a curriculum can form different types of relationships with external stakeholders. This is an important consideration when assessing ways to increase societal relevance in a curriculum and to enhance students' employability without sacrificing on academic quality.

In relation to the central model of the book, we position our chapter in section four – Learning Outcome/ Curriculum Design Outcome – since we address curriculum designs and specific learning outcomes – with an emphasis on student-employability.

Employability is a topic of considerable priority in the political debate around higher education in Europe (Commission/EACEA/Eurydice, 2014). This urges universities to give explicit attention to student employability. This challenge sometimes leads to universities offering extra- and co-curricular activities to students (e.g., see Hui *et al.*, 2017) in order to prepare them for work life after graduation – or in other words, "to enhance their employability".

The approach of this chapter is that we ought not to consider the demand for employability as an additional one that might come at the expense of academic quality when prioritising within the limitations in the curriculum. Instead, we should consider employability as the consequence of an explicit emphasis on quality and relevance within the curriculum.

In the literature, outcomes-based curriculum models form a bridge between the professional contexts in which the students are going to operate and curriculum design by translating competencies of skilled practitioners into specific learning outcomes that curriculum designers intend students to accomplish. These learning outcomes are translated into courses, which entails content, activities, and assessments, amongst other things (Harden, 1999). However, Grant (2006) argues that the underlying theory behind this perspective is flawed, since the competencies cannot be separated from performance in the complex practices in which students are expected to engage in. Therefore, there is a need for discussing curriculum design in a way that highlights the integration of relevant professional contexts into learning activities within the curriculum. Reading this chapter, you ought to gain at least three insights:

1. a new perspective on curriculum design emphasising professional, external environment integration into learning activities in order to promote employability;

2. a framework for designing specific course activities;

3. two inspirational examples that illustrate how this new perspective and this framework translates into curricula in different ways.

We have structured our chapter in four sections. In section one, we briefly elaborate on established perspectives about curriculum design, emphasising these perspectives' relations to the external environment. In section two, we develop three metaphors that challenge the way we look at an academic curriculum. The three metaphors conceptualise the curriculum as either a:

1. closed tube with an external environment at the end of the tube;

2. glass tube with windows through which students can get glimpses of the outside world without getting "messy"; and

3. perforated tube with holes enabling real-life exchanges with the outside world, with all the "messiness" this involves.

The metaphors are characterised by their perspective on learning, quality, relevance, and thereby ultimately on their approach to enhancing employability. In section three, we present a model for conceptualising how we can design specific learning activities that involve different forms of exchange with contexts outside the control of higher education institutions. In the fourth and final section, we discuss these elements in relation to contemporary work on curriculum design at two different campuses with the same overall curriculum but with different challenges regarding the academic environment, external environments, and student body.

Section I: The Role of the External Environment in Curriculum Design

In the literature, the term *curriculum* is used to describe either the design of individual courses (Biggs & Tang, 2007) or the design of programmes of study as a collection of courses. In this chapter, we refer to the latter perspective. Samuelowicz & Bain (1992) examined different conceptions of teaching held by academics within the fields of science and social science. One of the conceptions they identified concerned teaching as the transmission of knowledge within the framework of an academic discipline. If we translate this conception of teaching into a discussion about curriculum, it points towards designing curriculum around specific academic disciplines. This then results in discipline-based or subject-based curriculum design. In discipline-based approaches to curriculum design, the emphasis is on facilitating or transmitting knowledge on specific disciplinary subject areas to students. This approach links to external environments by considering the appropriate disciplines to be covered in order to develop academics with a relevant combination of disciplinary knowledge. Eventually, external stakeholders can play a role in deciding on disciplines to be covered through participation in advisory boards. Within medical education (Harden, 1999) suggested to change this relation to the external environment in curriculum design by advocating for an outcomes-based approach. The outcomes-based perspective is also found in other areas of higher education, such as in business (Brady, 2015), social work education (Ring, 2014), and entrepreneurship (Rezaei-Zadeh et al., 2014). Following an outcomes-based approach, the point of departure for curriculum design is an investigation of the knowledge, skills, and competencies required by professional practitioners of the corresponding field. The curriculum is then designed aiming to establish such knowledge, skills, and competencies. In the medical field, for example, Harden (1999) identifies three dimensions for describing outcomes for doctors:

1. what the doctor is able to do;

2. how the doctor should be approaching the task;

3. personal attributes.

In order to develop learning outcomes that can guide curriculum design, Harden (1999) suggested that learning outcomes should:

1. reflect the vision and mission of the institution;

2. be clear and unambiguous;

3. be specific and address defined areas of competence;

4. be manageable;

5. be defined at an appropriate level of generality;

6. assist with the development of "enabling" outcomes;

7. indicate the relationship between different outcomes.

However, the question that can be asked is that if we base our curriculum design on defined outcomes that follow the seven criteria above (e.g., are specific in a defined area, clear and unambiguous, and manageable), do we then address the complexity the students need to be able to meet when confronted with the real practice after graduation? The question regarding the complexity in the context of practice calls for new perspectives that approach the relation to outside context in radically different ways compared to discipline-based and outcomes-based approaches to curriculum design. Still within the field of medicine, Grant (2006) relates the outcomes-based approach to curriculum design to behaviourism and argues that contemporary approaches to curriculum design move beyond the assumptions and implications held in behavioural theories: *"The learning theories that inform today's curriculum design seem to be very far from the ideas of behavioural theories of learning, and from the idea that the knowledge base of the discipline must first be learned before its application can be attempted. Today's trajectory of learning is flatter, with integration being the hallmark throughout the course, and deep learning in the context of practice its aim."* (Grant, 2006:14). In discussing elements important for learning, Knight (2002) argues that student engagement is crucial when explaining the act of learning. He continues to argue that engagement cannot be reduced to merely equating time on a task:

> *"[Engagement] extends to learners' engagement in communities of practice, to their involvement in a variety of networks and to the amount and quality of interchanges with others.... According to Brown & Duguid (2000), participation in communities and networks regularly sustains learning that is not easily specified in advance, cannot necessarily be measured and is often unpredictable. Important things are learned in vibrant communities that lie outwith the formal curriculum and complement it."* (Knight, 2002:275).

Both of these examples point towards integrating learning into contexts of practice. However, the latter citation points towards learning in relation to communities as something that lay outside the formal curriculum. However, if learning in contexts of practice is important, then we need to develop models for considering this as an integral part of the formal curriculum. In the following section, we develop three metaphors for curriculum design that highlight the different forms of relationships with the external environment.

Section 2: Three Metaphors for Curriculum Design

In this section, we briefly describe three dimensions distinguishing the metaphors that we develop to describe curriculum designs. Thereafter, we present and elaborate on each of the metaphors related to the dimensions.

Perspectives on Relevance

Knight & Yorke (2004) have developed a simple, provocative, and insightful framework for increasing students' employability, namely, the USEM-framework. They argue that traditionally universities focus on developing students' understanding of specific content. They also argue that the quest for employability has led universities to supplement the understanding of content with the development of specific skills that are considered relevant to those workplaces that programme planners envisage graduates to enter. Many universities stop at this level. However, Knight and Yorke (2004) suggest that we need two additional levels. The first is a focus on developing students' self-efficacy. Bandura (1993:119) describes efficacy as follows: *"Among the mechanisms of agency, none is more central or pervasive than people's beliefs about their capabilities to exercise control over their own level of functioning and over events that affect their lives. Efficacy beliefs influence how people feel, think, motivate themselves, and behave."* In a meta-analysis, Robbins *et al.* (2004) found that among nine psychological and study skill factors, academic self-efficacy was the best predictor of college performance. Artino (2012) discusses how self-efficacy can be enhanced in education *"by providing students with authentic mastery experiences"* (Artino, 2012:81). The last element in Knight & Yorke's (2004) framework highlights the ability to question one's own learning and to question existing processes and existing courses of events. They term this *metacognition*. This element links closely to learning outcomes from research-based teaching, with its inherent critical stance towards existing knowledge as being temporary.

Perspectives on Learning

The second perspective, which distinguishes our metaphors, concerns perspectives on learning coming from Biggs' (2012) discussion of the stages in the development of perspectives of learning in higher education. At the first stage, it is believed that learning is an effect of "who the student is". At the second stage, the focus falls upon the role of the teacher. This is underpinned by the notion that learning is an effect of "what the teacher does". At the third stage, the focus falls upon the student. Here, learning is viewed as an effect of "what the student does". However, mindful of Knight & Yorke's USEM-model and focus on self-efficacy and metacognition as elements in providing competences relevant for employability, as well as the latter perspectives on curriculum design, we suggest adding a fourth stage highlighting relations with external stakeholders. The fourth stage suggests that learning is also an effect of "what students do in interaction with relevant external environments".

Perspectives on Quality

The last perspective distinguishing our three metaphors concerns issues related to quality. In higher education, it is ingrained in our culture that quality relates to research, which forms the foundation for teaching and learning. One commonly known model when discussing research-based teaching is presented by Healey (2005). This model uses two dimensions for distinguishing between four modes of research-based teaching. The one dimension considers the role of research in teaching: On the one hand, teaching can address the results of research (i.e., the "research content"), on the other hand teaching can address the "research process". The other dimension addresses the role of students in the teaching process. One can rightly ask: Are the students considered to be an audience or active participants during teaching? This results in four forms of research-based teaching. *Research-led* teaching describes teaching designs where the focus is on content/research results, and students are engaged in teaching as an audience (e.g., lecturing). *Research-tutored* teaching depicts designs with a focus on content, while the students are actively engaged in the processes as participants (e.g., through seminar activities discussing results of existing research). This might help students to develop a critical approach towards knowledge.

In *research-oriented* teaching, the focus of teaching moves from results or content to a focus on the research process. In research oriented teaching, the students are engaged as an audience, where they, for example, attend lectures on methodology. The term *research-based* teaching refers to designs where students are actively engaged in a research or knowledge-production process as participants themselves.

Three Caricatured Metaphors

The table below suggests three metaphors for curriculum design that apply these perspectives as distinguishing features. The metaphors are purposely caricatured to highlight specific features of each of them. Hayes (in this volume) points out that the word "curriculum" is derived from the Latin verb *currere*, meaning to run. This implies the idea that a curriculum is about motion. In the metaphors presented here, this idea of motion is illustrated by the idea of a tube. A tube is designed to channel a flow in certain directions.

The first metaphor considers a curriculum as a closed tube in relation to the external environments. In this metaphor, the students engage with the environment at the end for the tube. The second sees curriculum as a glass tube, where links to external environments are shown to students throughout the curriculum. The last metaphor envisages the curriculum as a perforated tube, with holes that allow access to the external environment. This means openings for real-life interactions with stakeholders in order to practice mastery and relevance in authentic settings.

The metaphors are not mutually exclusive, meaning that a curriculum inspired by the perforated tube metaphor can have elements recognised from the other two metaphors. The metaphors are briefly summarised below.

Image of Curriculum		Closed tube (Discipline-based)	Glass tube (Outcomes-based)	Perforated tube (Integrated)
Perspectives on	Learning — Learning is an effect of	What the teacher does	What the student does	What the student does in relevant professional contexts
	Quality — The role of research in learning	Research-led	Research-tutored Research-oriented	Research-led Research-tutored Research-oriented Research-based
	Relevance — Relevance in learning goals	Academic content is relevant (U)	Academic content is relevant (U) Skills are practiced (S)	Academic content (U) Skills (S) Efficacy (E) Metacognition (M)
	Relevance — Relevance in learning processes	Relevance is "explained". Relevance through input.	Relevance is "shown". Relevance through input.	Relevance is "practiced". Relevance as output.

Table 1: Three metaphors for linking curriculum design to the external environment.

An image of a curriculum as a *closed tube* describes a discipline-based curriculum with a series of courses aimed at research content and with students primarily taking part in learning as an audience. A curriculum as a closed tube gains its relevance from a specific selection of theoretical content (understanding) that is selected in order lead to a portfolio of knowledge and skills that employers are envisaged to demand. In this way, relevance is built into the curriculum as an *a priori* input. However, when developing a discipline-based curriculum, the specific disciplines and content might also be a result of internal university politics and negotiations between research disciplines rather than a collection developed with the external environments in mind. An image of a curriculum as a *glass tube* opens the curriculum in a way that makes it possible for the students to see the professional environment that the curriculum is designed to prepare them for. In relation to the established perspectives on curriculum design that were discussed above, we relate this broadly to the outcomes-based approach for curriculum design. According to the outcomes-based approach, links to the external environment can be made through explicit outcomes and skills that are demanded by the professional environment. However, links to the environment can also be made through the use of examples in the classroom, case-based teaching, and maybe even guest lectures or company visits. In addition to building relevance and employability into the curriculum through selection of content (understanding) and skills, this metaphor of a curriculum aims at showing students how content and skills can be relevant rather than just explaining, as suggested in the closed-tube metaphor.

The metaphor of a curriculum as a *perforated tube* takes the relationship to the external environment to a new level in highlighting that relevance and employability can be designed directly into the curriculum by designing learning experiences with actual interaction between students and professional environments that is relevant for future employment. These forms of committed interactions make more advanced and diverse learning outcomes possible in comparison to what can be narrowed down as outcomes in the outcomes-based approaches. Through actual interactions, the students also develop their abilities to act professionally based on their knowledge, skills, and competencies and reflect upon their knowledge in different types of situations. As a result, students may enhance their self-efficacy as well as their ability to reflect upon their own knowledge (metacognition) (Knight & Yorke, 2004). In this way, relevance is practiced and developed as an output of learning processes in the curriculum. The metaphor of the *perforated tube* emphasises the interaction with the external environment. However, it should be noted that the metaphor also suggests that a curriculum has closed elements where students can focus on specific disciplines without an emphasis on its immediate relevance, as well as elements from the glass-tube metaphor, which entails strictly guided interactions with stakeholders through cases and examples.

The next section will elaborate on a model for developing different types of learning experiences that involve interaction with external environments. Curriculum designers can use this model as an inspiration for developing more advanced learning experiences that involve a gradual increase in complexity of interactions with stakeholders. The last section gives examples of how these gradually more advanced learning experiences can be included in a curriculum.

Section 3: How to Develop Learning Experiences in Collaboration with External Stakeholders

In this section, we discuss a framework that propagates ideas for how learning experiences involving external stakeholders can be designed. The framework is inspired by one that has been put forward by Piihl *et al.* (2014). It has been developed to highlight different aspects related to learning experiences that involve interaction with external stakeholders. The framework has two dimensions, and on each dimension responsibility is gradually transferred from the teacher towards the students. The one dimension focuses on responsibility for selecting the specific academic content within a given learning experience. In the one extreme, the responsibility resides with the teacher, and as we move towards the other extreme, the responsibility is gradually given to the students. The other dimension focuses on who holds the responsibility for interaction with external stakeholders. Again, at the one extreme, the responsibility resides with the teacher, and as we move along the dimension, the responsibility is gradually handed over to the students. In this way, the framework aspires to develop a curriculum that allows students to gradually take over responsibility for the content and also the interactions. Within the framework, this means that the curriculum should gradually move students from the upper-left to the lower-right corner:

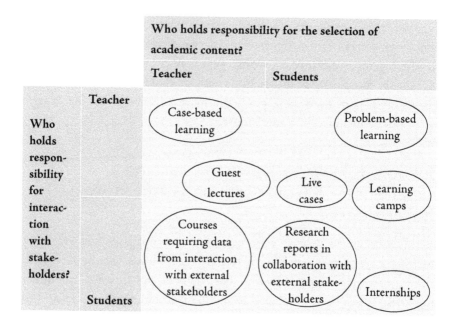

Table 2: Framework for learning experiences with interactions with external stakeholders.

In the upper-left corner, the teacher has responsibility for selecting the specific academic content. Likewise, the teacher has responsibility for interaction with stakeholders. Learning experiences in this area can include praxis-oriented cases, guest-lectures, company visits, etc., where the responsibility for interactions with stakeholders are primarily held by the teacher and the interactions are focused on exemplifying or giving perspective to specific elements of the academic content. In this way, the primary emphasis is on academic content (i.e., "Understanding" in the USEM framework). These learning experiences give the students windows through which they can get glimpses of the world outside the university (see the metaphor of curriculum as a glass tube).

If we stay in the left side of the framework, where the teacher holds responsibility for the content, but transfer some of the responsibility for interactions with stakeholders to the students, we move towards the lower-left corner. In this area, we work with, for example, courses that require the students to produce data in collaboration with external stakeholders of their choice. This requires students to engage with external stakeholders, which develops their self-efficacy and helps them practice skills in communicating around academic content and issues with externals.

In the centre of the framework, we have placed what we call "live cases". Live-cases are distinguished from written cases or guest lectures by the level of involvement with stakeholders during the learning experiences. For example, this could be stakeholders exhibiting real-life issues/problems/questions related to the subject area being studied in a course. If they participate as a live case, they not only show up as a one-time guest lecturer but also participate several times during the course, during which time different aspects of various issues are present. They allow students to work with the problems over longer periods of time as well as allowing for more direct and closer interactions. In this way, opportunities become available for the development of skills in relation to addressing specific real-life issues. This also gives students the opportunity to practice interacting professionally with stakeholders, which can enhance students' skills and efficacy. Furthermore, students are forced to relate their disciplinary knowledge to real-world problems, and communicate their ideas outside the classroom context.

Moving towards the right side of the framework, the responsibility to make decisions about the academic content is gradually transferred from the teacher to the students. This move creates more advanced learning experiences where students are responsible for defining relevant issues and selecting appropriate theoretical frameworks for addressing these issues. This opens opportunities for learning experiences, which address what Knight and Yorke (2004) term *metacognition*, as discussed above. Problem-based learning is one way of organising learning experiences in the right side of the framework. Savery (2006:12) describes problem-based learning as an approach: "...*that empowers learners to conduct research, integrate theory and practice, and apply knowledge and skills to develop a viable solution to a defined problem. Critical to the success of the approach is the selection of ill-structured problems (often interdisciplinary)."* This description of problem-based learning does not explicitly address the relationship between students and external stakeholders, which is the vertical axis in the framework. However, applying this dimension to the design of problem-based learning adds a structured way of designing learning experiences that also involves external stakeholders. Problem-based learning can be designed around (ill-structured) problems defined by the teacher and can involve interaction with external stakeholders to varying degrees. This also means that the levels of responsibility for the interaction and the form it takes vary in terms of the role of the teacher and the students.

In the right-hand side of the framework – towards the middle on the axis regarding responsibility for interaction – we have placed what we term *learning camps*. Camp Get Closer, as discussed by Piihl *et al.* (2016), is just one example. Camp Get Closer is a four-day event where students are grouped across semesters and educational programmes from social sciences, engineering, and the humanities to work on issues held by local companies and institutions. The external stakeholders (companies and institutions) are selected by the camp organisers, while students are responsible for the interaction during the camp. During the camp, the students are responsible for making the final interpretations of the issues at stake and practicing how they can apply their theories in ways that make them relevant. Since the students are grouped across semesters and educational programmes, there are no predefined approaches or academic content. When students need to select, and negotiate the content and approaches, they are provided with an opportunity where they can practice how they can be relevant with their knowledge in interactions with others. In this way, relevance is practised as an output of the learning experience rather than an input, which is in accordance with the perforated-tube metaphor's approach to relevance.

Moving to the lowest part of the framework, where students have responsibility for interactions with stakeholders, we have positioned *research reports developed in collaboration with external stakeholders* around the middle regarding responsibility for academic content. Research reports could, for example, be bachelor or master theses. These types of learning experiences are placed in the middle of the dimension on responsibility of content, since specific requirements as well as methodologies, which are considered appropriate for developing a scientific report, influence the issues and topics that can be addressed as well as the working procedures.

Towards the bottom right corner, the responsibility for interaction with stakeholders as well as responsibility for the selection of academic content are transferred to students in interactions with external stakeholders. One way to organise learning experiences in this area of the framework is internships. Piihl *et al.* (2014) discuss a model for organ-ising internships in accordance with the approach to relevance as an output, as suggested by the perforated tube metaphor. The approach asks students to develop experiences related to what it means to be an academic in practice. The point of departure in the internships is involve-ment in ongoing processes in host organisations or problems stakeholders ask the intern to look into. From this departure, the students are asked to critically reflect on processes and problems in the organisational setting in order to negotiate definitions of problems with the stakeholders as well as selecting the specific knowledge areas/academic content appropriate for the engagement. Facilitated by supervisors, students are required to practice their ability to engage and interact actively with stakeholders (efficacy), and they practice their ability to question unfolding events and acquire the skills necessary for engaging in problem-solving in real-life contexts (metacognition).

This list of examples is by no means complete and only serves to inspire new forms of learning experiences based on the framework.

Section 4: Two Tales of the Perforated Tube Metaphor and Curriculum Design

This section briefly discusses how the metaphor of a perforated tube can inspire curriculum design through a conscious variation in learning activities that emphasise employability through learning experiences incorporating interaction with the external environment. The section is based on an example from business studies, while du Plessis (in this volume) provides another example of a curriculum involving external stakeholders, but in a very different context, namely, the context of primary school teacher education in South Africa.

The example here is taken from the University of Southern Denmark, which offers a BSc in Economics and Business Administration at five distinct campuses. The core of the six semesters and 180 ECTS curric-ulum (see Branch & Hartge, in this volume, for a description of the ECTS model) is built around a set of standardised disciplines that are widely expected to be included in this type of educational programme: micro-and macroeconomics, entrepreneurship, organisation, marketing, finance, accounting, mathematics, statistics, business law, strategy, and a bachelor thesis. This core equals 120 ECTS, leaving 60 ECTS for campus-specific courses and electives. These 60 ECTS are developed independently at each campus to draw upon the strengths and possibilities in the research groups at the campus as well as the specific opportunities the campus can develop together with external stakeholders in proximity to each campus. The 60 ECTS that vary between the campuses is divided into 10 ECTS on the second, third, and fourth semester and 30 ECTS on the fifth semester. An overview of the curriculum is given in the table below. The table has the first semester at the bottom, progressing to the sixth semester at the top.

6	**Bachelor Project (20)**				**Strategy (10)**
5					
4	Macroeconomics (10)	Accounting (10)	Advanced Quantitative Analyses (5)	Business Law (5)	60 ECTS for campus-specific activities and electives
3			Finance (10)		
2	Microeconomics (10)	Mathematics and Statistics (10)	Marketing (10)		
1			Organisation with Theory of Science (10)		Entrepreneurship and Understanding Business (10)

Table 3: Curriculum for the BSc in Economics and Business Administration.

To illustrate the perforated tube metaphor and the accompanying framework, we briefly illustrate how they inform the curriculum design at two of the campuses.

At the first campus, there is a long-standing tradition for learning experiences involving external stakeholders. Here, the students are expected to find opportunities for collaboration with a local business and spend one day a week at the company during the second to fifth semester. The university offers some degree of facilitating assistance in connecting the students to companies, but students are ultimately responsible for closing the agreement with a company. In this way, the university does not guarantee a company agreement for each student (see Klein & Weiss, 2011, for an analysis of the effects of forced internships).

During each semester, the students attend at least one course, where the teacher decides the academic content, whereas the students are responsible for drafting a report concerning the themes related to the specific companies where they are working. Gradually, these assignments become more and more open-ended, thus moving the learning experience towards the lower-right corner in Table 2. This means that the students gradually become responsible for negotiating problems and processes with stakeholders as well as selecting academic content to guide the work towards solutions.

The second campus under consideration is characterised by a large proportion of international students. However, the political discourse is increasingly questioning the contribution that international students make to the national labour market. In a recent press release (UFM, 2017), the Ministry of Higher Education and Science has announced that due to this issue, they will reduce the intake of international students by 25% at non-research-based higher education institutions.

Consequently, the unique challenge at this campus is to create relations between international students and local companies and other institutions in order to turn incoming international students into a skilled workforce that can offer their skills to the region after graduation.

The local business community is very open to creating opportunities for collaboration – however, the students' interest is not to be taken for granted. Therefore, the idea of the perforated tube and the framework of forms of relationships suggest that we integrate interaction with stakeholders in gradually more advanced forms during the curriculum in a way that makes it a natural way of learning, by starting with guest lectures and moving into live cases and courses with requirements of data. The relations that students create with local business can then be used as a channel for developing internships, collaboration on bachelor projects, and hopefully getting a job at a company after graduation.

Conclusion: Quality and Relevance in Curriculum Design

The growing concern for employability after completing a qualification at a higher education institution requires new ways of working with quality and relevance in curriculum design. The perspective we have taken in this chapter is that relevance should be considered as an effect of the way we view the notion of quality during curriculum design.

Existing approaches to curriculum design hold different conceptions on the relationship between quality and relevance. We developed the metaphor of curriculum as a closed tube to illustrate how discipline-based approaches to curriculum design consider relevance through a portfolio of disciplines that are included in the curriculum. Outcomes-based models are described through the metaphor of a glass tube and design for relevance by translating the competences of skilled professionals into learning outcomes that need to be developed through a curriculum.

Apart from these models, this chapter suggests a metaphor for curriculum design that turns the relation between relevance and quality on its head. Whereas the discipline-based and outcomes-based approaches assure relevance through the careful selection of elements that are designed into the curriculum, the metaphor of curriculum as a perforated tube suggests an integrated approach to curriculum design and emphasises real-life interaction through professional networks within the curriculum.

The aim of these integrated real-life experiences is to let students practice how to become relevant based on quality academic content and methods within the curriculum.

About the Authors

Jesper Piihl is an associate professor at the Department of Entrepreneurship and Relationship Management at University of Southern Denmark. He can be contacted at this e-mail: jpi@sam.sdu.dk

Anna Marie Dyhr Ulrich is an associate professor at the Department of Entrepreneurship and Relationship Management at University of Southern Denmark. She can be contacted at this e-mail: amdu@sam.sdu.dk

Kristian Philipsen is an associate professor at the Department of Entrepreneurship and Relationship Management at University of Southern Denmark. He can be contacted at this e-mail: kp@sam.sdu.dk

Bibliography

Artino, A. R. (2012). Academic self-efficacy: from educational theory to instructional practice. *Perspectives on Medical Education*, Vol. 1, No. 2, pp. 76–85.

Bandura, A. (1993). Perceived Self-Efficacy in Cognitive Development and Functioning. *Educational Psychologist*, Vol. 28, No. 2, pp. 117–148.

Biggs, J. (2012). What the student does: teaching for enhanced learning. *Higher Education Research & Development*, Vol. 31., No. 1, pp. 39–55.

Biggs, J. & C. Tang (2007). *Teaching for Quality Learning at University* (3rd ed.). Maidenhead: Open University Press.

Brady, N. (2015). 'Epistemic chaos': the recontextualisation of undergraduate curriculum design and pedagogic practice in a new university business school. *British Journal of Sociology of Education*, Vol. 36, No. 8, pp. 1236–1257.

Commission/EACEA/Eurydice, E. (2014). Modernisation of Higher Education in Europe: Access, Retention and Employability 2014, *Eurydice Report*. Luxembourg: Publications Office of the European Union.

Grant, J. (2006). *Principles of curriculum design*. Edinburgh: Association for the Study of Medical Education.

Harden, R. M. (1999). AMEE Guide No. 14: Outcome-based education: Part 1-An introduction to outcome-based education. *Medical Teacher*, No. 21, Vol. 1, pp. 7–14.

Healey, M. (2005). Linking research and teaching: exploring disciplinary spaces and the role of inquiry-based learning. In R. Barnett (Ed.), *Reshaping the University: New Relationships between Research, Scholarship and Teaching*, pp. 67–78. Berkshire, GBR: McGraw-Hill Education.

Hui, V.; H. Mercer; C. Nickel & M. Cestra (2017). *Expanding the Zones: Fostering Innovation and Entrepreneurship in Post-Secondary Institutions*. Paper presented at the INTED2017 Conference, Valencia, Spain.

Klein, M. & F. Weiss (2011). Is forcing them worth the effort? Benefits of mandatory internships for graduates from diverse family backgrounds at labour market entry. *Studies in Higher Education*, Vol. 36, No. 8, pp. 969–987.

Knight, P. T. (2002). Summative Assessment in Higher Education: Practices in disarray. *Studies in Higher Education*, Vol. 27, No. 3, pp. 275–286.

Knight, P. T. & M. Yorke (2004). *Learning, Curriculum and Employability in Higher Education*. London: RoutledgeFalmer.

Piihl, J.; J. S. Rasmussen & J. Rowley (2014). Internships as case-based learning for professional practice. In C. Nygaard; J. Branch & P. Bartholomew (Eds.), *Case-Based Learning in Higher Education*, pp. 177–196. Oxfordshire: Libri Publishing.

Piihl, J. & K. B. Munksgaard (2016). Using Assessment Couplings to Engage Stakeholders in Co-curricular Activities. In C. Nygaard; P. Bartholomew & J. Branch (Eds.), *Assessment of Learning in Higher Education*. Oxfordshire, UK: Libri Publishing Ltd.

Rezaei-Zadeh, M.; M. Hogan; J. O'Reilly; B. Cleary & E. Murphy (2014). Using interactive management to identify, rank and model entrepreneurial competencies as universities' entrepreneurship curricula. *The Journal of Entrepreneurship*, Vol. 23, No.1, pp. 57–94.

Ring, C. (2014). Social Work Training or Social Work Education? An Approach to Curriculum Design. *Social Work Education*, Vol. 33, No. 8, pp. 1101–1108.

Robbins, S. B.; K. Lauver; H. Le; D. Davis; R. Langley & A. Carlstrom (2004). Do psychosocial and study skill factors predict college outcomes? A meta-analysis: American Psychological Association.

Samuelowicz, K. & J. D. Bain (1992). Conceptions of teaching held by academic teachers. *Higher Education*, Vol. 24, No. 1, pp. 93–111.

Savery, J. R. (2006). Overview of problem-based learning: Definitions and distinctions. *Interdisciplinary Journal of Problem-based Learning*, Vol. 1, No. 1, p. 3.

UFM (2017). Opbremsning i optaget af studerende på engelsksprogede uddannelser. [Slowdown in admission of students on English-taught educations]. Online resource: http://ufm.dk/aktuelt/pressemeddelelser/2017/opbremsning-i-optaget-af-studerende-pa-engelsksprogede-uddannelser [Accessed on 31 May 2017].

Lightning Source UK Ltd.
Milton Keynes UK
UKHW022224151020
371652UK00005B/571